Indonesian Company Law

This exceptionally useful book successfully clarifies Indonesian company law with keen insight and rigorous research. Few books have been written about contemporary Indonesian company law, so with a critical analysis based on cumulative research and comparative studies of corporate law in a number of foreign jurisdictions, this book will be of assistance both to legal practitioners and to market players seeking to conduct business in Indonesia.

—Sartono S. H., M. H., *Partner of Hanafiah Ponggawa & Partners*

In modern countries, a company is commonly categorized as either public or privately held, depending on whether securities are publicly traded on the open market, into a government-owned company or private company, depending on government ownership, or a financial company or non-financial company, depending on its main business, and so on. Of course, these categories are generally used in Indonesia as well. A unique aspect in Indonesia is that a well-settled legal practice mainly uses a dichotomy of company types that is rarely popular in foreign countries: a company with foreign direct investment (*penanaman modal asing*, or PMA) or company with 100 percent domestic direct investment (*penanaman modal dalam negeri*, or PMDN). Government plans concerning how to differently regulate these companies frequently becomes a national issue, as it is one of the main standards to evaluate how effectively and willingly the Indonesian government develops its economic policies. Laws, regulations, and actual legal practice also treat the two types of companies differently, based on whether a company has a foreign shareholder. Although many foreign countries are also equipped with similar regulations over companies with foreign direct investment, Indonesia distinctively applies this dichotomy for much wider uses for several reasons.

This book is designed to assist students, practitioners, and researchers with clear and comprehensive treatment of key concepts in Indonesian company law. Significant business, economic, and policy issues are highlighted together with a thorough analysis of the important statutory provisions and cases used in the study of Indonesian company law. The book includes the major theoretical approaches used in current company law literature, and statutory issues are covered under both the 2007 Indonesian Company Act and the 2007 Indonesian Capital Investment Act. The book will be an essential reference for investors and businesses contemplating entering the Indonesian Market.

Soonpeel (Edgar) Chang is a legal manager at Korindo Group and director of a company in the Netherlands.

Routledge Research in Corporate Law

Available titles in this series include:

For more information about this series, please visit: www.routledge.com

Indonesian Company Law

Soonpeel Edgar Chang

Routledge
Taylor & Francis Group

LONDON AND NEW YORK

First published 2018
by Routledge

2 Park Square, Milton Park, Abingdon, Oxfordshire OX14 4RN
52 Vanderbilt Avenue, New York, NY 10017

Routledge is an imprint of the Taylor & Francis Group, an informa business

First issued in paperback 2020

British Library Cataloguing-in-Publication Data
A catalogue record for this book is available from the British Library

Library of Congress Cataloging-in-Publication Data
Names: Chang, Soonpeel Edgar, author.
Title: Indonesian company law/Soonpeel Edgar Chang.
Description: New York, NY: Routledge, 2018.
Identifiers: LCCN 2018003795 | ISBN 9781138588042 (hardback)
Subjects: LCSH: Corporation law—Indonesia. | Business enterprises—
    Law and Legislation—Indonesia.
Classification: LCC KNW1050 .C43 2018 | DDC 346.598/066—dc23
LC record available at https://lccn.loc.gov/2018003795

ISBN: 978-1-138-58804-2 (hbk)
ISBN: 978-0-367-59045-1 (pbk)

Typeset in Galliard
by Apex CoVantage, LLC

Contents

Figures and tables

Figures

Tables

Preface

I vividly recall how disappointed and sad I felt when I realized the shallowness of the accumulated literature on Indonesian corporate law.

When I moved to Jakarta in 2014, the first thing that I did on the following day was go to the second largest bookstore in Jakarta at the Grand Indonesia Mall and purchase all the corporate law books sold there. While the text books I used back at my U.S. law school generally cost 200 dollars or more, thankfully, these books in Indonesia were only one- or two-twentieth the price, but there were not many books about company law. Despite my lack of speed in learning the language, it did not take too long to understand them, because all the books turned out to be almost just a copy and paste of the 2007 Company Act without any theoretical, conceptual, or analytical aspect to them.

A corporate law text book in my home country, South Korea, is usually about a thousand pages in general, and reading one requires substantial time to appreciate and ponder it even if the reader is legally savvy. This is because the book summarizes the cumulative studies of numerous researchers, the constant changes of corporate law, and the jurisprudence developed from a considerable number of cases. In contrast, at least in relation to Indonesian company law, it is extremely difficult to find any systematic collection of major cases or a monograph with the necessary rigor and originality that the academic world generally requires.

In other words, Indonesian company law seems to have developed without a systematic collection of court rulings or a rigorous review of prior studies compared to other developed jurisdictions. Meeting with judges at the Supreme Court, partners at large law firms, and professors in famous schools assured me that each individual's intelligence, wisdom, and talent are undoubtedly strong. What the practice of Indonesian company law lacks is presumably a "collective intelligence," a systematically organized collection of their wisdom. As a result, Indonesian company law appears to have been developed by practitioners dealing with public institutions such as Ministry of Law and Human Rights, the tax office or Indonesia Investment Coordinating Board, rather than widely accepted theories or interpretations by the court. Nevertheless, even these administrative interpretations and practices have been rarely collected and published.

This book, *Indonesian Company Law*, has been written against this background. I attempt to present a description of the positive law with a black-letter approach, hoping that it will contribute a foundation, at least in part, to the literature of Indonesian company law. Also, I try to introduce how actual practitioners interpret and use the law in the absence of relevant clauses in stipulations or court decisions in a number of essential company law topics. Still, the readers outside of Indonesia may feel that some important topics lack any exploration on approaches taken by the judiciary, academic explications, or theoretical developments in the field. Some direct quotations of statutory provisions with little explications on their practical utility may look unsuccessful in bringing out simplicity from a challenging subject. Then, it is the point where the readers get to grip with my frustration over the current stage of the accumulated literature on Indonesian corporate law.

Most importantly, this book cannot guarantee the result of any legal proceeding, and the author cannot take any responsibility for any decision contrary to the conclusions herein. Given the practice of law in Indonesia, it is difficult to say that a similar outcome will be reached in every case, even if the main facts and circumstances look the same. Also, my personal interpretations and conclusions have been explicitly stated as my own thought.

Lastly, the examples and cases described in this book can be easily searched in news, books or articles, or obtained by consultation with an expert. No materials of this book are related or based on work done for any companies or corporations with which I have been managing or consulting.

Acknowledgements

The process of preparing this book was eased by the hospitality from Routledge and Apex CoVantage. I have had the great benefit of the efforts of the peer reviewers at Routledge. I owe heart-felt thank to Andrey Mario, Dauri Lie, Efraim Asa Nainggolan, Jonathan Eliezer H Gultom, Masri Gunardi, Sang Min Choi, Sartono, Yi Seung Min, Wimbanu Widyatmoko and legal professors at the Pancasila University for their legal advices and intelligence and all Korindo members for their support.

I am very fortunate to have a supportive and loving family who enable and inspire my work. I am blessed by my parents, He Sook Kim and Kyung Jin Chang, honored to be the husband of Eunji Park and proud of my child, Dojun Chang. I thank to Professor Ko Dong Won at Sung Kyun Kwan University School of Law, Choon Sung Kim at Korea Exchange, Ji Woong Seok at Korean Securities Depository, Woo Joo Lee at Korean Development Bank, Jeffery Kwon at Woori Bank and my nearest and dearest friend, Yu Min Wook, all of who make me me.

1 Introduction

1. A dichotomy of company types: PMA and PMDN

In the vast majority of modern countries, a company is commonly categorized as either a public company or privately held company, depending on whether its securities are publicly traded on the open market; a government-owned company or private company, depending on government ownership; or a financial company or non-financial company, depending on its main business; and so on. Of course, these categorizations are generally used in Indonesia as well.

Unique to Indonesia, however, is a well-settled legal practice which distinguishes between companies with foreign direct investment (*penanaman modal asing*, or PMA) or companies with 100 percent domestic direct investment (*penanaman modal dalam negeri*, or PMDN). Government proposals concerning how to differently regulate these companies frequently become a national issue, as they are one of the main standards to evaluate how effectively and willingly the Indonesian government develops its economic policies. Not only that, but laws, regulations, and actual legal practice also treat the two types of companies differently. Although many foreign countries are also equipped with similar regulations of companies with foreign direct investment, for several reasons, Indonesia distinctively applies this dichotomy in many more situations.

The first reason is because of the historical catastrophes affecting the national economy in 1997 and 1998, which saw massive withdrawals of foreign investment. Indonesia has the lowest foreign inbound investment among the Association of Southeast Asian Nations (ASEAN) countries after the Asian economic crisis of 1997–1998, collapsing from its previous rank of 5th.[1] This was the

---

1 Indonesia recorded US$2.985 billion of inflow in annual averages from 1991 to 1996 and US$1.296 billion outflow from 1998 to 2002. The latter is the only case of withdrawals of investment outweighing inflow of inbound investment among ASEAN countries. For details, see United Nations Conference on Trade and Development, *World Investment Report*, New York and Geneva, 2003, p. 251.

only net outflow among ASEAN countries.[2] Employees who did not receive their full retirement allowance from withdrawing foreign companies violently protested, and by cutting off work to Indonesian companies, foreign project holders triggered a series of harsh demonstrations by Indonesian laborers. The notorious May 1998 riots of Indonesia, known as the 1998 Tragedy, brought on the resignation of President Suharto and the fall of the New Order government. Under these circumstances, the government, legislature, and public workers bitterly perceived the need for encouraging foreign investment as a more stable source of foreign capital than regular short-term financial investment.[3] Naturally, this scathing historical lesson resulted in a political climate that stressed foreign direct investment in the private sector. The 2007 Capital Investment Act (*UU No.25 Tahun 2007 tentang Penanaman Modal*) that defines and governs PMAs and PMDNs, directly mentions that its legal authority is the Decree of the People's Consultative Assembly concerning Economic Policy in the Context of Economic Democracy, which was legislated in 1998 as a result of these events.

The second reason is very ironic. As a world treasure trove of natural wildlife, Indonesia also has a history of ineffectively regulating foreign investment, bringing up substantial external diseconomies, particularly environmental exploitation, pollution, and negative impacts on indigenous people.[4] Due to the geographic and physiographic setting of Indonesia, the importance of environmental protection, particularly against damage caused by alien or foreign capital, has become an issue that cannot be emphasized enough. The 2007 Capital Investment Act sets forth the principle of environmentally sound investment (Article 3 Paragraph 1 Subsection h) and requires corporate social responsibility from every direct investor (Article 15). Interestingly enough, even the 2007 Company Act explicitly mandates a company conducting business related to natural resources must

2 The contrast between on the one hand, Indonesia, and on the other Thailand and South Korea, the two other East Asian countries most severely affected by the Asian economic crisis, is evident. The latter two countries never experienced net foreign direct investment outflows in any one year after the crisis. Hence, Indonesia endured the worst experiences of any large country in the East Asian region during the post-Asian economic crisis period. Thee Kian Wie, *Policies for Private Sector Development in Indonesia*, ADB Institute Discussion Paper No. 46, March 2006, p. 21.

3 After this sharp history lesson, Indonesia declared 2003 as the "Indonesia Investment Year," with a number of favorable policy changes to promote foreign direct investment and increase investor confidence. United Nations Conference on Trade and Development, 2003, p. 48. See also Je Seong Jeon, The Changing Relation between Indonesian State and Foreign Capital: Focusing on the Formation of the International Business Chamber after Democratization, *Korean Association of Southeast Asian Studies, the Southeast Asian Review*, Vol. 20, No. 1, p. 267; Thee Kian Wie, *supra* note 2, pp. 22–26.

4 Regarding the detailed history of how political interests and opening up foreign investment without effective regulations contributed to the external diseconomy, see Onkar Prasad Dwivedi, *Environmental Policies in the Third World: A Comparative Analysis*, Greenwood Press, 1995, pp. 91–104; and Ronnie D. Lipschutz & Judith Mayer, *Global Civil Society and Global Environmental Governance*, SUNY Press, 1996, pp. 179–181.

implement social and environmental responsibility policies under Article 74. Although corporate self-regulation and guidance standards on social responsibility, such as ISO 26000, recently began mandating social responsibility for corporations, it is still not very common to see a modern Company Act explicitly and mandatorily require corporate social responsibility.[5]

Lastly, Indonesia is also very well aware that generous treatment in favor of PMA companies may have negative impacts on its own development. Since independence in 1945, policies towards the private sector have often been influenced by considerations to promote the development of indigenous (*pribumi*) Indonesian entrepreneurship. These policies involved affirmative policies to promote *pribumi* entrepreneurship by restricting, and occasionally even banning, the economic activities of ethnic Chinese.[6] Even today, to upgrade its main economic engine from primary industry to secondary and tertiary industry, Indonesia still feels it needs to foster domestic business and guard its own small and middle-sized enterprises (SME) against foreign attempts to target the Indonesian market, or from "vulture capitalists" backed by giant funds. Article 13 of the 2007 Company Act also explicitly stipulates that the Government must establish business sectors that are reserved for SMEs, and guide and enhance its SMEs. This motive for industrial protectionism is directly contrary to the interests of encouraging the aforementioned foreign direct investment.

Yet this is not just a story of Indonesia. Professor Ha-joon Chang of Cambridge University indicates that all of today's rich countries use tariffs, subsidies, licensing, regulation, and other policy measures to promote particular industries over others, with considerable degrees of success. And, in the second half of the twentieth century, the governments of countries such as France, Finland, Norway, and Austria shaped and directed industrial development with great success through protection, subsidies and investments by state-owned enterprises.[7] Asian countries are no different. South Korea completely restricts foreign direct investment in more than 60 business fields, and it limits foreign direct investment from dozens more business fields through the Foreign Investment

---

5 There are some jurisdictions that stipulate corporate social responsibilities in company law. UK Companies Act 2006 requires directors to have regard to community and environmental issues when considering their duty to promote the success of their company and by the disclosure to be included in the Business Review. India has recently enforced the Companies Act 2013 to mandate the Corporate Social Responsibility in much detailed level. It requires that one-third of a company's board comprise independent directors; at least one board member be a woman; and the companies to disclose executive salaries as a ratio to the average employee's salary. The striking requirement is "2 percent rule": the board committee must ensure that the company spends at least 2 percent of the average net profits of the company made during the 3 immediately preceding financial years.

6 Thee Kian Wie, *supra* note 2, p. 4.

7 Ha-joon Chang, *23 Things They Don't Tell You about Capitalism: Thing 12–Governments Can Pick Winners*, 2011, Penguin Books.

Promotion Act and its enforcement decree.[8] Japan also maintains market entry barriers for protection of its own corporations.[9] Given that even these developed countries, already armed with their own behemoth corporations, are taking advantage of industrial protectionism, Indonesia seems to have good reason to differentiate between PMA companies and PMDN companies.

The 2007 Capital Investment Act and its enforcement regulations reflected strong demands to attract foreign investment and deep concerns over its side effects. Here, capital investment does not mean financial investment in the capital market, but instead direct investment in a business entity, such as a cash contribution for share subscription. Indeed, this Act and its regulations directly govern the practice of establishment, operation, change and dissolution of a company.

With this background, the Indonesian regulatory system governing privately held companies is largely divided across the 2007 Company Act (and related regulations) and the 2007 Capital Investment Act (and its related regulations). While the latter also governs purely native PMDN companies,[10] it has greater influence over PMA companies with foreign shareholders. Therefore, both academic discussion and legal practice regarding Indonesian companies require a thorough understanding of the 2007 Capital Investment Act. For these reasons, this book explains the Capital Investment Act in the wake of the Company Act.

2.   A brief history of Indonesian company law

The origin of *perseroan terbatas* (PT) is a European company model that stems from the beginning of the nineteenth century. The sparse 20 articles (Articles 36–56) of the initial Indonesian Commercial Act of 1847,[11] better known as

---

8 In the Organisation for Economic Cooperation and Development (OECD's) foreign direct investment restrictiveness index of 2016, Japan recorded 0.052, South Korea 0.135, and Indonesia recorded 0.315 (0 = open, 1 = closed).

9 "We have to guard against any unwarranted designation of issuers and we must seek to have this special restriction discarded as soon as possible. At the same time, I hope that foreign investors will conduct adequate investigations before entering the Japanese market. It is unfortunate and unfair if they regard some of our business practices as discriminatory just because they are unfamiliar with them. . . . Employees regard their jobs as life-long positions and feel as though they belong to a family. They are likely to be resentful of an invasion from outside the company; and customers and suppliers have similar feelings. These facts cannot be altered by legislation or government policy." Misao Tatsuta, Restrictions on Foreign Investment: Developments in Japanese Law, *Journal of International Law* Vol. 3, No. 357, 2014, pp. 163–164.

10 PMDN are governed by this law because the 2007 Capital Investment Act (*UU No. 25, 2007 tentang Penanaman Modal*) is a law unifying both the PMA Act (*UU No. 1, 1967 tentang Penanaman Modal Asing*) and PMDN Act (*UU No. 6, 1968 tentang Penanaman Modal Dalam Negeri*).

11 *Wetboek van Koophandel Staatsblad*, 1847, p. 23.

the Dutch East-Indies Commercial Code, introduced the initial company model with shareholder's limited liability, *naamloze vennootschap*. The term *naamloze vennootschap* originates from the French term *société anonyme*, which literally means anonymous society.

Thus, Indonesian company law has roots in French law via Dutch law, as the initial Indonesian Commercial Act was simply an Indonesian version of the Netherlands' Commercial Act of 1838, which itself had been developed from French Commercial Code of 1809, part of the Napoleonic Code. This initial company model, separating management from ownership, was innovative from a historical perspective, yet without a doubt was completely different from the corporate model widely used nowadays.[12]

After 1939, Indonesia began using the term *joint stock company* (*maskapai andil*) in the Ordinance of Indigenous Joint Stock Company.[13] This type of company had a short lifespan, and had a restriction on its ability to own land. It was originally limited to Java and Madura, yet was little used in actual practice.[14] Regardless, this dualism of having both the Commercial Code articles on the NV and joint stock companies continued until they were both superseded by the 1995 Company Act.

Although the Indonesian Commercial Code has been amended often since the country's independence in 1945, it originally merely restated Dutch law and lacked substantial elements of contemporary corporation law including merger and acquisitions, liquidation, protection of minority shareholders, management responsibilities, etc. Naturally, the gaps between law and actual practice became substantial as time went by. Finally, Indonesia legislated a new superseding law, the preface of which declares:

> The previous regulations regarding Limited Liability Companies, Wetboek van Koophandel, Statute 1847: 23, is no longer relevant to the development of economy and business area rapidly developing in an national and international level.

The term *perseroan terbatas* then began to be used. The new law was much more comprehensive than the old version and covered many of the conventions of modern corporate law, including rules on capital increase and decrease, and minority shareholder protections. Clearly, it was substantially influenced by the

---

12 The Code was composed of some basic rules, such as there being no personal liability for directors in management and crude articles such as substantially limited voting rights for shareholders depending on the total number of shares in company. For more details, see Introduction of the Dutch Commercial Code in 1848 in Petra Mahy's 2013 article The Evolution of Company Law in Indonesia: An Exploration of Legal Innovation and Stagnation, *American Journal of Comparative Law* Vol. 61, No. 2, pp. 384–389.

13 *Ordonnantie op de Indonesische Maatschappij op Aandeelen, Staatsblad 1939:569 jo. 717.* In Indonesian, *Ordonansi Maskapai Andil Indonesia.*

14 Mahy, *supra* note 12, p. 398.

U.S. law, with aspects including mergers and acquisition, piercing the corporate veil, directors' duties and business judgment rules, etc.[15] Finally, by introducing new company laws in 2007 (the 2007 Company Act), Indonesia filled in some details missing from the previous law, adding laws regarding special shareholders' meetings, creditor opposition against acquisition, additional director liabilities, the board of commissioner's authority to temporarily dismiss a director, and others. Some unique features distinctive from company law in other countries were also introduced in the Shariah Supervisory Board (*Dewan Pengawas Syariah*) as an additional board for all Islamic businesses governed by *shariah*, and a mandatory corporate social responsibility requirement for companies engaged in natural resource exploitation. In the end, this new law is appraised as additionally adopting a rough sketch of contemporary corporation laws.

In sum, Indonesia transplanted the Dutch company model from the nineteenth century and finally adopted the modern civil law corporation model, with substantial influence from the U.S. law. Although some Dutch heritage may still be found, such as the use of the Board of Commissioners in Dutch style,[16] the current PT is undeniably a corporation.

The Indonesian legal practice of translating PT as "limited liability company" often misleads foreigners from common law countries. In English legal terminology, Indonesia's limited liability company is simply a corporation. A limited liability company in the United States normally means a private limited company that combines pass-through taxation of a partnership or sole proprietorship with limited liability, although it may have some variations depending on the state. Also, because PT literally means limited (*terbatas*) company (*perseroan*), and a literal translation of both the Korean *yuhan huesa* and Japanese *yuugen kaisha* also means limited company, PT also often misleads legal minds from South Korea or Japan.

Today's PT is simply a corporation. To be more specific, it is a type of C-corporation since Indonesia does not recognize S-corporations. Nonetheless, this book mainly calls a PT a company, since actual Indonesian practice has already used the term limited liability company for more than two decades. For the same reason, *PT Terbuka* (or PT Tbk) is also called a public company.

As this book mainly analyzes and studies the 2007 Company Act, the articles and paragraphs referred to without mentioning specific laws are from the 2007 Company Act.

15 Mahy, *supra* note 11, p. 412.
16 Mahy, *supra* note 11, p. 418.

2 Establishment of a company

Article 1 of No. 25 2007 Capital Investment Act[1] defines domestic investment (*penanaman modal dalam negeri*, or PMDN) as investment to conduct business in Indonesia by a domestic investors using domestic capital, and foreign direct investment (*penanaman modal asing*, or PMA) as investment to conduct business in Indonesia by foreign investors with foreign capital, which may also include domestic investors. In general, as noted above, under the 2007 Capital Investment Act, a purely domestic enterprise is called a PMDN company (or simply a PMDN), and those companies with foreign direct investment are called PMA companies (or just a PMA).

Whether a PMDN or PMA, the establishment of a company is subject to the 2007 Company Act and relevant regulations. A PMDN can be established much faster and more simply than a PMA, as it does not need to comply with laws and regulations related to foreign direct investment. This section explains in general the relevant regulations regarding the establishment of a company according to the 2007 Company Act, and the next section subsequently describes the separate and additional regulations in regard to establishing a PMA.

1. Founder

The founder, or *pendiri*, is a person who creates the corporation and undertakes the preliminary work incidental to the formation of company.[2] At least two (or more) persons are required to establish a company and, most importantly, shall become shareholders of the company by acquiring the initially issued shares. The exception is where such incorporation is made by consolidation of two different companies.

1 UU No. 25 Th. 2007 tentang Penanaman Modal
2 Generally in the United States, "incorporator" means the person who creates the corporate existence by signing and filing the articles of association, while "corporate promoter" means a person who does the preliminary work incidental to the formation of company, such as soliciting people to invest money into a corporation. In Indonesia, *Pendiri* means a founder who does both or either of incorporator's and promoter's work and, most importantly, purchases some of the initially issued shares.

Thus, the founders are the actual owners of the business in principle, and employees or members of the law firm handling the establishment process are not referred to as either founders or incorporators. It is also noteworthy that a single-shareholder structure is not allowed at the establishment stage. If only one shareholder remains after the establishment stage, the company must find a new shareholder within 6 months. Should the company still be owned by a single shareholder after 6 months from establishment, he or she should personally assume all the rights and obligations of the company, and the company is then liquidated.[3]

The founder shall be an Indonesian citizen or legal entity in principle. A foreigner, or foreign entity, can only become a shareholder in certain situations allowed under separate laws and regulations.

1.1. *Founder's responsibilities in the establishment of a company*

Article 7 (2)

Each founder of a Company must subscribe shares at the time the company is established.

Article 9 (1)

To obtain the Minister's Decree with regard to the ratification of the Company as a legal entity as stated in Article 7 Paragraph (4), the founders shall jointly submit an application . . .

Article 10 (9)

In the event that the application to obtain the Minister's Decree is not submitted within the period stated in Paragraph (1) (i.e. 60 days from the signing date of the deed of establishment), the deed of establishment will become void by the lapse of time and the Company which has not retained a legal entity status shall be liquidated by operation of law and the founders shall be responsible for its affairs.

---

3 Whether the law allows single-shareholder structure or not, a company has the nature of a group entity. Etymologically, *company* means a number of people eating a bread (pane) together (com-), corporation is from *corporare* (combined in one body) in Latin, and either *gongsi* in Chinese, *hwesa* in Korean or *kaisha* in Japanese all mean a group. Allowing a single-shareholder structure as is done nowadays in many jurisdictions is simply for convenience only, not to change the nature of the company itself.

Article 12 (1)

The founders' legal acts in relation to the ownership and payment of shares prior to establishment of the Company shall be recorded in the deed of establishment.

Article 13

(1) The founder's legal acts for a Company's interest prior to establishment shall be binding the Company after the Company becomes a legal entity if the first general shareholders' meeting of the Company explicitly states that it accepts or assume all the rights and obligations out of such a legal act performed by the founders or their proxies.

(2) The first general shareholders' meeting in Paragraph (1) shall be held not more than 60 days from date when the Company obtains a legal entity status.

(3) The resolution of the general shareholders' meeting in Paragraph (2) shall be lawful if the general shareholders' meeting is attended by those shareholders representing all the voting-rights shares and approved unanimously.

(4) In the event that the general shareholders' meeting is not held within the period as stated in Paragraph (2) or the general shareholders' meeting does not adopt the resolution as stated in Paragraph (3), each of the founders who performed such legal acts shall be personally liable for the consequences thereof.

(5) The general shareholders' meeting's approval in Paragraph (2) is not required if the legal act has been performed or approved in writing by all of the founders before the establishment.

Article 14

(1) Legal acts on behalf of a Company which has not obtained a legal entity status may only be performed by all the members of the Board of Directors, all the founders and all the members of the Board of Commissioners of the Company and all of them will be jointly and severally liable for the legal acts.

(2) In the event that the legal acts in Paragraph (1) are performed by the founders on behalf of a Company which has not obtained a legal entity status, the founders shall be liable for such legal acts and the legal acts shall not bind the Company.

(3) The Company shall by operation of law be liable for the legal acts in Paragraph (1) after the Company becomes a legal entity.

(4) The Company shall only be bound by and liable for the legal acts in Paragraph (2) after the legal acts are approved by all the shareholders

in a general shareholders' meeting attended by all of the Company's shareholders.

(5) The general shareholders' meeting in Paragraph (4) is the first general shareholder meeting which shall be held no later than 60 days after the Company obtains the legal entity status.

Article 94 (2)

The first members of the Board of Directors shall be appointed by the founders through the deeds of establishment stated in Article 8 (2) b.

Article 111 (2)

The first members of the Board of Commissioners shall be appointed by the founders through the deeds of establishment stated in Article 8 (2) b.

Among those involved in establishment of a company, founders have pivotal functions and strict responsibilities. These responsibilities are divided into when the company has been established and when it has not, and the responsibilities in the former case are again divided into the responsibility for capital repletion and the responsibility to remedy a damage. The responsibility of capital repletion means the responsibility to acquire issued shares with payment in full.

1.1.1.   *Before establishment of a company*

Even if the founder had begun preparation for establishment, such as drafting a deed of establishment, a company may not actually be established, and it may fail to receive a written approval from the Ministry of Law and Human Rights (MLHR) for several reasons. If the deed of establishment has not even been drafted, there seems to be no need to refer the 2007 Company Act at all. It would be simply a matter to claim a personal responsibility between the founder and the third party. Therefore, the provision about a founder's responsibility in failing to establish a company would become applicable only where a deed of establishment has been made.

Should the founders fail to establish a company (i.e. a *de jure* corporation), the founders remain liable for related acts. If there is more than one founder, all related founders are considered jointly and severally liable, although the 2007 Company Act does not explicitly state this. This provision about founder liability aims to prevent a founder's hasty acts in preparation of establishment and to fully protect share subscribers and creditors of the company being established (i.e. allowing the formation of a *de facto* corporation or corporation by estoppel) where there is no better relevant party to take responsibility. Therefore, when claiming the founder's responsibility pursuant to this article, the founder's negligence is not an element.

In circumstances that a business organization has failed to become a *de jure* company (a company by law), the founder should return any deposit, cash, or property given for share subscription and either perform or restitute the contracts for establishment of company including employment, office lease, etc.

1.1.2. After establishment of a company

The date of establishment is the date when the MLHR issues written approval of the company's legal entity status. This is the same for a PMA or PMDN.

1.1.2.1. RESPONSIBILITIES TO THE COMPANIES

Founders are responsible for subscription and payment in regard to all issued shares for repletion of the company's capital. Each founder takes this responsibility at the time of establishment. Article 7 Paragraph 2 of the 2007 Company Act merely states: "Each founder of a Company must subscribe shares at the time the company is established." This does not explicitly presume the founders' joint ownership of the shares,[4] thus, a question remains as to the ownership of any unsubscribed shares.

First, if any shares are not subscribed due to any fault by the founders, these shares will not be regarded as owned by either the company or any third party. Thus, theoretically, all the founders will presumptively have a deemed joint ownership and payment responsibilities thereof pursuant to Article 13 Paragraph 4 and Article 14 Paragraph 2. Despite this theoretical foregone conclusion, the ownership would be waffling and noncommittal in practice, which always requires documents formally specifying the subscription with the subscriber's signature, and the subscriber's possession of the share certificate.

What if share subscriptions become invalid due to the subscriber's incompetence, fraud, or representation without authority? While many countries solve this issue with an explicit statute,[5] the 2007 Company Act remains silent. Insofar as the law does not state otherwise, Article 13 Paragraph 4 and Article 14 Paragraph 2 would still govern subscription, and ultimately the founders would be the main parties to take over responsibility. Even in this case, where in theory

---

4 An example of an explicit presumption is Paragraph 1 of Article 321 (Liability of Incorporators for Subscription and Security for Payment) of the Korean Commercial Act, which stipulates: "Where, after a company comes into existence, any shares issued at the time of incorporation of the company are found to have not been subscribed to or the subscription for certain shares has been cancelled, incorporators *shall be deemed to have jointly subscribed to such shares*" (emphasis added).
5 An example of such an explicit statute is Paragraph 1 of Article 320 (Restrictions on Asserting Invalidation or Cancellation of Share Subscription) of the Korean Commercial Act which stipulates: "Once a company comes into existence, no subscriber may assert the invalidation of his/her subscription by reason of deficiency in the requirements for the share subscription form, nor may cancel his/her subscription on the ground of fraud, duress or mistake."

the stocks must have been jointly owned by the founders, stock ownership would fall into "neither flesh nor fowl" under Indonesian formalism, which always requires specific documents and subscriber possession of stock certificates.

What if share subscriptions are cancelled for reasons of a subscriber's mistake or a third party's coercion or fraud? The end result would be the same as the above in the absence of a relevant provision in the 2007 Company Act.

This approach to shift the subscription and payment responsibility to the founders is consistent with civil law. In a number of common law jurisdictions, such a responsibility belongs to the party who agreed to purchase the shares, not a founder. Hence the company in these jurisdictions can directly seek proper remedies from the very party in default.[6]

1.1.2.2. RESPONSIBILITIES TO THIRD PARTIES

If a third party is damaged or harmed because a contract becomes invalid due to a failure to receive an approval from the general shareholders' meeting as required by Article 13 and 14, the founders become personally liable for the damages and harms. This founder liability is for the protection of third parties, and it is similar to the director's liability to a third party in Article 97.

This legal responsibility, specifically recognized by 2007 Company Act for the protection of third parties, should be viewed as separate from torts liability. Thus, if the founder's act also satisfies the legal elements of a particular tort at the same time, the damaged party can claim responsibility under both tort law and the 2007 Company Act, in which case the statutes of limitation of each responsibility should be applied in parallel.

Protected third parties include share subscribers, shareholders, or contractors to the company, and yet it seems hard to accept shareholders damaged by a drop in stock price of the company caused by a founder's wrongful behavior as protected third parties.[7]

1.2.   *Personal benefits to the founders*

Where the founders make an arrangement or form a contract in the process of establishing a company, it may run the risk of harming other shareholders or creditors of the company upon establishment. Thus, each country generally

---

6 For example, New York Business Corporation Law §503 (Subscription for share; time of payment, forfeiture for default) (d): "In the event of default in the payment of any install-ment or call when due, the corporation may proceed to collect the amount due in the same manner as any debt due the corporation or the board may declare a forfeiture of the sub-scriptions . . . "

7 No successful claim based on a drop in stock price has been found. The difficulties in this claim among others is proving a direct causation between exact price drop and founder's wrongful behavior, and the calculation of precise price drop itself.

regulates these types of transactions through company or corporation law. For example, Germany names these transactions as *qualified establishment* (*qualifizierte Gründung*) under Articles 26–35 of the Stock Corporation Act (AktG), and South Korea collectively calls them *abnormal incorporation* (*byunte sullib*) under Article 290 of Corporation Act. The following are examples of these sorts of transactions:[8]

- Granting special benefits[9]
- Cost and expenses in establishment[10]
- Transfer of property to a company after establishment[11]
- In-kind contributions[12]

Special benefits mean the founder's certain gains from his dedication and service provided to the company even despite the risk that he may take all the responsibilities upon failures. Thus, even if the founder took an extremely high risk and contributed considerable effort, he or she still cannot enjoy any special benefits from the repletion-of-capital requirements (i.e. exemption of obligation to pay for the acquired shares), from the principle of equality in same stock (i.e. no special arrangements for a founder shareholder's voting rights), or the nature of corporate governance (e.g. arrangement to remain as a perpetual director without any limitation). Thus, special benefits are stipulated as one of qualified, or abnormal, establishment.

Cost and expenses in establishment means any foundation costs incurred to the founder, such as fees to lease an office, costs to solicit potential investors, payment to officials working on the establishment of the company, advertising costs, etc. Under German and South Korean law, for example, because overvaluation may overburden the company and give the incorporator or promoter excessive payment, this sort of transaction should also be explicitly recorded on the certificate of incorporation in order for the company to assume the responsibilities incurred in the transaction.

Transfer of property to a company after establishment means a special arrangement between the founder and another founder or a third party that the company should purchase a certain asset from the founder or the third party after the

---

8 There are other qualified transactions depending on the country. For example, an audit report for incorporation created by a founder and not an independent external auditor (§34 AktG 1965) and acquisition of shares by a member of a supervisory board or board of directors who was also a founder (§33 AktG 1965).
9 §26 AktG 1965 and §290 (1) Korean Commercial Act.
10 §26 AktG 1965.
11 §290 (3) Korean Commercial Act. This transaction is also often called *ex post facto* incorporation, because even a lawful and legitimate incorporation at the time may be retrospectively regarded as unlawful and void depending on whether such an arrangement is lawfully performed.
12 §27 AktG 1965 and §290 (2) Korean Commercial Act.

company is fully established. This arrangement aims to simply avoid all the hassles regarding in-kind contribution. For example, the arrangement may state "all the equipment recorded as assets of the company's financial statements shall be purchased from stationary store ABC 60 days after the deed of establishment is issued." This type of transaction is virtually the same as in-kind contributions, and thus any establishment agreement or contract containing such a transaction would be regarded as a qualified or abnormal establishment.

In-kind contribution means a subscription of shares with non-cash consideration. Any overvaluation of in-kind property would matter as well. Because Indonesian company law has separate provisions governing this type of transaction, the details are explained in the next section on in-kind contributions.

The genius of Indonesian company law is found here. Except for some types of in-kind contribution, it does not regulate each of the above transactions separately. Instead, it simply forbids "founder's personal benefits" (*pemberian manfaat pribadi*) to be written into the deed of establishment, so that such an arrangement cannot bind the company once established. This approach seems fresh, because this simple sentence, "*the articles of association may not contain provisions concerning the grant of personal benefits to the founders or other parties,*" effectively frustrates the very aim of all the above qualified transactions (e.g. giving personal benefits by overvaluation of in-kind property, reimbursement agreements for the cost and expense of foundation, or stating special rights, thereby potentially harming creditors and other shareholders of the company). Moreover, this also frustrates all the other types of potential qualified transactions without specifically listing them one by one. Undoubtedly, this single article could be deemed too comprehensive and thus too obscure for an ordinary person, particularly the actual founders or related individuals who may not understand challenging and difficult legal terms. Therefore, it may have been better to state each potential problematic transaction in a manner similar to the approach of German and South Korean law, and then use Article 15 Paragraph 3 Item b to cover any other potentially problematic transactions.

In conclusion, the point of Article 15 Paragraph 3 Item b is that any arrangement to give special benefits to the founder or a third party – including potentially overvalued foundation costs or property – should not be included in the deed of establishment and that a company will not be thereby bound. Because all those qualified or abnormal establishment transactions can be assumed by the company only when the requirements in Article 14 are satisfied in full, the actual practice in similar transactions do not seem very different from South Korea or other countries.

In the case that a company forms such a contract before establishment (i.e. before receiving the declaration of establishment issued by the MLHR), every single director, founder and commissioner of the company must approve or agree to such a transaction, as a result of which they will all be jointly and severally liable for the transaction pursuant to Article 14(1). To interpret Article 14 Paragraph 1 and 3 congruously, those contractual rights and obligations obtained in the name of company are thought to temporarily belong to the *persekutuan perdata* (or *maatschap*), composed of directors, founders and commissioners, and only be transferred to the company at the time when the company becomes a legal entity by obtaining the declaration of establishment.

In the meantime, in the event that the founder forms a contract on behalf of the company before its establishment, he or she should receive approval from all the shareholders at the first general shareholders' meeting within 60 days after the issuance date of establishment declaration. Otherwise, the contractual liabilities and obligations will solely belong to the founder or *persekutuan perdata* of the founders, whereby the founders shall be jointly and severally liable for the contract. Because the transaction cannot be written into the deed of establishment, the founders cannot claim against the company.

In the event that the founder fails to receive an approval from all the shareholders in the first general shareholders' meeting, it remains unclear whether the company can still voluntarily assume the contract by a separate procedure, such as mutual transfer and assumption agreement, or the company's unilateral ratification of the unauthorized representation.

2. Minimum capital

In general, minimum capital of 10 billion Indonesian rupiah (IDR) is required upon establishment of a company (BKPM Regulation 13/2017). This minimum capital requirement may be higher, however, depending on the type of business the company will conduct, such as banking, insurance, freight forwarding, etc. For example, a company that desires to conduct freight forwarding (*jasa pengurusan transportasi*) is required to have at least IDR 25 billion of initial authorized capital.

A minimum 25 percent of the initial authorized capital should be subscribed and paid.[13] These can be proven by the company's bank accounts, or in financial statements, either fully audited or signed by the company's board of directors and board of commissioners. In the case of a PMA, opening a bank account under the company's name is impermissible before establishment is completed. Thus, a public notary's formal statement of the plan for capital remittance upon establishment should be alternatively submitted.

According to Article 31, Paragraph 1, a share acquirer may make an investment *in kind* as well as in cash. Since an overvalued in-kind contribution may harm not only the company's capital value, but also creditors and cash investors,

---

13 In principle, an inquiry regarding the third party's bank account balance is not allowed. Thus, those who desire to establish a small company with limited funds often use a record of repeated deposits and withdrawals of small amounts in order to create a supporting document. Given that certain types of companies, such as application developers or consulting businesses require only a small amount of initial operating funds, the trend in company law internationally is to remove this minimum capital requirement. For example, South Korea removed it in 2009.

the company should (i) receive a valuation from an independent expert, particularly where such in-kind contribution is not a cash equivalent, and (ii) record the contribution in the deed of establishment. In-kind contribution is explained in detail in a later section on founder personal benefits.

3.   Deed of establishment

Akta Pendirian is the equivalent of a Certificate of Incorporation in the United States; however, in practice, "Deed of Establishment" is the more widely used English translation. The Deed should contain (i) the articles of association and (ii) other information related to establishment of the company, as stated in Paragraph 2 of Article 8 of the Act. However, "legal acts performed by the prospective founders in relation to the ownership of shares and paying in before the Company is established" are not necessarily required to be recorded, and thus the establishment of the company remains valid and effective without such a record, although the rights and obligations related the founder's activities that are not recorded would not belong to the company.

3.1.   *Articles of association:* Anggaran Dasar

A Company's articles of association should contain all the following (Article 15, Paragraph 1):

- The Company's name and domicile
- The purposes and objectives and field of business of the Company
- The Company's period of incorporation
- The amount of the authorized capital, subscribed capital, and paid-up capital
- The number of shares, classifications of shares (if any, including the number of shares for each classification), the rights attaching to each share, and the nominal value of each share
- The name, position, and number of members of the Board of Directors and Board of Commissioners
- The determination of the place and procedure for holding a shareholders' meeting
- The procedures for the appointment, replacement, and dismissal of members of the Board of Directors and Board of Commissioners
- The procedure for the use of profits and allocation of dividends

If any of the above items are omitted, the entire articles of association becomes invalid and ineffective. Particularly, Article 107 requires the following items to be recorded in terms of Board of Directors:

- Procedures for the resignation of members of the Board of Directors
- Procedures for filling vacant positions on the Board of Directors

- Names of parties who have the authority to undertake the management of and represent the Company in the event that all of the members of the Board of Directors are prevented from doing so or have been suspended

Insofar as observing laws and regulations, the articles of association may also contain other provisions apart from the aforementioned mandatory items. However, even in this case, it should not contain:

- Provisions concerning receipt of fixed interest on shares
- Provisions concerning the grant of personal benefits to the founders or other parties[14]

Although the law remains silent on this issue, undoubtedly any items contrary to the nature of the company or any matters infringing shareholders' intrinsic rights should not be included. A clear example of such an inclusion would be the receipt of fixed interest on shares.

3.2. Other information related to the establishment of the company

Article 8 Paragraph 2 requires the recording of the following items:

- Where the founders of the company are individual persons, the full name, date and place of birth, occupation, residence, and nationality of the individual founders.
- Where the founder of the company is a legal entity, the domicile and full address and number and date of the Minister's Decree regarding the ratification of legal entity founders.
- The full name, date and place of birth, occupation, residence, and nationality of members of the first Board of Directors and Board of Commissioners to be appointed.
- The names of shareholders who have subscribed shares, details of the number of shares, and the nominal value of the shares subscribed and paid up.

3.3. Submission of the deed of establishment

Application for legal status can be made by a public notary's submission of the Deed of Establishment on behalf of the founders to the MLHR within 60 days from the signing date of the deed. Once all the relevant documents are completed and the MLHR approves the use of the corporate name, the notary public should submit the Model Format I called *Isian Akta Notaris: FIAN* via MLHR's

---

14 Paragraph 3, Article 15. Therefore, an arrangement providing a founder personal benefits when establishing the company, related to the cost and expenses or acquisition of assets, also cannot be recorded. For further details, see the section on personal benefits to founders.

administration system (*Sisminbakum*).[15] The result can be seen on MLHR's webpage. If the submission is made after 60 days from the signing date of the deed, the application will be rendered invalid, and the *de facto* company will automatically fail to obtain legal status. Any omitted or unusual item may be sent back to the notary for further clarification. The notary should then directly submit the original copy of the application form and attached documents on behalf of the founders within 30 days from the date of the MLHR feedback.[16]

In order to issue the declaration of approval of the establishment of the company (*Keputusan Menteri Hukum dan Hak Asasi Manusia untuk Pendirian Perseroan Terbatas* or simply *Surat Keputusan*), the MLHR should publish the announcement (*Pengumuman*) of the declaration through the state gazette, called *TBN RI*,[17] within 14 days of the approval date. Because this is the MLHR's obligation, the company is not required to keep the copy of this approval in its office. Nevertheless, it is known as one of the typical documents for legal due diligence when the company is later sold, or if the company later desires to receive an external investment from or consolidation with a third party. Regardless, in practice, most Indonesian companies obtain and retain this document.

4.   In-kind contributions

4.1. Definition

"In-kind contribution" means a contribution of property, service, contractual rights, or any form other than cash. Indonesian company law does not explicitly regulate in-kind contributions. Nonetheless, it appears to be regulated as a type of transaction that could give a personal benefit to a founder, since overvaluation of the in-kind property may let the founder indulge inflated gains and consequently infringe the rights of other creditors or cash contributors. For public companies (*perusahaan terbuka*), Rule No. 32/POJK.04/2015 on Capital Increases in Public Companies with Pre-emptive Rights (POJK No. 32/2015)[18] is further applied.

Inasmuch as the economic value of any contributed property in other forms (*bentuk lainnya*) than cash is reasonably and sufficiently measurable, the type of form must not be limited pursuant to Paragraph 1 of Article 34. In other words, in-kind contributions generally include cash equivalents, property, labor, services, contracts to furnish cash or property at a certain time, and promises

---

15 Indonesian legal entity administration system information technology service (*jasa teknologi informasi sistem administrasi badan hukum*): http://eprints.undip.ac.id/16450/.
16 If required to check the types of documents in detail for submission, see Article 7 of Nomor: M-01-HT.01–10 Tahun 2007 Tentang Tata Cara Mengajuan Permohonan Pengesahan Badan Hukum Dan Persetujuan Perubuhan Anggaran Dasar, Penyampaian pemberitahuan Perubahan Anggaran Dasar Dan Perubahan Data Perseroa.
17 Tambahan Berita Negara Republik Indonesia.
18 Peraturan Otoritas Jasa Keuangan Nomor 32 /POJK.04/2015 Tentang Enambahan Modal Perusahaan Terbuka Dengan Memberikan.

to provide certain services in the future, as long as it has some economic value. It would therefore exclude any consideration whose economic value is too small to recognize, such as watered stock with an artificially inflated value, or a stock subscribed without payment. Importantly, it is extremely hard to accept technology or know-how transfer as an in-kind contribution because of the difficulty in objectively measuring its value.

In addition to in-kind payments, POJK No. 32/2015 allows financial receivables to be used as payment for shares of a public company, provided that such receivables have been disclosed in the public company's most recent audited financial statements.

4.2. Requirement of shareholder ratification

A founder's acts related to share subscription prior to establishment of company must be written in the deed of establishment (Article 12 Paragraph 1 of the 2007 Company Act). Thus, a founder who contributed property, service, or promises instead of cash should specify this on the deed. Even though establishment of company itself would never be negated solely because of the founder's failure to list a contribution on the deed, any contribution not included would not belong to the company, nor could the contributor bind the company (Article 12 Paragraph 4 of the 2007 Company Act).

In order to bind such a contribution to the company without inclusion in the deed, the first general shareholders' meeting must ratify the contribution. The company is required to hold its first shareholders' meeting within 60 days from MLHR's issuance of establishment approval (i.e. the date when the company obtains legal entity status). At this meeting, the contribution should be agreed to by shareholders representing the entire voting rights of the company. A founder will be solely responsible for the contribution should the first general shareholders' meeting not be held within 60 days, or the quorum not be satisfied, or the vote not be agreed to by all shareholders.

4.3. Preemptive rights

Except for the all-encompassing but vague Article 15 Paragraph 3 Item b, and valuation of property contribution, there is no particular requirement or procedure that specifically regards protecting shareholder preemptive rights against in-kind contributions to a privately held company under the 2007 Company Act. Neither a provision in articles of association nor a shareholder resolution is needed for a company to receive an in-kind payment for shares. Nor is there a particular qualification to be an in-kind contributor. This implies the possibility that a general shareholder's preemptive rights may not be applied to an in-kind contribution. However, at least for a public company, POJK No. 32/2015 prevents this problem by explicitly necessitating a majority shareholder's declaration whether it intends to exercise its rights or to assign them to a third party. Nonetheless, in the absence of a referable precedent for a privately held company, opinions are divided.

One opinion is that preexisting shareholders' preemptive rights would not be applied in the case of a property contribution to a privately held company. This view maintains that Indonesian company law does not necessitate approval or agreement from shareholders on in-kind contributions, and thus these are matters to be decided solely at the board's discretion. The view further claims that preexisting shareholders will not be damaged or harmed simply because of decreased ownership rates because, in the general practice of in-kind contributions, the property contributor has already been specified in advance. For the same reason, preemptive rights are not applied when it comes to a share subscription due to corporate restructuring, such as statutory merger (Article 43 Paragraph 3 Item c), securities converted into shares such as bond with warrants, convertible bonds, convertible stock, etc. (Article 43 Paragraph 3 Item b), and employee stock ownership plans (Article 43 Paragraph 3 Item a).

If preexisting shareholders' preemptive rights are applicable to property contributions to privately held companies, another legal consequence to take into account is tax imposition. Let us suppose that PT *A* has a total of 100 issued shares at IDR 1 million per share, all of which are owned by 10 different shareholders. To receive a property evaluated at IDR 400 million as a contribution from a certain individual, PT *A* duly makes a shareholder resolution to increase the total issued shares from 100 to 500 shares, and further issue 400 shares to the property contributor. In this hypothetical case, 400 new shares are issued to the property contributor with the sacrifice of other shareholders' preemptive rights. Then, the newly issued shares over and above the other shareholder's proportional preemptive rights may be deemed a gift from the preexisting shareholders, upon which as a result gift tax could be imposed. The Indonesian tax authority seems to presume that in this situation preexisting shareholders have transferred their shares to the property contributor subscribing all the newly issued shares, and does not impose a gift tax.

In my opinion, preemptive rights must be applied to in-kind payments to a privately held company because: (i) in all three cases under Article 43 Paragraph 3, shareholders could reasonably expect the individual would subscribe to a certain number of shares in a specific time period, whereas they could not be certain in the case of in-kind payments (in other words, preexisting shareholders' rights could be harmed to a great degree when the board of directors decides at its sole discretion to approve a third party's in-kind contribution for shares, although the third party may be in fierce ownership competition against them); (ii) Article 43 Paragraph 3 excludes in-kind contributions for shares from exceptions to preemptive rights; and (iii) to hold the interpretation of regulations for a privately held company consistent with those for a public company.

4.4. *Valuation*

If the consideration for share subscriptions does not have a fair market value, a valuation from an independent appraiser is required (Paragraph 2 of Article 34). Wrongful valuation (i.e. overvaluation or undervaluation) may be then an issue.

Founders either establish a company by themselves or with other investors, which may not trigger a need for market value appraisal before making the deed of establishment, because a thorough check and good management alone can immediately detect and amend errors. In particular, Indonesia does not differentiate between the establishment process when it is only by founders or includes other investors. Nor, in situations where an appraiser is required, does Indonesia stipulate a specific appraiser appointment process by the court, nor does it stipulate the appraiser's reporting process to the inaugural meeting of the *de facto* company.

Instead, Indonesian law requires a shareholder register to contain information on shares paid up in other forms (Article 50 Paragraph 1 Item e) and enumerates certain conditions where a professional appraiser is required, who must be free from a conflict of interest as per elucidation of Article 34 Paragraph 2. Such an expert should not have any of the following:

- A family relationship either by marriage or lineage up to the second degree, horizontally or vertically, with an employee, a member of the Board of Directors or Board of Commissioners, or a shareholder of the Company
- A relationship with the company due to a similarity with one or more members of the Board of Directors or Board of Commissioners
- A relationship to the control of the Company, whether directly or indirectly
- Shares in the company in the amount of 20 percent or more

There are several professional Indonesian companies who provide objective evaluation services.[19]

Where real property or other types of immoveable property are contributed for a share subscription, a public announcement should be made through one or more newspapers within 14 days after signing the deed of establishment or after a resolution issued by a general shareholders' meeting. Considering the substantial number of disputes around real property ownership in Indonesia, this article seems to allow any interest holder in the real property of interest time to oppose and to stave off any potential trouble. Because Article 1 Paragraph 14 states that the newspaper must be an "daily newspaper in the Indonesia language with national circulation," an electronic newspaper should be sufficient.

4.5. *Default on in-kind contributions*

Where a share subscriber defaults on the agreement to contribute property before the company is established, the subscriber's performance can be enforced pursuant to their contract. If the default is due to impossibility, one can simply

---

19 SGS, Sucofindo and other similar companies seem to be widely used for this type of service in Indonesia.
Sucofindo's website: www.sucofindo.co.id/; SGS's website: www.sgs.co.id/.

terminate the contract, proceed to amend the deed, and move on to the next step for establishment.

The problem is where the company has been already established. If termination of the contract causes rescission of the contract, thereby placing the parties in the position they would have been had the contract never been entered into, then a substantial part of the company's capital will be withdrawn. Indonesian company law does not allow this situation, in order to protect the other interest holders. If the contract is enforceable, the company should seek enforcement. Otherwise, the founders should be personally liable for the default in the event, for example, that the promised property becomes irrevocably valueless, or a share subscriber becomes incompetent or incapable of performing.

4.6.   Advice for practice

It is advisable to consider whether (i) to directly contribute the asset, (ii) to sell the asset to the company and then subsequently purchase the company's shares with the payment made, or (iii) to sell the asset to the company without receiving payment, and then swap the debt to equity in the company. If the asset is from a foreign country, the imposed tax could be substantially different depending on the country and the type of asset; for instance, Indonesia may impose tax while the foreign country exempts it. Therefore, it is desirable to obtain advice from tax experts in both Indonesia and the foreign country.

A valuation report for the asset contributed from a foreign country should be made in English, by a certified document translation and notarization service.

5.   Miscellaneous

5.1.   Date of establishment

The effective date of establishment of the company is the date the declaration (*Surat Keputusan*) of approval (Article 7 Paragraph 4 of the Company Act) is obtained.

5.2.   Nationality of directors

There is no requirement that a director's nationality or citizenship be Indonesian, whether a PMA or a PMDN. That is, the board of directors may be composed entirely of foreigners in general.

5.3.   Principle license (Izin Prinsip) and Registration of Capital Investment

Prior to the BKPM Regulation 13/2017, the Principle License or *Izin Prinsip* was required for establishment of a PMA company. It was approval of the Indonesia Investment Coordinating Board (BKPM) of a share subscription (i) where a company was established as either a PMA or PMDN, (ii) where a PMA wanted to convert its status to a PMDN, or (iii) where a PMDN wanted to change its status to a PMA. Thus, the shares were required to be subscribed within the terms of the Principle License. Although the 2007 Company Act is silent on this issue, this formality have been a mandatory requirement under BKPM Reg. 14/2015, authorized by 2007 Capital Investment Act requirements.

Now, however, the BKPM Regulation 13/2017 has removed this license requirement and instead has introduced a new type of license, the Registration of Capital Investment. It only applies to the PMA companies in certain type of business: (i) construction business; (ii) business that is entitled to investment facilities; (iii) business that has potentials of environmental pollution; (iv) business involved in national defense; or (v) natural resources management, energy, and infrastructure. These business can only begin after obtaining a business license.

5.4. *Opening a bank account*

Because a founder of company has virtually no option but to open a bank account to receive cash contributions for shares in today's legal practice, the founder's responsibilities of capital repletion stated in the 2007 Company Act seem to be legislated under the assumption that opening a bank account for the new company is inevitably necessary. Still, opening a company's bank account is not a requirement of establishment, but simply preparation for business.

To open a bank account for a company being established, the following documents should be submitted to the bank: (i) the declaration of establishment (*Surat Keputusan*) issued by the MLHR; (ii) the Deed of Establishment; (iii) NPWP from the tax authority; and (iv) business registration (*Tanda Daftar Perusahan*, or TDP) issued from the regional government (*Pemerinta Daerah*, or PEMDA). While some Asian countries such as South Korea and Japan require a registered corporate seal and relevant certificate, Indonesia does not. A bank account will usually be opened within 7–10 Jakarta business days once all documents have been adequately prepared and submitted.

If for some reason foreign investors have an urgent need to establish a company as early as possible, they may attempt to alternatively establish a PMDN, namely an Indonesian local company, with support from an Indonesian citizen or entity, as this does not require examination by BKPM, business approval, or research about minimum investment requirements. A PMDN can later become a PMA by issuing shares to the foreign investor. To schedule or provide a starting date for the commencement of a company's business ventures, both the time spent to satisfy all the legal requirements in company law and practical preparations – including opening a bank account – should all be taken into consideration.

5.5. *Permits and licenses*

In any country, it is a par for the course for a startup company to have to obtain a relevant business license and industrial permit and comply with specific regulations depending on its business field and purpose. Nonetheless, the majority opinion among experienced entrepreneurs suggests that business preparation in Indonesia is more rigorous than most. While some entrepreneurs maintain that market competition is comparatively endurable (or less harsh) because the threshold to enter the market at the beginning is so high, others refute this, saying the market is also studded with other types of difficulties.

A PMA should obtain a relevant business permit (*Izin Usaha*), depending on its business field, either from Indonesia Investment Coordinating Board (BKPM) or a regional board (BKPMD). For example, a construction company should obtain a construction license, and a production company should obtain a relevant industrial license. In particular, obtaining a relevant import license takes considerable time and effort in preparation, because the details governing requirements and limitations are substantially different depending on the type of items imported. Some industries, such as plantations, may require significant costs in preparation of these approvals. The complexity of regulations concerning permits and licenses is as notorious as tax law in the United States.

5.6. *Trademarks*

The use of a trademark is subject to the No. 15 2001 Trademark Act,[20] and it requires registration in advance. Unregistered trademarks are not protected. A trademark is protected within the scope of its own specific business field, or "class." If a third party in the same business field uses the trademark already registered in the class, he is subject to civil and criminal sanctions.

Certain procedures, including inspection for similarity with previously registered trademarks and distinctiveness, are required upon application for trademark. Once the procedures are completed, the new trademark should be published in a trademark magazine for 3 months to allow adequate time for potential opponents to object to its registration. A trademark registered in Indonesia is valid for 10 years and may be renewed.

5.7. *Patents*

Patents are protected under the No. 14 2001 Patent Act.[21] In principle, a patent is protected within the territory of a sovereign state in which its inventor or assignee files it. However, thanks to the development of the Patent Cooperation Treaty (PCT), which provides a unified procedure for filing patent applications, inventions in each of the PCT's contracting states, including Indonesia, now may be protected in other contracting states than the one in which it is filed. To explain, on filing a patent with the PCT in another country, the application

---

20 UU RI No.15 Th. 2001 tentang Merek.
21 UU RI No.14 Th. 2001 tentang Paten.

and filing date should have the effect of a regular national application in Indonesia, as well as in all other designated states of the PCT. This is correct, at least in theory. It is also true that the laws and regulations of Indonesia fully respect the PCT and develop their own protections pursuant to the international trends.

Nonetheless, it is yet to be shown that an applicant in another contracting state can expect a full and timely protection of his invention in Indonesia. In practice, a patent filed in another country necessitates at least 3–5 years, or possibly longer, to complete all of the procedures required to obtain suitable protection in Indonesia. Foreign patent applicants often designate all the ASEAN countries, roughly expecting the possibility to enter these markets, but this is not a good strategy. The best way to retain timely protection in full is to directly file a patent in Indonesia.

5.8. *Report of Beneficial Owners*

The President Regulation No.13 of 2018 on the Implementation of the Principle of Knowing Beneficial Owners of Corporations in Relation to the Prevention and Eradication of Money Laundering and Terrorism Financing Crimes (the "Regulation on Beneficial Owner") is infamous for its vagueness.

Under this Regulation on Beneficial Owner, a company must determine at least one person as its beneficial owner, appoint an employee to implement the principle of knowing the beneficial owners, and report to the government authority accurate information on the beneficial owner.

The beneficial owner is a person:

a   Who possesses more than 25% of the shares in the company as stated in its article of association;
b   Who possesses more than 25% of the voting rights in the company as stated in the article of association;
c   Who receives more than 25% of the profits earned annually by the company;
d   Who possesses authority to appoint, replace and dismiss members of the board of directors and board of commissioners of the company;
e   Who possesses authority or power to influence or control the company without the need to obtain authorization from any party;
f   Who receives benefits from the company; or
g   Who is the actual owner of the fund used to subscribe for the shares of the company.

An individual who satisfies the criteria in e, f and g is an individual who does not fulfil the criteria in a, b, c and d. Any company that does not comply this report obligation may be sanctioned. This notorious stipulation is so vague that anyone can interpret it in a way that he wants.

3 PMA specifics

1. Establishment of a PMA

As explained earlier, Indonesian companies are largely divided into purely domestic companies (PMDN) or foreign capital companies (PMA), based on whether they have any foreign shareholders. The latter are subject to separate regulations and procedures on their establishment, operation, and liquidation, including BKPM Regulations.

Foreign capital investment should be made only via a PMA, pursuant to Article 5 Paragraph 2 of the 2007 Capital Investment Act, and the proportion of foreign capital may be limited anywhere from 0 percent to 100 percent, depending on the provided list of closed and open business fields, with certain requirements in the field of investment (Negative Investment List) under the Presidential Decree.[1]

When a PMDN receives foreign direct investment, it must be understood that once the parent PMDN becomes a PMA via share subscriptions by a foreign investor, all its subsidiaries will also be automatically converted to a PMA and be subject to the Negative Investment List. Furtive share subscription under a borrowed name from an Indonesian citizen to circumvent the Negative Investment List is rendered void and ineffective. Nonetheless, in reality, many companies seem to use several loopholes to circumvent these regulations. The details are explained later in the section on the 2007 Capital Investment Act.

If a business is totally new and unprecedented, or if a concrete business model has not yet been decided, finding an exact business sector in the Negative Investment List may be difficult. In the event that the business can be classified into two or more sectors depending on interpretation, considerable time may be spent on deciding the appropriate business sector due to different interpretations at BKPM.

---

1 Peraturan Presiden Republik Indonesia tentang daftar bidang usaha yang tertutup dan bidang usaha yang terbuka dengan persyaratan di bidang penanaman modal.

1.1. Establishment process and requirements

To establish a PMA, two or more founders are required to subscribe the shares and become shareholders, in the same manner as for a PMDN. Additionally, establishment of a PMA requires any shareholder to pay IDR 10,000,000 or more for share subscription (Article 12 Paragraph 3 Item b of BKPM Regulation 13/2017).

Establishment of a PMA generally follows the process as illustrated in Figure 3.1.

Although a foreign shareholder's payment for shares subscription is not a mandatory requirement to obtain BKPM's approval, the foreign investor may remit the price for shares in advance. Nevertheless, it seems safer to remit the payment after obtaining the approvals from BKPM, given (i) the risk that the cash may be unnecessarily tied up until BKPM's approval, which could possibly be delayed or postponed; and (ii) the submission of the BKPM's approval to the relevant authority in the foreign investor's country can act as evidence to show that the cash movement is for a legitimate purpose.

Recently, the BKPM Regulation 13/2017 has been enacted by replacing the BKPM Regulations in 2015, which previously necessitated a principle license. Now, the principle license is no longer regulated, and instead, a new type of license, the Registration of Capital Investment is required depending on the applicant's business industry. Under the BKPM Regulation 13/2017, the Registration of Capital Investment only applies to PMA companies that satisfies any of the below criteria: (i) business that needs time for construction activities; (ii) business that is entitled to investment facilities; (iii) business that has medium

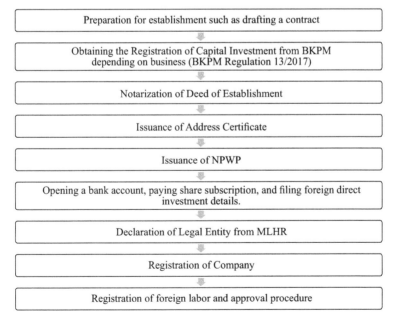

Figure 3.1 Establishment of a PMA process

to high potential of environmental pollution; (iv) business related to national defense, natural resources management, energy, and infrastructure; or (v) other business as determined by specific regulations. There are two types of business licenses for PMA companies under the BKPM Regulation 13/2017: (a) a 1-year business license for PMA companies that are unable to satisfy certain requirements; and (b) a permanent business license.

Since the Registration of Capital Investment should be issued from the BKPM for certain PMA companies before the deed of establishment is made, some may question whether there is a danger in not officially having a name during this period, such as losing the name to a third party, being disallowed to have the name due to the same name of another preexisting company, etc. This concern can be relieved by a public notary's advance investigation and reservation of the company name for 60 days. It is better to consult with a public notary in early stages in any case, as the application for legal entity status requires the notary's participation in the submission of the FIAN (*Isian Akta Notaris*) through the administration system (*Sisminbakum*).

The effective date of establishment of a PMA is the issuance date of the MLHR's declaration (*Keputusan Menteri Hukum dan Hak sasi manusia untuk pendirian Perseroan Terbatas*) – the same as the situation for a PMDN. The subsequent registration process has nothing to do with the effective date.

Should there for some reason be a need to establish a new Indonesian company urgently, a foreign investor may seek help from an Indonesian citizen so as to alternatively establish a PMDN first, as this is not subject to the hurdles of a PMA, such as the minimum investment requirement, the Negative Investment List, or BKPM's review and approval. Once the domestic partner duly establishes the company, the PMDN can later be switched to a PMA by issuing shares to the foreign investor, or converting foreign investor bonds to shares.

1.2.   Documentation and presentation for BKPM's approval

The following documents are mandatorily required for BKPM's approval of the establishment of a PMA:

- Foreign parent company's articles of association
- Relevant details about the members of board of directors
- Power of attorney for an Indonesian agency
- A copy of signatory's identification

The documents should be (i) translated into English by a notary who provides a certified translation service; (ii) stamped or confirmed from a consulate in the foreign country, and (iii) notarized by a consular official at an Indonesia embassy. Because a contract or agreement among shareholders to establish a PMA is not required to be submitted, the draft and review of the shareholders' mutual contract may proceed at the same time as preparation for BKPM's approval.

After submission of the above documents, a presentation with further detail should be made to BKPM. Although the requirements for the presentation may be different from company to company, the matters to explain in the presentation are generally as follows:

- Profile of the company
- Details of shareholders
- Business activity
- Value-added and peculiar matters
- Details in investment
- Target consumers
- Labor
- Infrastructure to be used in business activity

Depending on the business aim, the involved person's background, resume, and experience may be further required.

After the company is duly established, BKPM does not proceed with any further due diligence or inspection to check whether the company is actually doing the business as explained in the presentation. The company may add a business activity via amending the articles of association. However, the immigration and tax authorities do perform due diligence or inspection of company activities.

1.3. Minimum capital investment

The establishment of a PMA requires investment of IDR 10 billion (Article 3 of the 2007 Capital Investment Act),[2] only 25 percent of which should be proven at the time of conversion. This amount should be paid in cash, exclusive of property.

In principle, irrespective of whether an individual or corporation, a foreigner can establish a company as a founder only if allowed to participate in the particular industry or business sector. As discussed earlier, each founder should subscribe the initial shares, except in the case of establishment by consolidation of two or more companies.

1.4. Filing foreign direct investments in a foreign country

Generally, each country has its own authority and regulations to capture inbound and outbound cash flows. Although the specific requirements vary depending on the country, a foreign investor may be required to submit relevant

---

2 This requirement seems to consider protection of domestic small–middle enterprises, because a capital standard for small–middle enterprise in Indonesia requires IDR 10 billion. Chaji Hoon & Leehe Wang, *Indonesian Investment Act: Investment & Business Guide*, South Korean Ministry of Justice, 2013, p. 26.

documents to those authorities regarding the outbound cash movement for tax purposes, or to meet other policies. In general, this includes written documents with some evidential values such as contracts, business plans, appropriate completed forms, tax receipts, financial statements, identification, etc. This is the same when an established Indonesian company later desires to pay dividends to foreign investors.

1.5. Registered address

To obtain approval from BKPM, the company must locate at an office building whose name includes a sign of being an office, such as *Wisma, Gedung, Menara, Tower, Center*, or *Building*. BKPM does not approve company office locations in residential areas. Special attention should be paid to the fact BKPM's approval is not allowed if the office is located in a mixed residential-commercial complex called a *Ruko* or *Rumah Toko*, but it is allowed for residential-office complex called a *Rukan* or *Rumah Kantor*.

There have been several problematic cases where (i) the classification of the estate has changed without the estate owner's notice after the owner and a company's founder had already formed an office lease contract; or that (ii) the extension of office registration is not allowed for the same reason, although the company is in active business.

2.   Converting a PMDN to a PMA

If a PMDN issues new shares to a foreigner, or a PMDN's shareholders transfer or sell its shares to a foreigner, the company's legal status is converted from a PMDN to a PMA. The first question at this point is not "What is the maximum share rate permitted to the foreign shareholder of the company subject to the Negative Investment List?" but "Does the PMDN have a subsidiary?" This is because all subsidiaries are immediately subject to the Negative Investment List upon the issuance of its parent company's shares to a foreigner. Purchasing shares using a domestic nominee (i.e. a borrowed name) to avoid the Negative Investment List is illegal, void, and ineffective. To check the details in practice and legal analysis, see the later section "Warnings against attempts to end run around regulations in direct inbound investments."

BKPM Reg. 13 of 2017 Article 10

(1) Starting a business includes activities . . .

> Starting business activities in order to change its status to PMA, as a result of the entry of foreign capital in the ownership of the whole/part of the company's capital; . . .

(2) To start the business activities referred to in Paragraph (1), both in the context of domestic investment and foreign investment that fulfills

certain business activities shall have the Registration of Capital Investment (*Pendaftaran Penanaman Modal*).

Article 20

(1) (1) A company that begins the business and fulfills the business criteria under Article 10 Paragraph (4) in accordance to Article 10 Paragraph (1) Item a, d, e, f and g shall have Registration of Capital Investment.

(2) In case of any change from a PMDN company to a PMA company under Article 10 Paragraph (1) Item b must apply for Registration of Capital Investment with a registration type of conversion status.

2.1. Documentation and presentation

The documents for BKPM's approval of a shift from PMDN to PMA are the same as the documents required to submit when establishing a PMA. Since it is not mandatory to submit contracts such as a joint venture agreement or share subscription agreement, it does not matter if both the application for BKPM approval and contract draft and review occur simultaneously.

The order to change a PMDN to a PMA is presented in Figure 3.2.

Because the BKPM's approval is not conditional on a foreign shareholder's payment, the foreign investor may remit the investment earlier. However, it is safer to advance the payment after the BKPM's approval, given the possibility that the funds may be unnecessarily tied up due to delays in the BKPM approval, and the need to submit that BKPM approval as a proof of foreign direct investment to the foreign authority.

While the effective date of a conversion to a PMA is the issuance date of the MLHR's approval, the effective date of a foreign investor's share subscription is still obscure, in the absence of a clear stipulation in the 2007 Company Act

Figure 3.2 The order to change a PMDN to a PMA

and the 2007 Capital Investment Act. Due to bureaucratic practice, people generally regard the share subscription date as the issuance date of the MLHR's approval (*Surat Keputusan Menteri*). See also the section "Effect and validity of capital increase."

For the timing of issuance of Registration of Capital Investment, see the earlier section "Principle license (*Izin Prinsip*) and Registration of Capital Investment."

2.2.   Capital

Conversion from a PMDN to a PMA still requires investment of IDR 10 billion, only 25 percent of which must be proved at the time of conversion. This amount should be paid in cash exclusive of property.

2.3.   Filing investment

The bank account remains valid irrespective of the conversion from a PMDN to a PMA. When the company's name has also been changed in the process of conversion, changing the name of bank account owner is not a complicated task. The onerous task is explaining the change of name to the foreign remittance bank at the time of outward remittance, because many countries require its citizens to file notification of a foreign direct investment. Generally, joint ventures or share sales and purchase agreements are used to explain the different company name before and after conversion.

3.   A PMA's divestment obligations

According to Government Regulation No. 20 of 1994 (Shares Ownership in a PMA Company) and its amendment through Government Regulation No. 83 of 2001, a PMA wholly owned by a foreign investor is obliged to ensure that a certain portion of its shares is divested to a native Indonesian within 15 years after the PMA commences its commercial operations.

When the 2007 Capital Investment Act was enacted without any mention of divestment obligations, this brought out questions as to whether it cancelled the divestment obligation in previous regulations or contracts. Legal experts at a leading law firm initially understood that "it was the intention of the drafters . . . to eliminate all preexisting divestment requirements, except those contractually agreed by parties, which by virtue of freedom of contract principles will be deemed as the law governing the parties."[3]

However, subsequent BKPM regulations and practices have directly contradicted this initial interpretation. First, the BKPM has consistently applied

---

3 Hadiputranto, Hadinoto & Partners, *Indonesia's New Capital Investment Law*, 2011, p. 4.

Government Regulation No. 20 of 1994, which states a divestment requirement of some portion of the existing shareholding after 15 years. After the BKPM Regulation No. 5 of 2013 (Guidelines and Procedures for Investment Principal License) was enacted, explicitly enforcing the divestment obligation, experts in the market expressed concerns.[4] In defiance of these concerns from sophisticated market players, the BKPM Regulation No. 14 of 2015 further required that a minimum IDR 10,000,000 value of shares be shifted to an Indonesian participant through direct ownership or domestic capital market. This requirement has survived under Article 16 of the new BKPM Regulation No. 13 of 2017.

In sum, the divestment requirement survived the 2007 Capital Investment Act, subject to the BKPM regulations and other industrial regulations such as those for mining or oil and gas. It is also formally stated in the foreign investment approval (*Izin Prinsip*) that was used to be issued in old days and business permit (*Izin Usaha*). The BKPM can grant a maximum 2-year extension for completion of divestment.

Failure to divest results in a range of possible sanctions against the PMA, such as

- Temporary suspension of the company's activities
- Revocation of all or part of its investment facilities
- Partial revocation of permits
- Revocation of investment approval

To satisfy this notorious condition, many investors are still forced to reluctantly divest its shares to an Indonesian individual or company shortly (and purchase back to reinstate its position).

4 "It might jeopardize the interests of Indonesian public companies and their public shareholders because information on divestment can be very sensitive, and publicity announcing that a public company's shares will be (mandatorily) divested may significantly affect the price at which the divestment can be conducted." Hadiputranto, Hadinoto & Partners, *Amendment to BKPM Regulation on Guidelines for Investment Licensing: A Sigh of Relief or More Frustration for Public Companies?*, 2013, p. 2.

4 Shares

1. Issuance of shares (capital increase)

An increase in the size of a company's equity capital may be made either through a hike of par value of its capital stock, or the issue of new shares. The latter may be made with or without consideration. An example of issuance with consideration is a rights issue – that is, a dividend of subscription rights to purchase additional shares in a company made to the company's existing shareholders. When the rights are for equity securities such as shares, it is a conducted in non-dilutive *pro rata* manner to raise capital. Thus, the company's capital increases as much as the nominal value of the newly issued shares, whereby the company's total assets increase as its capital increases, or sometimes more, except in the case where stocks are issued at a discount. Often, new shares may be issued without consideration. In other words, shares may be distributed as fully paid shares free of charge. Bonus issues or stock dividends are examples of such an issuance. In addition, exchangeable shares or convertible bonds are also commonly used in Indonesia. In these examples, a company may issue new shares via its shareholders exercising the right to exchange shares for another class of shares pursuant to Article 53 (4) of the 2007 Company Act, or the right to convert bonds to shares, an act about which 2007 Company Act is, however, silent. This section explains only issuance with consideration.

If a PMDN is to be converted to a PMA by issuing new shares to a foreign investor, see the later section "Converting from a PMDN to a PMA," in addition to this section.

1.1. Procedures for share issuance

1.1.1. Resolution of share issuance

An increase in a company's capital may be approved by a shareholders' meeting (Article 41 Paragraph 1), or alternatively the board of commissioners to which the shareholders' meeting has delegated authority for not more than 1 year. In either case, the capital increase is limited to the authorized capital, the maximum amount of share capital that the company is authorized by its articles of association. For issuance of shares with a resolution of approval from a shareholders' meeting, shareholders who together own more than half of the company's shares should be present or represented at the meeting, and more than half of those present or represented should agree on the issue. Again, to avoid any doubts, the shareholders' meeting may entrust the authority of the approval of share issuance to the board of commissioners for not more than 1 year, and it may revoke the approval at any time.

The solicitation or offer of share subscriptions to the company's preemptive right holders (Article 43 Paragraphs 1 and 2) may be undertaken after the shareholders' meeting approving the share issuance. It would not matter if this agenda item was notified to the shareholders in advance or not. Normally a shareholder's meeting should be held, but at times meetings are not actually held in practice. Instead, shareholders make a written resolution to leave as a formal document as if the meeting had been held. Thus, in the event that the shareholders' written resolution operates as an alternative to the actual meeting, this draft should include whether the shareholders exercised preemptive rights and other relevant matters in detail.

1.1.2. *Share subscription agreements*

Many Indonesian legal experts advise to proceed with legalization (*legalisasi*) of the contract with a public notary at the time of signing. Basically, their concerns are based on many actual cases in which an Indonesian party to a contract later insists that he did not sign it, bringing a forged contract and stubbornly persisting that it is the right one, or where the party turns out to be an unauthorized signatory. Foreign lawyers or business persons often draw a long breath listening to this sort of advice.

However, unless making a contract with a person who disregards his own dignity by insisting on this sort of formalization – to which a court would not listen in any case – this legalization is thought to only waste time and costs. The supporting documents and evidence automatically collected in general contract practice already provide sufficient proof. The parties to the contract normally are present with witnesses at the signing ceremony, and each give and take a copy of each signatory's ID card and articles of association showing their authority. Undoubtedly, there is other evidence which shows the parties' genuine intent to the contract, such as emails and other correspondence for mutual contract review, and a bank's remittance confirmation from the share purchaser. If the parties remain concerned, they can simply email each with a message such as "I have duly signed the contract on this date," with an attachment of the contract draft or copy of signed version. In any case, legalization of contracts seems to be a naked example of the pervasive formalism spread throughout Indonesia.

1.1.3. *Payment and performance with in-kind contributions*

A share subscriber should pay the price of the entire subscribed shares on the payment date. An in-kind contributor should tender the subject matter and documents certifying ownership and registration on the payment date. However, an independent appraiser free from any conflict of interest should be appointed to appraise the subject matter of the in-kind contribution. For further detail, see the earlier section "In-kind contributions."

1.1.4. *Notarization of amendments to the articles of association and deed of share sales*

Issuance of new shares is valid and effective up to the number of shares subscribed and paid for. In theory, the unsubscribed and unpaid shares (i.e. forfeited shares) would become unissued shares. In practice, a public notary examines whether the shares have been fully subscribed and paid at the time of notarizing the deed of share sales and amendment of the articles of association, and the MLHR also checks and records these at the time of notice.

1.1.5. *Application for change of* Izin Prinsip *no longer needed*

In the event that a PMDN should be switched to a PMA by issuing shares to a foreign investor, see the section "Conversion to PMA." It is important to note that change of *Izin Prinsip* is no longer needed after the BKPM Regulation 13/2017.

1.1.6. *Financial and public companies*

Financial companies, including banks, should obtain an advance approval from Indonesia's Financial Services Authority (the *Otoritas Jasa Keuangan, or* OJK).

Public companies must make a public disclosure in the event that any share sale causes a party's share ownership to reach 5 percent of the entire ownership pursuant to the Capital Market Act. Once a party owns 5 percent or more shares in a public company, any change in his ownership of the shares should be notified to OJK insofar as ownership remains at 5 percent or more.

1.1.7. *Share issuance procedure*

The general procedure of issuing shares is as illustrated in Figure 4.1.

1.2.   *Effect and validity of capital increase*

In many foreign jurisdictions, share issuance becomes valid and takes effect on either the date of contribution, or the following day.

On the other hand, the Indonesian Company Act is silent about when the share issuance becomes duly effective. Because of "red-tapeism," which sticks to rigid conformity to formal rules now considered redundant or bureaucratic, the issuance date of the MLHR's approval (*Surat Keputusan Menteri*, or SK) regarding amendment of articles of association is deemed to be the effective date of capital increase, at least in actual practice.

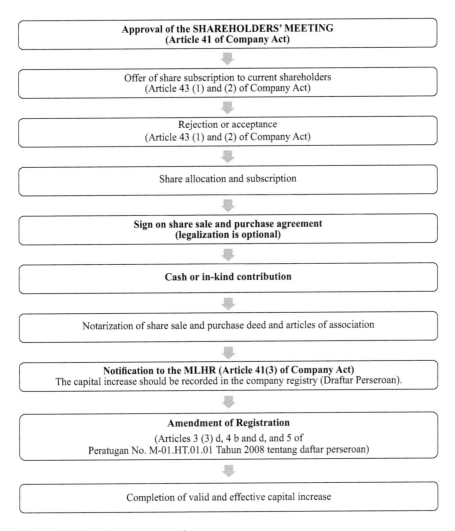

Figure 4.1 Share issuance procedure

In Indonesian accounting practice, for example, a payment of share purchase is entered as a suspense receipt or stock deposit at the time of payment (cf. a stock deposit account is used particularly where a foreign shareholder requires using this bookkeeping approach as an evidence showing that the aim of remittance is a foreign direct investment). Later this is credited to paid-in capital upon the issuance of SK as the following example shows:

Table 4.1 An actual example of accounting for share subscription

At the time of payment	Dr) Cash 110,000,000	Cr) Deposit (or suspense receipt) 110,000,000
At the time of issuance of SK	Dr) Deposit 100,000,000 (or suspense receipt)	Cr) Common stock (par value) 100,000,000
		Paid in capital in excess of par 10,000,000

Although the accounting method is a different matter to one with a legal effect or validity, the same conservatism seems to be applied due to the ambiguity in the law.

Thus, a share sale and purchase agreement should not be drafted as something like "the company shall obtain all the relevant approvals from the authority by the closing date when the payment is made." A safer draft would be, for example, "the company shall obtain all the relevant approvals from the authority within 60 days of signing date, or by a later date which the authority may require."

In my view, the vacuum in either the law or the court's judgment about this crucial matter is a serious problem, because it is unclear whether the party who has made the payment of stock but has yet to receive SK is a shareholder or not. That is, whether the party has a right to receive dividends is unclear if dividends are distributed between the date of contribution and the issuance of SK. Further, it is unclear whether the party has voting rights at a shareholders' meeting held after his contribution, but before the SK is issued.

2.　Preemptive rights

A preemptive right is a privilege that grants to shareholders or a certain non-shareholder third party the right to purchase additional shares in the company prior to shares being made available to other people to purchase.

In a company law context, preemptive rights are divided into two concepts: a preemptive right for shareholders, and a preemptive right for a non-shareholder party. These days, however, the term is more widely used for the former, while the contractual rights given to the third party to preemptively subscribe shares are more commonly referred to as a "right to first reject."

> ### Article 43 (1)
>
> All shares issued for the increase of capital must first be offered to each shareholder in proportion to their share ownership for the same classification of shares.

2.1. *Preemptive rights of shareholders* (pemegang saham yang berhak membeli terlebih dahulu)

2.1.1. *Definition*

If a company issues new shares to obtain investment, the preexisting shareholders' power to govern the company may be weakened, and the existing share value may be diluted. Accordingly, preemptive rights are required to allow the company to protect preexisting shareholder interests at the same time as satisfying the demands of investment.

A shareholder's preemptive right is the right, but not an obligation, to acquire new shares such that the shareholder can maintain proportional ownership of the company, thus preventing stock dilution.[1] In this context, the right is sometimes alternatively named anti-dilution provision rights.

While a preemptive right is not automatically provided for by statute in the majority of the United States at present,[2] Indonesia and many other countries have retained statutes to protect these rights for shareholders in their company laws.[3] In other words, a preemptive right is not shareholder's inherent right, but a mere statutory right given by the law in each jurisdiction.

2.1.2. *Preemptive rights before and after the board of director's resolution of stock issuance*

Shareholders are presumed to have preemptive rights even before a board's decision to issue shares. This is because, as explained, this statutory right is given by the jurisdiction's company law, and Indonesia's Company Act does not require a board's decision as a condition to recognize a shareholder's preemptive rights. Of course, the rights specifically arise upon a board's decision to issue shares, whether by moving its reserve into capital or by receiving investment. In U.S. accounting principles and practices, these rights when they become specific and reasonably measurable are named *stock rights* on entry into the financial statements.[4]

---

1 "*Yang berhak membeli terlebih dahulu*" in Article 43(2) is literally translated as "that have a right to purchase in advance."

2 Revised Model Business Corporation Act §6.30(a) (1984) is one example, while the N.Y. Business Corporation Law §622(b)-(c) (1986) is an example of the opposite. The former is in place in the majority of the United States, James D. Cox et al., *Corporations*, 1997, Aspen Law and Business, p. 474; John E. Moye, *The Law of Business Organizations*, 5th ed., 1999, NY West Legal Studies, p. 214.

3 §419 (1) of Korean Commercial Act and §561(1) of UK's Companies Act 2006.

4 Because a share price presumptively reflects the value of preemptive rights which may be appraised separately, the rights could be debited or credited apart from the share price. This price is thus recorded on the account as Stock Rights at the time when the value can be reasonably measured. "*Stock rights* are commonly used if a *preemptive right* is granted to common shareholders by some state corporation laws." Joanne M. Flood, *Wiley GAAP*, 2015, Wiley. However, actual practice does not differentiate any one term from the others.

The question is whether preemptive rights prior to a board's resolution are transferable to another person without transferrin stock ownership. Even if shareholders are deemed to have these rights before the board's decision, how can a shareholder effectively transfer the rights independently and separately from the stock when the board has not decided how many shares will be issued, at what price, and even when?

The laws and courts in Indonesia remain silent on this question. No actual case on a separate and independent transfer, assumption, or sale of preemptive rights before a board's resolution has been witnessed in Indonesian practice. It is clear, however Indonesia uses the term, that preemptive rights (or *hak membeli terlebih dahulu*) exist, irrespective of whether they are specifically declared, and whether the Board has resolved to recognize these rights. In the light of actual practice in Indonesia, only preemptive rights after the Board's resolution is considered to be a subject of transfer.

2.1.3.   *Stocks that cannot be the subject of preemptive rights*

Shareholders generally have a right to subscribe to all the shares issued in the future as explained above. Nevertheless, a share subscription is often prearranged to a certain person, in which case shareholders' preemptive rights may be an issue. Examples of this are (i) issuance by converting either convertible bond or convertible shares to new shares, or exercising a bond warrant,[5] (ii) an employee stock ownership plan,[6] (iii) issuance of shares to shareholders of a target company in a merger, and (iv) issuance of shares conducted in the context of reorganization and/or restructuring with the approval of a general shareholders' meeting.[7] As explained in the section on in-kind contributions, a share subscriber is not necessarily specifically predetermined in every in-kind contribution case, and the view of Indonesia's courts regarding whether a preemptive right is applicable also seems unclear.

While Article 43 Paragraph 3 does not state as much, there is no issue whether the subscription rights are predetermined to all the shareholders, because there is no offer or stock allocation. The examples are issuance of stock-by-stock split, reverse stock split (i.e. stock consolidation), stock dividends, or transfer of reserve to capital.

A public company can also make a private placement without any problem with preemptive rights. A private placement is the sale of securities to a relatively small number of private investors rather than as a part of a public offering to raise capital. By undertaking a private placement, a company can solve any problems related to preemptive rights in advance, avoid the time and expense of registering with the OJK, creating a prospectus, or obtaining a credit rating, and sell more complex securities for the benefit of investors. To make a private placement, the company's articles of association must set it forth, and the total value of newly issued shares must not be more than 10 percent of the company's capital over the past 2 years. In general, a resolution of general shareholders' meeting is required.

---

5   Article 43 Paragraph 3 Item b of the 2007 Company Act.
6   Article 43 Paragraph 3 Item a of the 2007 Company Act.
7   Article 43 Paragraph 3 Item c of the 2007 Company Act.

2.1.4. *Transfer of shareholder preemptive rights*

A preemptive right can be transferred or assumed by making a Transfer-of-Right Deed (*Akta Pemindahan Hak*) according to Article 56 of the 2007 Company Act. The board of directors should record this transfer to the list of shareholders and notify the MLHR within 30 days. One matter requires attention when a shareholder hands over his preemptive right to another person, apart from ownership of the stock. In many other jurisdictions, a transfer of preemptive right is valid provided the company has approved such a transfer, irrespective of whether the board of directors has resolved to approve it. In Indonesia, however, the statute explicitly requires the board to notify the MLHR of the transfer within a certain time period, and the MLHR will then reject or approve it, and such a transfer includes those transfers by mergers–acquisitions, bequests, and testations. Therefore, the reasonable interpretation of law seems to be that a transfer of preemptive rights in Indonesia requires both a decision of the board and notification to (and approval by) the MLHR.[8]

2.1.5. *Third-party preemptive rights*

When a third party other than shareholders is entitled to subscribe to new shares at the earliest point, it is generally through contractual arrangement such as a call option, a right to first offer, a right to negotiate, etc. Although it may be used for control defense by allocating new shares to a so-called white knight third party, there has been no actual case of hostile takeover in the Indonesian capital market,[9] nor is it common amongst private companies. This will be explained in depth in the later sections, "Limitations on share transfer by shareholder resolution and articles of association" and "Merger and acquisition."

2.1.6. *Relief for invasion to preemptive right*

There are not many options to give relief to damaged preemptive rights. Because there can be no injunction, or temporary injunction, against the issuance of new shares, one can only take ex post measures such as seeking annulment of a shareholder resolution, or invalidation of a share issuance. If the previous shareholder resolution also includes preemptive rights, a shareholder may further claim responsibilities in defaults.

8 Article 56 Paragraph 4 of the 2007 Company Act.
9 Generally, whether a takeover is hostile or not depends on the parties' agreement and purchaser's act. For example, a hostile tender offer by a purchaser to buy out shares from certain shareholders, or buying out listed shares in a capital market irrespective of the management's intent, are examples of a hostile takeover. Nonetheless, it is very uncommon to see this sort of hostile takeover. Theodoor Bakker & Herry N. Kurniawan, *Indonesia Mergers & Acquisitions*, ICLG, 2016.

> *PT. Kodeco Timber v. PT. Bintang Bengawan* (659/Pdt. G/2008/PN.JKT.Sel.)
>
> In a case where new shares were issued in disregard of shareholders' preemptive rights, the plaintiff, PT. Kodeco Timber, claimed voidance of shareholders' resolution based on (i) that the shareholders resolved other matters (a change of directors and commissioners, and issuance of new shares) than those matters given on the advance notice to the shareholders, on which the defendant, PT. Bintang Bengawan, declared only a readjustment of payables, share transfers, and accounting report, "etc. (*dan lain*)" as items to resolve; and (ii) the quorum of 66.66 percent was not satisfied due to the attendance of only 60 percent of the total voting rights shares. The court ruled out voidance of the shareholders resolution based on that the expression "etc." could not be an effective matter, inasmuch as it was not agreed to by all the other shareholders.

3.   Reduction of capital

Article 44

(1) The resolution of the Shareholders' Meeting for the reduction of the Company's capital shall be valid if adopted by taking into account the requirements of quorum provisions and the numbers of votes in favor for the amendments of the articles of association . . .

(2) The Board of Directors is obliged to notify the resolution as referred to in Paragraph (1) to all creditors by announcing it in one or more Newspapers, within the period of not later than 7 (seven) days.

Article 45

(1) Within the period of 60 (sixty) days as of the date of the announcement as referred to in Article 44 Paragraph (2), the creditors may submit written objection to the resolution on the capital reduction, together with the reasons therefore to the Company, with a copy to the Minister.

(2) Within the period of 30 (thirty) days as from the objection as referred to in Paragraph (1) are received, the Company is obliged to provide written response to the objection received.

(3) In the event that the Company:

   a   rejects the objection or fail to provide a settlement that the creditors agree to within the period of 30 (thirty) days as of the date of receipt of the Company's response; or

   b   fail to give any response within the period of 60 (sixty) days as of the date the objection is submitted by the Company,

   creditor may suit to the District Court whose jurisdiction covers the domicile of the Company.

Article 46

(1) The reduction of the capital of the Company constitutes the amendment of the articles of association which must have approval from the Minister.

(2) The Minister's approval as referred to in Paragraph (1) shall be provided in the event that

    a there is no written objection from the creditors within the period as referred to in Article 45 Paragraph (1),

    b a settlement of the objection raised by the creditor is achieved; or

    c creditors' suit is rejected by the District Court based on the judgment which has obtained absolute legal force.

Article 47

(1) Resolution of the SHAREHOLDERS' MEETING concerning reduction in subscribed and paid-up capital shall be carried out by means of a withdrawal of shares or a reduction in the nominal value of shares.

(2) The withdrawal of shares contemplated in Paragraph (1) may be carried out against shares which have been repurchased by the Company or against shares with a classification which may be withdrawn.

(3) Reductions in the nominal value of shares without repayment must be carried out in proportion against all shares of every classification of shares.

(4) Exemptions from the proportionality contemplated in Paragraph (3) must have the consent of all shareholders the nominal value of whose shares will be reduced.

(5) In the event of there being more than 1 (one) classification of shares, the resolution of the SHAREHOLDERS' MEETING concerning the reduction in capital may only be adopted after obtaining the prior consent of all shareholders of each classification of shares whose rights will be diminished by the resolution of the SHAREHOLDERS' MEETING concerning the reduction in capital.

3.1. *Introduction*

According to a number of Indonesian experts and professionals, the opinions about capital reduction of PMA seem divided. They view a reduction alternatively as:

- Not allowed – The BKPM does not generally approve a PMA's capital reduction despite the absence of any specific regulation or particular rationales.

- Generally permitted – There is no restriction in a PMA's capital reduction, and no particular limitation is placed in actual practice.

- Permitted but limited – The BKPM does not approve a PMA's capital reduction in the event that it views scaling down the business or retrieving capital as harmful to the national wealth.

In sum, although no particular laws and regulations apply, a PMA suffers substantial difficulties in reducing its capital in actual practice. For example, even one of the experts holding the view that capital reduction is "generally permitted" says: "The MLHR intentionally ignores the application of approval for a couple of months without any review." Whatever opinion is true, the following will not be applicable to a PMA if either the MLHR or BKPM do not approve capital reduction.

3.2. Definition

Capital reduction refers to the process of decreasing a company's shareholder equity through share cancellations or share repurchases. A company reduces its capital for numerous reasons, including losses that cannot be recovered from the company's earning and thereby permanently reducing a company's scale of operations, increasing shareholder value by having a more efficient capital structure, etc. In most cases, merely an effort for recovery and capital reduction are insufficient for a company to completely rehabilitate. Thus, capital reduction is often used with a debt–equity swap or other measures for survival. For example, in many cases, a company attempts to secure liquidity by issuing new shares after reducing its capital.

Depending on whether the result is a decrease of assets on the left-hand side of a financial statement, the reduction of capital is divided into paid-in capital reduction and one without refund. If a company returns the paid-in capital to investors, its assets decrease by as much as it repays to investors. In actual practice, a company sometimes pays a premium in addition to the paid-in capital, so that investors willingly return the stock to the company. Of course, the company may return less than the paid-in capital, thereby obtaining a margin. On the other hand, the company may reduce the capital without any refund to the stockholders. An absolute majority of capital reduction examples in the Indonesian market are ones without stockholder refunds. For example, if a company starting with stated capital of IDR 2 billion now has only IDR 1 billion value for the equity after burning retained earnings, it may reduce a half of the capital by consolidating shares (i.e. a reverse stock split) in order to improve its financial soundness.[10]

Either with a refund or not, any capital reduction should be done by a shareholders resolution, amendment of articles of association, and protection of the company's creditors in accordance with the 2007 Company Act.

---

10 Such consolidation must be in a way of returning stocks, as the Company Act allows only the return of stocks and reduction of nominal value of stock for capital reduction.

Since a company's capital is also related to creditors' interests, it must satisfy the strict requirements and procedures explained in the section "Procedures."

It is important to note that, for a capital reduction, an Indonesian company requires an amendment to the articles of association, a quorum for such an amendment, and approval of MLHR, while many foreign jurisdictions do not require an amendment to the articles of association.

3.3. Types

Article 47 of the 2007 Company Act allows two ways to reduce capital: returning stocks (*penarikan kembali saham*) and reducing the nominal value of stocks (*penurunan nilai nominal saham*). The former is a critical mistake under the legislation, as explained below.

Return of stock – an error in legislation

Article 47

(1) The resolution of shareholders' meeting to reduce the issued and paid-up capital of the company shall be conducted by way of withdrawal of shares (*penarikan kembali saham*), or reducing the nominal value of the shares.

(2) The withdrawal of shares stated in Paragraph (1) may be carried out to the shares which have been repurchased by the company or to the shares having a classification which may be withdrawn.

A return of stocks *does not* reduce the number of shares, nor does it decrease capital or equity. It only results in treasury stocks. In other words, if a shareholder returns stock to the company, the company then owns the stock. Apparently, the poor legislator mistakenly thought that the return of stock reduces the amount of stock owned by someone outside of the company, and therefore reduced the company's capital. Article 47 Paragraph 1 is a disastrous error, because the company can legally own treasury stocks in accordance to Article 36 Paragraph 2 of the 2007 Company Act, and thus, naturally, it should be able to reduce capital without any return of stocks by cancelling the treasury stocks. Probably, the legislature intended was not return of shares (*penarikan kembali saham*), but cancellation of shares (*penghapusan saham*). Due to this mistake in legislation, in an attempt to reduce capital, Indonesian companies are now forced to return the shares owned by unwilling stockholders whether they already have unsellable treasury stocks or not. Consequently, the company cannot even use a control defensive tactic against an outside takeover attempt, which increases a current shareholder's ownership rate by cancelling treasury stocks.

Regardless, because a return of stock does not automatically reduce capital, the company should cancel the returned stock for capital reduction. Upon cancellation of stock, both the number of total issued stocks and the amount of aggregated par value decrease as much as the of returned stock. If a company repurchases the stock and these treasury stocks are cancelled, earning per share (EPS) increases and dividends per share increase as the amount of stock decreases. On the other hand, the debt-to-equity ratio is resultantly negatively affected, as the equity value decreases.

Another problem with Article 47 is ambiguity as to whether it includes stock returns without any payment, involuntary cancellation, consolidation of stocks, etc. While the Article appears to suggest consolidation is excluded, many experts believe that Indonesian companies frequently consolidate stocks in actual practice.

At least a return of stock with payment is clearly included. The well-known pharmaceutical company PT. Kalbe Farma Tbk repurchased and cancelled 3,904,950 shares among a total of 46,879,027,060 issued shares in 2013.

A literal interpretation is that a return of stocks (*Penarikan kembali saham*) seems to include a return of stock without repayment. Nonetheless, there is a contrary opinion: Since shareholders receive no consideration for stock returns/cancellation and thus the company's assets do not decrease, following the creditor protection procedures is a needless cost without any benefit.

Undoubtedly, shareholders and a company can voluntarily cancel stocks by freely making a contract. On the other hand, it is questionable whether a company can cancel the stock using an equalitarian method such as a lottery or proportional cancellation, irrespective of shareholder intent. At least, no expert interviewed has said that he or she has seen such an involuntary stock cancellation.

3.3.1.   Reduction of nominal value

In the event that a company's deficit is so large that it cannot return any earnings to its shareholders, the shareholder may voluntarily give up a portion of paid-in capital and reduce the stated value of stock. Article 47 Paragraph 3 governs this capital reduction without return.

However, if the company desires to decrease its excessive capital, it may return a certain portion of paid-in capital to its shareholders. For example, PT. Matahari Putra Prima Tbk, an affiliate of a well-known Indonesian corporate group, reduced its nominal value per capital from IDR 500 to IDR 50, returning the difference to its shareholders on 26 November 2012.

In either approach, the stated value should remain equal. However, if all the equity holders owning the reduced capital agree, the company may decide otherwise (Article 47 Paragraph 4).

3.4.   Procedures

3.4.1.   Shareholders resolution on quorum

The 2007 Company Act does not provide a specific quorum for a shareholders' resolution on capital reduction. Thus, a shareholders' resolution satisfying the quorum requirement in the company's articles of association is required for capital reduction (Article 44 Paragraph 1).

3.4.2. *Protection of creditors*

The company should announce resolutions about capital reduction in at least one newspaper within 7 days (Article 45). That is, constructive notice is enough. Whether the company gives actual notice to the creditors, or intentionally does not give an actual notice to creditors where it could easily do so, constructive notice in a newspaper is required and is sufficient. Furthermore, an electronic newspaper seems to be permitted, given that Article 1 defines a "newspaper" as a daily newspaper in the Indonesian language with a national circulation. In other words, irrespective of whether anybody reads all types of newspapers every day, a company's creditors should not miss the notice in the 60-day objection period in any case. This is the same with creditor protections in a company split.

Any creditor having an opposing opinion should submit a written claim against the capital reduction to the MLHR and the company within 60 days of the company's newspaper announcement. The company should then reply in writing within 30 days of receiving the objection. If the company and creditor cannot reach a settlement within 30 days from that reply, or the company does not reply within 60 days of the creditor's objection, the creditor may file a lawsuit at the district court in the venue in which the company is located.

The company has no obligation to provide a security or payment to the creditor opposing capital reduction. Nor is it liable to entrust an asset to a third party's trust company for this purpose. Further, a bond holder opposing a capital reduction is not required to obtain an agreement with or resolution of other bond holders in order to submit a written claim.

3.4.3. *Amendment of the articles of association*

To reduce capital, a company should obtain the MLHR approval and amend the articles of association (Article 46). If no creditor submits a claim against the capital reduction within the stated period, or the opposing creditor and the company has settled, or the creditor's claim has been rejected by the court, the MLHR should approve the amendment of articles of association for capital reduction.

4. Pledge and fiduciary on shares

4.1. *Introduction*

Since stocks are regarded as personal property, they can be used for security purposes unless the company's articles of association contains contrary provisions. Offering stocks as security on a loan or other obligations is called a pledge (*gadai*). Generally, the debtor pledges the stocks as an asset against the amount of debt and promises to return the money.

A shareholder also can provide his stocks as another type of security, fiduciary. The legal term "*fidusia*" in Indonesia has different meaning to "fiduciary" in other jurisdictions. Because the word means "trust," given reciprocally from one to another, United States use the term to typically refer to the person who owes to the principal (or beneficiary) the duties of good faith and trust. In Indonesia, however, the word *fidusia* means the trust given reciprocally from one party to the other, in which what is "on the outside appears as transfer of property" in reality (inside) is merely "collateral" for a debt.[11] Thus, it is often alternatively translated to a mortgage by transfer, security by means of transfer, or a mortgage in which ownership of the property is transferred to the lender in external appearance. In this book, the term "fiduciary" is used to describe *fidusia* more widely than is done in actual practice.

Fiduciary security was initially intended for collateral in the form of movable properties, but also began being used for immovable properties. Fiduciary security for movable properties became regulated by Law No. 42 of 1999 on Fiduciary Security ("1999 Fiduciary Act"),[12] while fiduciary for immovable properties has been governed by Law No. 04 of 1996 on Mortgage on Land and Objects related to Land.[13] Since stock is regarded as personal movable property in Indonesia, fiduciary security over stocks is governed by both the 2007 Company Act and 1999 Fiduciary Act.

Because the 2007 Company Act regards stock as a movable property (*Benda bergerak*), Article 1150 to 1153 of Indonesian Civil Act in regard to a pledge for movable assets governs the pledge for stocks, and the 1999 Fiduciary Act governs the fiduciary. That is thought to be the reason why the 2007 Company Act mandates either a pledge or fiduciary for a security interest in stocks.

Both pledges and fiduciary over stocks can be used to withdraw injected money. As a security interest, the following are common features of both the pledge and fiduciary.

- It is better for the creditor to receive a power of attorney to dispose of the stocks, because it will allow him to proceed to auction without a court order. Of course, the creditor may end up paying a great deal for worthless shares.
- Because every issuance of shares must be known to the MLHR for registration purposes (*daftar*), providing unregistered stocks for security is not governed by the 2007 Company Act, as providing unissued stocks for security is also not covered.

---

11 Celina Tri Siwi Kristiyanti, Fiduciary Security Law in Collateral Material Law System in Indonesia, *US-China Law Review* Vol. 11, 2014, p. 986.
12 Undang-undang Republik Indonesia Nomor 42 Tahun 1999 tentang Jaminan Fidusia.
13 Undang-undang Republik Indonesia Nomor 4 Tahun 1996 tentang Hak Tanggungan atas tanah beserta benda-benda yang berkaitandengan tanah.

- Unless otherwise provided by articles of association, either a pledge or fiduciary must be written in the articles of association (Article 60 Paragraph 3). That is, a restriction, limitation, or condition can be placed in the articles of association.
- If it is a revolving credit facility and the initial loan has been repaid, the security needs to be re-created every time the facility is provided.[14] However, some experts hold contrary views to this in practice. Either way, the best solution is to draft a contract in a clear way that the security can be automatically extended in the event of it revolving.

4.2. Pledge of shares: **gadai**

4.2.1. How to pledge shares

A share pledge comes into force and is effective upon satisfaction of conditions under the Civil Act (i.e. a written agreement or instrument to pledge shares) and the requirement under the 2007 Company Act (i.e. the listing of names and address of the share pledgee in the list of shareholders). Importantly, a pledgee does not need to physically possess the share certificate.

Since a pledge of shares is to be registered (*daftar*) according to the 2007 Company Act, some often believe that an unregistered pledge of shares is ineffective. Registration is not a requirement to be effective, however.

4.2.2. Legal effects

Even if shares are pledged, the underlying voting rights are still exercisable by the pledger (Article 60 Paragraph 4).

Nonetheless, it is unclear whether the purpose of pledge is limited to the value in exchange of the pledged stock only, or extended to both "fruits" (i.e. dividend rights and preemptive rights) and modified forms of the preexisting stock (e.g. split, reverse split, cancellation, or conversion of stocks). That is, it is unclear whether a pledgee may enjoy dividend rights and preemptive rights, or whether a share pledge automatically survives after a split, reverse split, cancellation, or conversion of stocks.

Considering the practice in Indonesia, the purpose of a pledge is thought to be limited to the value in exchange of the pledged stock unless otherwise provided in the agreement or articles of association. Should the pledgee begin applying all these abstract rights into calculations of the pledge value, the calculation becomes tremendously intricate. Article 2.2.5 of the Indonesian Capital

---

14 Theodoor Bakker & Ayik Candrawulan Gunadi, *Indonesia Lending and Secured Finance 2016, 2.3: Is Lack of Corporate Power an Issue?*, 2016, ICLG.

Market Regulation[15] is a similar provision for listed companies, which explicitly excludes cash dividends (*dividen tunai*), stock dividends (*dividen saham*), preemptive rights (*saham bonus*), and other rights from the rights of a pledgee. There seems no good reason to treat unlisted companies differently. As Article 43 Paragraphs 1 and 2 state that all shares issued for capital increase must be first offered to each "shareholder," the purpose of a pledge is deemed to at least exclude preemptive rights.

In sum, if a pledgee thinks that the value of a security is diluted due to these provisions, he can claim in addition either these rights or other securities. In other words, claiming these rights in addition to the value in exchange is the same as compelling additional security to the pledger.

Either way, the contract should be drafted as clearly as the law is unclear. While it is easy to draft that a pledger still has a voting right, a contract drafter often omits preemptive rights or dividend rights in the draft.

4.2.3. Advice on drafting a share pledge agreement

Although expert opinions are varied, the best way to ensure enforcement for foreclosure is to set Indonesian law as the governing law, an Indonesian institution (either BANI or a court) as a settlement place, and Indonesian language as the contractual language.[16] Although the Singapore International Arbitration Centre (SIAC) appeals to Indonesian lawyers or apprehensive foreign investors, emphasizing that it has recently successfully obtained case judgment enforcement in Indonesia, an Indonesian court or BANI is ultimately the safest to secure foreclosure in accordance to the contract.

4.3. Fiduciary security (Jaminan Fidusia)

A fiduciary is the transfer of ownership of an object on trust, with the provision that the transferred ownership of the object remains in the control of the owner of the object for satisfaction of receivables, and the ownership returns upon full repayment. Thus, it looks like a transfer of ownership from the outside, but it in reality is merely collateral for a debt, so that the creditor can dispose it, satisfy his receivables, and give any remaining amount from a sale to the fiduciary provider. Thus, the fiduciary receiver cannot dispose of the property at any time he wants.

The kinds of receivables secured by fiduciaries are existing debt, a debt which is determined to be made in future, or a debt which can be determined at certain time in accordance with a contract.

---

15 Kustodian Sentral Efek Indonesia (KSEI) No: KEP-0013/DIR/KSEI/0612, June 2012.
16 "Can such security validly be granted under a New York or English law governed document? . . . A pledge of Indonesian shares can be enforced provided the governing law is Indonesian law." Bakker & Gunadi, *supra* note 14.

1999 Fiduciary act

The clauses in 1999 Fiduciary Act are useful to understand, in a rough manner, what a fiduciary is are as follows:

Law of the Republic of Indonesia, number 42 of 1999 on Fiduciary

Article 1

1 Fiduciary is a transfer of ownership of an object on trust with the provision that transferred ownership of the object remains in the control of the owner of the object.
2 Fiduciary is the right over moving objects . . . as collateral for the repayment of certain debt, which gives priority to the receiver's debt against other creditors.

Article 15

(3) If the debtor breaches the contract, the Fiduciary receiver has the right to sell the object of Fiduciary on his own behalf.

Article 17

Fiduciary giver is prohibited from encumbering with a Fiduciary an object which already has a registered Fiduciary.

Elucidation: . . . because the ownership of the object has been transferred to the Fiduciary receiver.

Article 27

(1) The Fiduciary has precedence over other creditors.
(2) The right that takes precedence referred to in Paragraph (1) is the right of the Fiduciary receiver to settle their claims against the proceeds of execution of the Fiduciary object.

Article 33

Any commitment that authorizes the Fiduciary giver to keep the object of Fiduciary if the debtor defaults is null and void.

Since a fiduciary is defined as "transfer of ownership of an object on trust" (*pengalihan hak kepemilikan suatu benda atas dasar kepercayaan*), the fiduciary receiver must obtain complete ownership and have an obligation not to exercise the owner's rights beyond the purpose of a trust.

Procedures and legal effect

Whether the object of a fiduciary is located in Indonesia or elsewhere, a fiduciary is formed through an official deed in Indonesian language by a public notary, and should be recorded in the Fiduciary Register Book (*Buku Daftar Fidusia*) at the Fiduciary Registration Office (*Kantor Pendaftaran Fidusia*). A fiduciary becomes effective at the time it is recorded in the book. Upon registration, the Fiduciary Registration Office issues a fiduciary certificate (*sertifikat fidusia*), which includes the date of application.

Whether by a pledge or fiduciary, a security provider still retains the voting rights (Article 60 Paragraph 4). If the fiduciary giver attempts to cancel, split, or consolidate without permission, the fiduciary receiver can be protected according to the Fiduciary Act, and foreclose using the certificate only without requiring a court judgment.

4.3.1. *Time and cost*

While a share pledge requires only preparing an agreement and the list of shareholders, a fiduciary requires registration, which takes, roughly, a month.

Registration fees for mortgages are normally based on the value of the secured amount under the mortgage, and the mortgagee can elect the actual value of the assets, or the advanced amount. Thus, the cost can be substantially increased, depending on the circumstances. There is also a registration fee for fiduciary transfers, which is a nominal amount.

Also, notary fees for preparing fiduciary transfers and pledges of shares vary and are negotiable.

5. Debt–equity swap

A debt–equity swap, or debt-for-equity swap, means a transaction in which a company's creditors cancel some or part of the debt in exchange for equity in the company. Because the creditor obtains shares instead of withdrawing cash, he becomes a shareholder – or if already holding shares, a larger shareholder – of the company, while the stake of original shareholders or other shareholders in the company is diluted. If both the debt and the remaining assets in the company are so large that there is no advantage for the creditor to drive the company into bankruptcy, the creditor may prefer to take control of the business as a going concern. As a consequence, the creditor can later sell the shares after stabilizing the company.

From the perspective of the original credit-swap shareholders, or other shareholders, however, it is hard to say losing control of the business is a good result. From the creditor's view too, it may worsen the situation by losing an opportunity to sell the bad loans, or to use asset-backed securitization (although the latter is as yet rarely used in Indonesia).

An example of a recent large size swap in Indonesia is the transaction where Bakrie & Brothers swapped its US$700 million debt as equity to Credit Suisse, Mitsubishi Corporation, and Eurofa Capital Investment.[17]

5.1. Procedures

Article 35

(1) Shareholders and other creditors having receivables against the Company may not set off these receivables against the payment obligation to pay the share price they have subscribed, except with the approval from the shareholders' meeting.
(2) The receivables towards the Company referred to in Paragraph (1) that may be set off against the payment of shares receivable on claims towards the Company which arise out of any of the following:

    a the Company has received the money or the surrender of tangible or intangible goods which have a monetary value.
    b a party who becomes the guarantor of the Company's debt has paid the Company's debt in full, for the amount guaranteed.
    c the Company becomes the guarantor of a third party's debt, and the Company has received benefits in the form of money or goods which have a monetary value which the Company has in fact directly or indirectly received.

A debt–equity swap may take place by transferring preexisting shares, or by issuing new shares to the creditor. As an Indonesian expert states:

> In the event that a creditor receives preexisting shares from a shareholder, it needs the company's guarantee of the debt. This is because of Article 35 Paragraph 2 Item c. Payment of the share purchase price can be relieved only when it comes under this provision.

To remove the company's debt, the shareholder must transfer as many of his shares as necessary to remove the debt. The agreement among the company, creditor, and shareholder must explicitly state that all the debt has been satisfied in consideration of the shares transferred. Of course, the share transfer must be

---

17 Linda Silaen, "Indonesian investor in $700M equity swap," *Asian Review* (10 February 2015): http://asia.nikkei.com/Business/Companies/Indonesian-investor-in-700M-equity-swap.

registered through the MLHR, pursuant to the procedures explained in the previ-ous section.

5.2.   *Legal effect*

A creditor becomes a shareholder – or if already a shareholder, a larger share-holder – upon the closure of the debt–equity swap, and is no longer able to claim the previous receivables against the company.

5   Shareholders' meeting

1.   Holding a shareholders' meeting

The shareholders' meeting is the highest mandatory organ of a company, making annual decisions regarding the company and important decisions to resolve specific issues concerning the company or shareholder interests.

1.1.   *How to call the shareholders' meeting of a closely held company*

A shareholders' meeting can be generally called by either the board of directors (Article 79 Paragraph 1), by one or more minority shareholders whose accumulated shares equate to at least 10 percent (or more if the articles of association provide) of ownership of the company (Article 79 Paragraph 2), by the board of commissioners (Article 79 Paragraph 6), or by court order (Article 80). Any resolution at a shareholders' meeting put by an unauthorized person is per se null and void without any special circumstances.

Articles 79 to 83 explain the procedures and administrative issues around the call for a shareholders' meeting in a closely held company.

The notice of the shareholders' meeting should be delivered to shareholders no later than 14 days prior to the convening of the meeting, and the notice must be sent by registered mail or announced in a daily newspaper. The notice must contain information on the date, time, place – and, specifically, the agenda – of the meeting. Also, the notice must inform shareholders that materials for the meeting are available in the office from the date of the notice until the date of the meeting. To resolve any issue which is not notified at the call, the requirement to notify shareholders in advance of the issue can be waived only with the unanimous agreement of all shareholders in attendance.

A closely held company's shareholder meeting can be held at the company's address or the main place of business specified in the articles of association within Indonesian territory, while a public company can hold the meeting at the Indonesia Stock Exchange (IDX). Alternatively, the meeting can be held at any place within Indonesian territory provided all the shareholders are in attendance or represented by a proxy (with a power of attorney, and who is not a director, commissioner, or employee of the company – Article 85), and the agenda is agreed (Article 76). Undoubtedly, a teleconference, videoconference, or any other electronic media that enables a shareholder located in foreign country or different region to attend the meeting may be used (Article 77). Thus, a foreign shareholder may exercise a voting right by attending the meeting in an electronic manner, or by being represented by a proxy.

When one or more minority shareholders who individually or together own 10 percent or more of shares want to convene a meeting, they may make a request to the board of directors. If the board of directors does not convene the meeting, the board of commissioners should do so. Therefore, to draft a request of a call for a shareholders' meeting, it is better to write to both the board of directors and the board of commissioners. If neither board convenes the meeting, the minority shareholder may take the request to the relevant court in the venue where the company is located.

1.2.   How to call a shareholders' meeting of a public company

For public companies, a notice of a general meeting of shareholders must be delivered to shareholders no later than 14 days prior to the convening of the meeting, and the notice must be sent by registered mail and/or announced in a daily newspaper. The notice must

- Contain information on the date, time, place and agenda of the shareholders' meeting
- Let shareholders know that materials for the meeting are available in the company's office from of the date of the notice until the date of the meeting

The notice of a shareholders' meeting can be waived if all shareholders attend the meeting and unanimously approve the resolution.

A meeting can be validly convened if attended or represented by parties holding more than 50 percent of the total shares with valid voting rights. If this quorum for the meeting is not reached, a notice for a second meeting can be sent informing shareholders that the first meeting failed to reach a quorum. The second shareholders' will be valid and entitled to adopt resolutions if attended by shareholders representing not less than one-third of all shares with valid voting rights. In the event the quorum for the second meeting is not reached, the company can request the chairman of the relevant District Court to determine the quorum for the third general meeting of shareholders.

A public company must convey notification of the agenda of the meeting to the OJK no later than 5 days before the announcement, which must be made at the latest 14 days before the invitation to the general meeting of shareholders is issued. The shareholders' meeting announcement must include the

- Eligibility requirements for shareholders to attend the meeting
- Requirements for eligible shareholders to propose agenda items

- Date of the meeting
- Date of the invitation

One or more shareholders who individually or collectively represent 5 percent or more of the total shares with voting rights can propose agenda items to the board of directors of the company, at least 7 days before the invitation for the meeting is issued. A company must invite shareholders to attend the meeting no later than 21 days before the meeting, excluding the date of the invitation and the date of the meeting. The invitation for the shareholder's meeting must at least include

- The venue, date, and time of the meeting
- Eligibility requirements for shareholders to attend the meeting
- The agenda with a summary of each item
- A statement that the agenda is available at the company's office or website from the date of the invitation until the date the meeting is held

Finally, the company must submit evidence of these announcements to the OJK no later than 2 days after the announcements are made.

These regulations apply to public companies within Indonesia. If a company is listed outside Indonesia, or issues a repository receipt in a foreign capital market, separate regulations in that country should be applied.

1.3.   Quorum and matters to be reserved

The shareholders' meeting is not an omnipotent organ. However, it has the authority to resolve those matters that are beyond the authority of the board of directors or the board of commissioners, and those matters required under the 2007 Company Act or the company's articles of association.

The quorum and minimum votes required for resolution of matters is stipulated in the 2007 Company Act, unless the articles of association state a higher

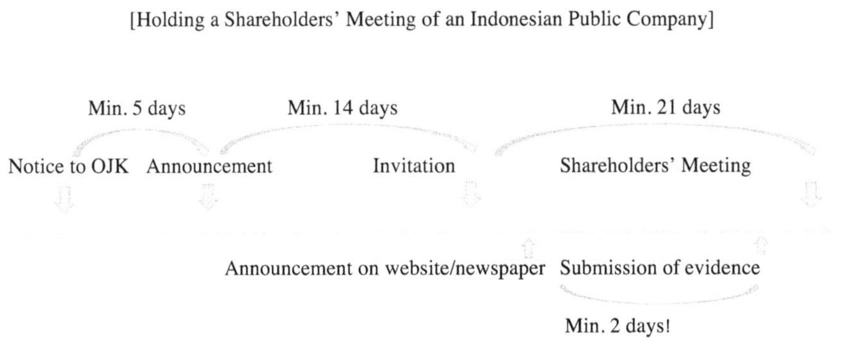

[Holding a Shareholders' Meeting of an Indonesian Public Company]

Min. 5 days	Min. 14 days	Min. 21 days
Notice to OJK Announcement	Invitation	Shareholders' Meeting

Announcement on website/newspaper   Submission of evidence

Min. 2 days!

Figure 5.1 Holding a shareholders' meeting of an Indonesian public company

quorum or minimum votes. In the event the quorum for the first shareholders' meeting is not met, the company must then hold a second shareholders' meeting (Article 86 Paragraph 2). The quorum and minimum vote requirements of each of the first and second shareholders' meeting are as follows:

A public company's shareholder meeting is also basically governed by the same quorum and principles. That is, if one-half of shareholders having voting-rights shares attend or are represented, the shareholder meeting is deemed valid. If such a quorum is not reached, a second shareholders' meeting can be held with a quorum of one-third of shareholders (or representatives) having voting-rights shares. The only difference is that if the quorum for the second shareholders' meeting is not reached again, a third shareholders' meeting can be held, with a quorum as stipulated by the OJK at the request of the public company.

Therefore, in general, a shareholder owning 50 percent or more of the total issued shares can in its sole discretion control most of an agenda that does not require amendment to the articles of association; and a shareholder owning 66.67 percent or more can in its sole discretion decide most matters, which may also include an amendment to the articles of association; and a shareholder owning 75 percent or more can its sole discretion also decide a significant change concerning the company's existence. Of course, a higher standard of protection for minority shareholders can be conceived in the articles of association.

Table 5.1 Quorum and minimum vote requirements for shareholder's meetings

Matter	First shareholder meeting	Second shareholder meeting
General matters		
Not explicitly stipulated (Articles 86–87)	Quorum: One-half of total voting-right shares present or represented.	Quorum: One-third of total voting-right shares present or represented.
	Approval: One-half of total voting-right shares.	Approval: One-half of total voting-right shares.
Special matters		
Amendment of the Articles of Association (Article 88)	Quorum: Two-thirds of total voting-right shares present or represented.	Quorum: Two-thirds of total voting-right shares present or represented.
	Approval: Two-thirds of total voting-right shares.	Approval: Three-fifths of total voting-right shares.
Merger, Consolidation, Acquisition, Separation, Bankruptcy, Extension of Life, and Liquidation (Article 89)	Quorum: Three-fourths of total voting-right shares present or represented.	Quorum: Two-thirds of total voting-right shares present or represented.
	Approval: Three-fourths of total voting-right shares.	Approval: Three-fourths of total voting-right shares.

If the agenda in an invitation of shareholders' meeting states "other matters," those additional agenda items can be resolved provided all shareholders at the meeting approve.

A case which annuls the resolution of shareholders' meeting about an agenda item omitted in the invitation *PT. Kodeco Timber vs. PT. Bintang Bengawan* (659/Pdt. G/2008/PN.JKT.Sel.)
The plaintiff, PT. Kodeco Timber, claimed that PT. Bintang Bengawan unlawfully obtained a shareholder resolution to issue new shares in defiance of the existing shareholders' preemptive rights. The plaintiff argued the resolution was per se void because (i) the actual meeting additionally resolved a change of directors and commissioners and issuance of new shares, although the defendant's shareholders' meeting invitation stated that the agenda of the meeting was to be debt restructure, share transfer, an accounting report, "and others" (*dan lain*); and (ii) the quorum of 66.66 percent was not satisfied because only the owners of 60 percent of total voting-right shares attended the meeting. The Court viewed the resolution void because "and others" could not be resolved insofar as all the shareholders agreed.

If the board of directors resolves any reserved matter of a shareholders' meeting without a shareholders' mandate, shareholders can invalidate such a resolution or resolve to the contrary. However, even if shareholders give the board's decision their mandate, the board of directors cannot take the place of shareholders' meeting for the matters that the 2007 Company Act specifically indicates must be resolved by a shareholders' meeting.

1.4. Proxy voting

A shareholder may exercise voting rights at a shareholders' meeting by delegating his power to a person with a power of attorney (Article 85). The person so designated is called a *proxy*. Proxy voting can remove a shareholder's burden to physically attend the meeting, yet still assist in providing a quorum. Because using a proxy for either convenience or need is a shareholder's inherent right, articles of association should not be able to restrict this ability.

A director, commissioner, or company employee cannot vote as a proxy of a shareholder (Article 84 Paragraph 4). Therefore, if a director, commissioner, or employee is present on behalf of a shareholder, he or she cannot not be included in the counting of votes to satisfy any minimum required. However, whether he or she can be included in counting to determine a quorum is arguable, because Article 84 Paragraph 4 states that they are not allowed to act as a proxy of the shareholder "in the voting" (*dalam pemungutan*), not "in the shareholders' meeting."

To be duly presented, a proxy should present the delegation of power of attorney. If he fails so, the company can reject his representation. If such delegation has been duly established, the company should not reject the proxy's representation merely because the power of attorney is a copy. If the company still rejects his representation despite the duly established delegation, such undue or unfair rejection constitutes a cause of unlawful resolution.

Advice for foreign investors residing outside of Indonesia who cannot attend a shareholders' meeting

A parent company of a PMA having only foreign directors, all residing outside of Indonesia, may find itself unable to resolve a matter. In this case, as mentioned earlier, a power of attorney with a proxy for every single agenda item should be provided. Solving this problem requires breathtakingly pesky procedures.

Although bureaucratic red tape varies according to each country, in Indonesia in 2017, a foreign shareholder was required to (i) notarize his signature with a notary public, (ii) obtain proof of the notary's registration and authority at a court, (iii) obtain a signature affirming this from the Ministry of Law, (iv) obtain confirmation and sign this at the Court, the Ministry of Law and before a notary at the Ministry of Foreign Affairs, and finally, (v) receive a signature from the Indonesian Embassy. It seems an extreme and yet actual example of "red-tapism."

1.5. Deadlock in shareholders' meeting

A deadlock situation arises when contrary or conflicting opinions on a significant issue reach a stalemate with equal number of votes for each side (e.g. 5:5 or 1:1:1). The deadlock should be broken in a commercial manner or via a contract, since the law leaves such a resolution up to the parties. Thus, a shareholders' agreement or joint venture agreement should generally determine how acute disagreement on significant issues should be resolved.

The majority of contract drafters in Indonesia seem to choose to resolve the deadlock or dispute at an arbitration center or a court after some cooling-off period, or an amicable settlement period. Still, deadlock provisions vary depending on what matters the parties want to ensure consensus upon, whether the parties are of equal standing in the venture, and other factors.

The following are examples of some common deadlock provisions:

- **Mediation** is a provision that a deadlock should be resolved by appointing a mediator who helps resolve it in an amicable way within a certain period. However, such a deadlock provision is likely to only waste time. The fact that a deadlock has arisen at all suggests the parties have an acute conflict of interest and are sharply divided over a thorny issue. Even if the president were appointed as intermediary, it would be still difficult to resolve. Even if the mediator makes a reasonable determination like the judgment of Solomon, an unsatisfied party may still question its reasonableness to the court.

- A **deterrence approach** is a provision to deter a deadlock situation in the first place by providing a punitive element for the party initiating the dead-lock procedure. The punitive element may require the party initiating the procedure to either purchase the other party's shares at a specified high price, or to sell its own shares at a specified low price. The downside is that it does not help resolve the issue causing the deadlock at all.
- **Winner-takes-all** is a draconian provision in which each party bids the price to *purchase* the opponent's shares, and the highest bidder "wins," purchasing all the other party's shares at that highest bid price.
- A **Dutch auction** is the opposite provision of winner-takes-all. The parties instead bid the minimum price to *sell* its shares. Again, the winner who bids the higher sell price must buy the loser's shares at the price bid by the loser.
- **Multi-choice procedure** is a provision to put forth a set of fixed options. The parties must agree on one option to break the deadlock. The downside is that those options drafted into the articles of association may not quite fit the actual situation when a deadlock occurs some years later. Thus, the parties are likely to remain at loggerheads, at which time a third non-interested party (or mediator) comes in to select one of the options on their behalf.

1.6.   *Defects in shareholders' meetings*

Since a shareholders' meeting is intertwined with many stakeholders' interests, a defect in procedures of the meeting or in the substance of the resolution needs to be treated strictly. The 2007 Company Act does not provide a spectrum of gravity or type of such defects. In other words, Indonesia does not differentiate between a suit seeking cancellation or amendment of a resolution, affirmation of the absence or illegality of a resolution, nullifying a voidable resolution, etc. In Indonesian practice, accordingly, to argue any defect in a shareholders' meeting, a plaintiff always claims that the shareholder meeting or a resolution is null and void (*batal demi hukum*), and rarely maintains the absence of a meeting or the withdrawal of a resolution.

2.   List of shareholders

The list of shareholders refers to company's internal document clarifying the shareholders and their rights in shares pursuant to company law.[1] There is a general list of shareholders specified in Article 50 Paragraph 1, and a special list of shareholders in Paragraph 2. Each should be stored at the company for shareholders to find and read. Indonesia does not have any codified exception to this rule for foreign companies.

---

1 To see an example of the list of shareholders for financial companies distributed by Bank Indonesia, see www.bi.go.id/id/peraturan/perbankan/Documents/Lampiran_se_154914. PDF.

The rationale of this requirement is not only to protect shareholders and the company, but also to capture share flows which are related to inheritance tax, gift tax, income tax, transaction tax, dividends tax, or any other relevant tax.

2.1.   *General list of shareholders*

The general list of shareholders should describe the following items:

- Name and address of shareholders
- Amount paid-up for each share
- Name and address of any individual or legal entity having a pledge over the shares or the fiduciary guarantee of the fiduciary over shares, and the acquisition date of pledge on shares or registration date of the fiduciary security
- Description of the payment for shares in other forms, as referred to in Article 34 Paragraph (2)

A company must update the general list of shareholders for its investors to exercise rights as shareholders (Article 50 Paragraphs 1 and 2). In other words, the person named in the general list of shareholders is presumed to be a shareholder of the company, and thus able to exercise their rights as such without further showing that he is the valid owner of a share certificate. Thus, the list of shareholders establishes the named person's entitlement. If the company still desires to reject a shareholder exercise of his rights, it should produce contrary evidence that he is not a valid shareholder. If the company accepts his exercise of preemptive rights, voting rights, dividends rights, or any other shareholder's right as written in the general list of shareholders, the company should be exempt in general should his ownership of shares later be found to be invalid or void.

In contrast, if the company knew, or had a reason to know, that the person recorded in the list of shareholders was not an actual valid shareholder, or if the company could reject such an illegal attempt to exercise voting rights by easily proving such an invalid ownership but did not do so, or allowed him to vote, such an exercise of voting rights is illegitimate. For example, let us suppose that shareholder A and outsider B made a share sale and purchase agreement, and subsequently a company listed B as a shareholder without proper examination before the conditions precedent for ownership transfer were satisfied. In this case, the company should not allow B to exercise any shareholder rights despite B's shareholder status being recorded in the general list of shareholders.

2.2.   *Special list of shareholders*

Article 50 (2)

Apart from the general list of shareholders as referred to in Paragraph (1), the Board of Directors is obliged to make and keep a special list of shareholders containing information regarding the shares of the members of the Board of Directors and the Board of Commissioners, together with their families, in the Company and/or other Company, as well as the date acquisition of such shares.

This article seems to aim at reducing an agency cost[2] by specifying the fiduciary duty of directors and commissioners to the company. However, such a well-intentioned aim has been shadowed by the rough-and-ready legislation, which mandates a list be kept of all shares owned by directors, commissioners, their spouses, and parents.

To see how unrealistic this approach is, think about trading securities or available-for-sale securities which are momentarily or temporarily owned for margin. Scalpers own shares at times only for seconds, literally. To see this requirement is utterly ignorant of legal principles, let us suppose that a director's spouse has some shares in a closely held company which has nothing to do with the director's company at all, that she does not want to let her husband know of her ownership of these shares, and that the company also desires to protect its ownership status as a commercial secret. What is the prevailing benefit of infringing her privacy and causing the unrelated company to breach its confidentiality?

Undoubtedly, whether a closely held or a public company, it seems extremely rare to see a company thoroughly updating its special list of shareholders and maintaining it (of course, all companies insist that they do). As can be imagined, the cost of this requirement severely outweighs any benefit, as no sanction is imposed on negligence in updating any special list of shareholders, and seeking a remedy for any direct damages based on an incomplete special list of shareholders is far-fetched.

3. Shareholder's rights

3.1. Definition

Shareholder's rights refer to the legal status and rights of shareholders in a company based on ownership of the stock. Because a shareholder's right is based on stock, these rights cannot be transferred or seized separately from the stock. In many other countries, if a final and conclusive assignment order is made by

---

2 An agency cost is an economic cost to a principal, when the principal uses an agent who may have a conflict of interest or moral hazard. Although agency cost is present in any agency relationship, the term is most used in a business context between shareholders and directors. While shareholders are concerned with increasing share value, management may be more concerned with increasing personal wealth using more information than available to shareholders, and imperfect supervision. Agency cost is not only this inherently associated risk, but also the cost to mitigate the risk.

the court, the seized claim is immediately transferred to the execution creditor in lieu of the payment. Thus, it is deemed that the debtor has reimbursed his or her debts when the assignment order was served on the garnishee. Unfortunately, Indonesian civil procedure law does not provide the assignment order and, thus, stock cannot be subject to the assignment order. Of course, the right does not expire due to time passing, and should be differentiated with a specifically decided receivable, such as a right to claim dividends receivable, which has already been specifically agreed in a resolution of the board of directors.

3.2.   *Rights in economic interests*

An investor's direct economic interest should be secured for withdrawal of his investment and the right to enjoy gains in return for the investment.

The 2007 Company Act recognizes the right to receive a distribution of remaining assets at liquidation (Article 150), and a right to claim correction of the list of shareholders (Article 50 Paragraphs 1 and 2) so that investors can withdraw their investment. Further, it protects a shareholder's right to join a return of gains, such as the right to claim dividends (Article 71 Paragraph 2) and preemptive rights (Article 43 Paragraph 2).

3.3.   *Minority stockholder and single-stock owner's rights*

Minority shareholder rights require a certain minimum shareholding rate, while single-stock owner rights are protected even if they own only one share.

Minority shareholder rights in an Indonesian closely held company that necessitate at least 10 percent ownership: the right to claim a derivative suit against directors who has incurred damages (Article 97 Paragraph 6: 10%), the right to adjourn the shareholders' meeting for special matters (Article 79 Paragraph 2: 10%) and the investigation right (Article 138 Paragraph 1: 10%). These rights can be exercised by either one shareholder or a number of shareholders who own 10 percent or more issued outstanding shares in total.

A single-stock owner's rights include the rights to claim a remedy of damages against the company (Article 61 Paragraph 1), to examine the company's books (Article 67 Paragraph 1), to offer stock subscriptions (Article 62), etc. Although the 2007 Company Act does not specifically stipulate a "golden" stock which has absolute veto rights over all the other stockholders, it is possible to give a voting right to only one stock, leaving all the other stocks lame.

The protection of minority stockholders in Indonesia is substantially different from that in other countries. For example, in New York, discriminative oppression by majority shareholders against minority shareholders has long been harshly criticized as bad faith and dishonest purposes under the court's view. Furthermore, majority shareholders have a fiduciary duty to minority shareholders.

In Indonesia, the likelihood of a minor shareholder's triumph is far lower, unless some influential factors join any action. First, Indonesia does not recognize a major shareholder's fiduciary duty to minor shareholders, similar to most civil law jurisdictions. Second, a minor shareholder's right to retrieve his investment is not guaranteed, either by stipulation or case law. For example, a contract requiring advance approval from other shareholders for a share sale is unlimitedly permitted, and thus valid and enforceable. Third, the shareholder may demand the company buy back his shares at a reasonable price if damaged by company's act, which is limited to the following acts only:[3]

- Amendment of articles of association
- Transfer or giving a security over the company's assets which occupy 50 percent or more of the total net assets
- Merger, consolidation, acquisition, or separation

Instead, however, the minority shareholder has one last resort to protect himself or herself, which is the powerful investigation right (Article 138). A minor shareholder owning 10 percent or more total shares can request a court to investigate the company with experts (details are explained later in the section *Inspection of the Company.*) Because the court may approve such an investigation even if the request is based on mere suspicion without any evidence, a minor shareholder may simply request an investigation if a plausible reason is provided. Because any honest and diligent business man in Indonesia can still be caught because of a slight mistake in administration, bureaucratic interpretation of vague law, or for whatever other misguided reason, this strategy actually operates much like a corporate suicide or a "poison pill." No doubt if a minor shareholder uses any data and information obtained from this investigation, nobody can guarantee that a court will not determine the majority shareholder's actions are a tortious act against the plaintiff. Eventually, the majority shareholder is likely to accept the minority shareholder's demands.

Widely accepted hearsay among foreign businessmen is that this inspection right is often misused by a local shareholder who is not actually engaged in business at all, instead participating as a stockholder solely because of the Negative Investment List or divestment requirement. Since both the Negative Investment List and the notorious divestment requirement necessitate an Indonesian stockholder, foreign businessmen inevitably seek a domestic partner, who may however later change his mind and demand some commissions. Then, even if the local stockholder does not directly raise the topic of inspection, the foreign major shareholder cannot easily ignore the demand for commissions when aware of all the aforementioned risks. Even worse, whether the minority shareholder has a strong case or not, the company and majority shareholder would suffer considerable stress dealing with such a demand.

3 Ira A. Eddymurthy & Tengku Almira Adlinisa, *Shareholders' Rights in Private and Public Companies in Indonesia: Overview, Q. 16, Practical Law*, A Thomson Reuters Legal Solution, 2015.

In a nutshell, the investigation right is the last resort for protection, but at the same time, it also incentivizes minor shareholders to behave badly.

3.3.1.   *The right to file a derivative suit against a director*

Article 97

(3) Each member of the Board of Directors shall be fully and personally liable over the loss of the Company if it resulted from its fault or negligent in performing its duties. . . .

(4) In the event the Board of Directors consist of 2 (two) members or more, the responsibility as referred to in Paragraph (3) shall jointly and severally apply to each member of the Board of Directors.

(6) On behalf of the Company, the shareholders representing at least 1/10 (one-tenth) from the total number of shares with voting right, may submit a claim to a District Court against member of the Board of Directors which causes loss to the Company due to their fault or negligence.

The details are explained in the later section "Derivative suits."

3.3.2.   *Investigation rights*

Article 138

(1) Inspection over the Company may be performed with the purpose to obtain data or explanation in the event that there are suspicions concerning the following:

   a the Company has committed an illegal action which may cause adverse effect to the shareholders or the third party; or

   b the members of the Board of Directors or the Board of Commissioners has committed an illegal action that may cause adverse effect to the Company or shareholders or the third parties.

(2) Inspection as referred to in Paragraph (1) shall be performed by submitting an application in writing together with the reasons to the District Court with jurisdiction covering the domicile of the Company;

(3) The application as referred to in Paragraph (2) shall be submitted by:

   a 1 (one) shareholder or more representing at least 1/10 (one-tenth) of the total number of shares with voting rights . . .

(4) The application as referred to in Paragraph (3) shall be submitted after having requested the Company to provide the data or

---

information in the Shareholders' Meeting, and the Company does not provide such data and information;

(5) The application to obtain data and information of the Company or application for inspection to obtain data and information shall be on the basis of a reasonable reason and with good faith.

(6) The provision . . . shall not preclude the possibility of the capital market regulation to stipulate otherwise.

3.3.3. The right to claim a remedy from the company

Article 61

(1) Each shareholder shall have the right to file a suit against the Company to the District Court if they suffer losses due the action of the Company which is considered to be unfair and unreasonable as a result of a resolution of the Shareholders' Meeting, the Board of Directors, and/or the Board of Commissioners.

Official Elucidation

Suits filed must basically contain a request that the Company cease the harmful action and take specific steps to deal with the consequences which have already arisen and to prevent similar action at a later date.

3.3.4. The right to claim a buy-out

Article 62

(1) Each shareholder shall have the right to request the Company to purchase its shares with a reasonable price if the shareholder concerned does not agree with the action of the Company which harm the shareholders or the Company in the form of

a amendment to the articles of association;
b the transfer or the encumbrance of the Company's assets, having a nominal value of more than 50 percent of the net assets of the Company; or
c merger, consolidation, acquisition, or separation.

(2) In the event that the shares requested to be purchased as referred to in Paragraph (1) exceed the limit of the buy-back requirements by the Company as referred to in Article 37 Paragraph (1) letter b, the Company is obliged to endeavor that the remaining shares be purchased by a third party.

Article 37

(1) the Company may buy back the shares which have issued under the following conditions:

  b the amount of nominal value of all shares bought back by the Company and the pledge of shares or the fiduciary security on shares held by the Company itself, and/or other Company which shares are directly or indirectly owned by the Company does not exceed 10 percent from the amount of issued capital in the Company, except otherwise regulated in the legislation in the field of capital markets.

Shareholders must be allowed to exit by selling out their shares to somebody if brutally ignored in making an important corporate decision that can change the entire nature of the company, whether the actual damages have been already incurred or not. Therefore, the draft of the article stating "act of Company that incurs damages to the shareholder or the Company (*tindakan Perseroan yang merugikan pemegang saham atau Perseroan*)" seems erroneous. It should instead be "act of Company that 'may' incur damages to the shareholders or the Company (*tindakan Perseroan yang 'dapat' merugikan pemegang saham atau Perseroan*)."

Because an acquiring company should issue new shares to shareholders of a target company in the process of a merger-acquisition, the acquiring company must increase the authorized capital if not sufficient. Should a shareholder of the target company oppose the merger-acquisition and request a buy-out of his shares, there is no need to issue new shares to this opposing shareholder. Therefore, a side benefit of allowing shareholders to exercise the right to claim a buy-out is that the company can know in advance whether to increase authorized capital.

Restriction on transfer of shares and shareholder's right to retrieve investment in a closely held company

Although courts in common law and civil law jurisdictions have less doubt on the assumption that stock in a corporation is personal property, each jurisdiction has a different view whether a restriction on transfer of shares should be regarded with disfavor as if it was a restraint on alienation of personal property.

Let us suppose the following cases in a closely held corporation:

Case 1: Shareholders have made a contract that a shareholder should obtain advance approval from the board of directors to sell shares within 5 years from the share purchase. Also, the same limitation has been placed in the articles of association.

Case 2: A shareholder and a company have made a contract that the shareholder cannot sell his shares for 5 years. Also, the same limitation has been placed in the articles of association.

In New York, the consent requirement is likely to be null and void, because the corporation could refuse for no reason. A 5-year restriction is also likely to be deemed undue restraint on alienation.

In South Korea, such a mandatory approval requirement is likely to be effective, but the 5-year limitation would be null and void. Arguably, the mandatory holding period could have been effective if it had been less than 5 years (Supreme Court 99Da4842).

In Indonesia, both the advance approval requirement and the 5-year limitation are legitimate and effective in the absence of a contrary court judgment.

4. Shareholder duties and responsibilities

Shareholder duties generally refer to the liability to contribute the price of subscribed stocks to the company. In principle, a shareholder should not be liable for anything other than his investment. Because this limited liability is the very nature of company, the company should not increase it. Nonetheless, this does not bar a shareholder's additional cash injection, or payment of the company's debt on its behalf with his own free will.

One arguable issue is whether a shareholder also has a fiduciary duty to other shareholders in exercising voting rights or acting for the company. U.S. case law has been developed in such a way that the director's fiduciary duty is extended to the major shareholders, thereby obligating a major shareholder to consider other shareholders' interests as well if he desires to sell his shares. Some other countries have a similar position in either case law or stipulated law.[4]

In Indonesia, however, fiduciary duty is difficult to extend to the shareholders, because the 2007 Company Act does not explicitly state it, and the concept of fiduciary duty itself is unclear about its requirements, consequences, effects, etc.

4.1. *Duty of contribution*

A creditor to a company cannot set off his receivables and contribution liability without shareholders' advance approval (Article 35 Paragraph 1).[5] That is, creditors cannot reduce his contribution for share subscription even if he has receivables due from the company. However, it is unclear whether the set-off is not allowed, even if both the company and creditor desire it and such a set-off does not harm any interest holder of the company.

4 For Germany, see RG 132, 149, 162; BGH 103, 194: Lutter, "Die Treupflicht des Aktionars," ZHR 153 (1989), S. 447.
5 In some countries, a debt–equity swap or a set-off between receivables and contributions obligations is allowed only in reorganization procedures for corporate safety. However, the double-dip recession triggered by subprime mortgage crisis of 2008 in the United States changed these jurisdictions' approach in a way that a set-off or debt–equity swap could be used more easily, so that a company in recession could write off its debt. Unfortunately, Indonesia's Company Act has not been amended in the same way.

4.2.   Shareholder's responsibilities

In principle, shareholders are not responsible for corporate governance or company actions beyond their investments in the company. One exception to this rule is tax liability: Indonesian tax authority invoices a shareholder if his company does not fully pay an imposed tax, and it will not issue any approval related to the company's liquidation until the imposed tax is paid in full.

In addition, an ultimate beneficial owner controlling an insurance company may be directly liable for the company's responsibility according to the 2014 Insurance Act No. 40, and the shareholders of a bank may be responsible in accordance to regulations concerning shareholding levels of banking governance.

4.3.   Piercing the corporate veil

The general principle of limited liability may be inapplicable in some situations, and as a result the shareholders may be held personally liable for the company's action or debt. The very well-known example of such an exception is where the legal entity status is permanently or momentarily deprived.

"Piercing the corporate veil" or "lifting the corporate veil" is the legal theory explaining when this exception is applicable. It treats the rights or duties of a company as the rights and obligations of its shareholders if certain conditions are satisfied. However, the corporate veil (i.e. the separate legal entity status) is not completely removed even in this case. Instead, it may be temporarily pierced (i.e. disregarded) in a particular case to shift the responsibility to the person responsible.

Indonesia has codified what events lift the corporate veil and hold shareholders unlimitedly liable as follows:

Article 3

(1) The Company's Shareholders are not personally liable for agreements made on behalf of the Company, and they are not liable for the Company's losses in excess of their prospective shareholding.

(2) The provision as referred to in Paragraph (1) does not apply if

   a   the requirements for the Company as a legal entity have not been or are not fulfilled;
   b   the relevant shareholders, either directly or indirectly, with bad faith, exploit the Company for their personal interest;
   c   the relevant shareholders are involved in illegal actions committed by the Company; or

   d   the relevant Shareholders, either directly or indirectly, illegally utilize the assets of the Company, which result in the Company's assets become insufficient to settle the Company's debt.

To lift the corporate veil via the previous Article, nevertheless, the plaintiff must overcome a substantial burden of proof because the dominant principle of limited liability should only fail to govern in exceptional circumstances. The mere fact that a company has no financial capacity to repay a debt, or has no intent to repay, is insufficient. Although the codified Article is not specific, courts and legal scholars list the circumstances to prove one or more of the following:

- The company has been controlled by an individual shareholder.
- If the company's act is not regarded as the individual shareholder's act, it results in substantial unfairness.
- An individual shareholder has abused the company's legal entity and company law with intention or aim to acquit himself or herself of its responsibility in bad faith that consequently damages another party.[6]

Since the court considers a totality of circumstances, to successfully show the above circumstances, the plaintiff should prepare considerable data on all of these items that apply:

- False or incomplete entries in the company's establishment deed or articles of association
- Undercapitalization
- Concealment by directors or officers
- Absence of any employees or offices
- Absence of dividends
- Absence of participation of business or commercial activity
- Mixed use of company's assets and main owner's assets
- Main owner's misappropriation of company assets
- Size and extent of the assets appropriated to the third party
- Whether an appropriate value has been given as a compensation for asset transfer, if any
- Whether the company is used as a mere conduit of cash flow or personal asset

Besides these, all or any relevant facts should be substantiated to successfully show the main owner's use of corporate structure for personal transactions.

---

6 *"Itikad buruk yang menimbulkan kerugian kepada pihak lain" PT. Bank Perkembangan Asia v. PT. Djaja Tunggal*, No. 1916 K/Pdt/1991 (1996).

> A case that the court lift the corporate veil on directors and commissioners: *PT. Bank Perkembangan Asia v. PT. Djaja Tunggal* (Supreme Court of Indonesia No. 1916 K/Pdt//1991 (1996)
>
> The plaintiff bank advanced a loan to the defendant borrower without credit analysis, and the defendant provided a mortgage of real estate with cultivation right (*hak guna usaha*). At the time, the bank's directors and commissioners were also the directors and commissioners of the defendant borrower. When the defendant fell in default and the plaintiff bank attempted to foreclose, the mortgage turned out to be impossible to foreclose due to the expiration of the cultivation right. The plaintiff bank subsequently dismissed the involved directors and commissioners and immediately brought a claim against the company and all the dismissed directors and commissioners. The Supreme Court determined that those directors and commissioners had constructive knowledge and conspiracies because they advanced the loan without credit analysis, despite the document showing that the cultivation right would expire in a few years. Therefore, the Supreme Court pierced the corporate veil and decided the joint and several liabilities among the defendants.

5.   Change of shareholder (transfer of shares)

A transfer of shares in Indonesia requires more time, a heavier process, and more tolerance compared to other countries. Even for a transfer of only a small number of shares, the articles of association must be still amended as it is mandatory to identify shareholders in the articles of association. Further, a deed of share transfer should be signed because shares are transferred by the deed of transfer of rights (Article 56 Paragraph 1), not by the tender of share certificate. As an option, a so-called legalization process (*legalisasi*) is often used to prevent parties later fraudulently claiming they did not sign a deed. The share transfer must be delivered to the company as a notification (Article 56, Paragraph 2). Subsequently, the company must issue a share certificate (*sertifikat*) as the proof of share ownership pursuant to Article 51. Upon the issuance of new *sertifikat*, it is advisable to shred the previous share owner's *sertifikat*, as it does not show whether it has been nullified.

In sum, a share acquirer should receive shares and the deed of share transfer from the previous share owner, and a *sertifikat* from the company. Legalization of the share transfer is optional.

As discussed earlier, the board of directors should record shareholder details including name and address, subscription date, class of shares, subscription price, share pledger's name and address, etc. on a list of shareholders pursuant to Article 50. To update this company registry, the MLHR should be notified of any share transfer within 30 days of the date when it is recorded on the list of shareholders (Article 56 Paragraph 3). If the 30-day period elapses without timely notification, the MLHR can refuse to approve the share transfer (Article 56 Paragraph 4).

An important issue to note about share transfers and assignments in Indonesia is that agreement from a seller's spouse is a mandatory condition to validly acquire shares. All assets obtained after marriage are subject to joint ownership between the husband and wife in the absence of a prenuptial agreement to the contrary under Article 120 of Indonesia Civil Code. A share purchaser should be advised that any assumption of shares may be voidable without agreement from the seller's spouse. Further, in the event of inheritance of a shareholder's assets upon his death, the deceased's oldest spouse and descendants become joint owners of the shares. To acquire such shares, a purchaser must have agreement from all the descendants and the spouse. Because it may be too difficult to personally visit many descendants, a power of attorney is often used, so that an appointee signs on behalf of a group of descendants. However, the share purchaser should proceed with great care in this case. It is possible the principal may argue he did not actually sign the power of attorney, and thus the share sale is invalid. Normally, he can subsequently command a substantial premium as a settlement fee.

The transfer of listed shares is governed by the Capital Market Act.

5.1. The sequence of share transfer

Share Sale and Purchase Agreement

In general, the closing of the sale is conditional onnecessary approvals and permits from authorities and terms set by parties.

If the contract is governed by Indonesian law, the contract must be made in the form of notarized deed (*akta*) pursuant to Article 56. In the meantime, if the contract is made by foreign entity or persons, and governed by foreign laws, it remains valid without making an *akta*.

The following process should be prepared at the same time and notarized.

(a) Preparation of shareholder resolution

The quorum for a shareholder resolution (Article 88) should be satisfied for any amendment of articles (with presence of two-third of total shares issued with voting rights, and two-third of total votes cast at the meeting)

(b) Change in articles of association and shareholders list

The board of director should record the items at Article 50 on both the general and special lists of shareholders.

(c) Pay for share subscription and tender share certificate

Nullifying pre-existing shareholder certificate (*Sertifikat Saham*). Subscription of share and certificate.

Notification to the MLHR and record at the company registry

The board of directors should notify the change to the MLHR to record in the company registry within 30 days. Otherwise, the MLHR may reject the application.

MLHR's Final Approval and Record on the Company Registry

Figure 5.2 The sequence of share transfer

5.2.   *Example of Indonesian share certificate*

SURAT SAHAM KOLEKTIF
COLLECTIVE SHARE CERTIFICATE
No: 001

PT ABC
("Perseroan")
(the "Company")

Berkedudukan di Jakarta, didirkan dengan Akta Pendirian No.[***] tanggal [***] dibuat di hadapan [***] di [***], yang telah disahkan dengan Persetujuan Menteri Hukum dan Hak Asasi Manusia No. [***] tanggal [***] dan telah diubah terakhir kali dengan Akta Pernyataan Keputusan Pemegang Saham Perseroan No. [**] tanggal [***] dibuat di hadapan [***] di [***] yang telah disetujui oleh Menteri Hukum dan Hak Asasi Manusia berdasarkan Surat Keputusan No. [***] tinggal [**] dan Perbuahan Anggaran Dasarnya telah diterima dan dicatat berdasarkan Surat No.[***] tanggal [***].

Domiciled in Jakarta, established by Deed of Establishment No. # dated [***] made before [***] Notary in [***], which has been legalized by Ministry of Law and Human Rights No. [***] dated [***] and lastly amended by Deed of Resolution of Shareholders No.[***] dated [***] made before [***] Notary in [***] which has been approved by Ministry of Law and Human Rights under Decree No. [***] and the Change of Articles of Association has been accepted and recorded based on Letter No. [***] dated [***].

MODAL DASAR PERSEROAN
AUTHORIZED CAPITAL OF THE COMPANY
Rp.[***]

MODAL DITEMPATKAN PERSEROAN
SUBSCRIBED CAPITAL OF THE COMPANY
Rp.[***]

MODAL DISETOR PERSEROAN
PAID-UP CAPITAL OF THE COMPANY
Rp.[***]

Terbagi atas:
[***] saham masing-masing dengan nilai nominal Rp. [***]

Dividend into:
[***] shares each with a nominal value of Rp. [***]

SURAT KOLEKTIF BUKTI PEMILIKAN SAHAM
COLLECTIVE CERTIFICATE EVIDENCING SHARE OWNERSHIP

No. 000001

Sebagai bukti pemilikan   As evidence of ownership

Sampai dengan

Up to and including

No. *****

Tedaftar atas nama

Registered under the name of

[***]

Pemilik/ pemegang [***] saham

Owner' holder of [***] shares

[Date]

Name:_____   Name:_____

Title:_____   Title:_____

6. Restriction on transfer of shares

6.1. *Restriction on transfer of shares by shareholders agreement and articles of association*

6.1.1. *Introduction*

Preventing a shareholder from selling his shares to an unknown outsider is a problem for the initial shareholders of closely held company. Shareholders of the closely held company usually operate in intimate contact with one another, and shares are sold not so much to raise money as to bring capable personnel into the company. A new shareholder without managerial capacity, understanding, and determination may be a real detriment. Hence, closely held companies often seek to impose restrictions upon the transfer of shares.

Generally speaking, a restriction on stock transfer in a closely held company is any condition or limitation which qualifies the right of a shareholder to alienate his interest in the company. It may take the form of an absolute prohibition of transfer, a prohibition of transfer to designated individuals or members of class, or a condition that any share transfer will be void unless the shareholder first offers the shares to the company or the other shareholders.

It is now settled throughout Indonesia that restrictions may be imposed on a shareholder's right to transfer shares. Restriction may be imposed by Articles of Association (Article 57 Paragraph 1) or by an independent shareholders' agreement. Additionally, the 2007 Company Act does not require that the stock restriction must appear on a stock certificate to bind purchasers.

6.1.2. Kinds of restrictions on share transfer

Article 57 Paragraph 1 states that any or all of the following restrictions may be applied to share transfers, where shareholders must mandatorily

- offer the shares to shareholders with a particular classification, or other shareholders;
- seek prior approval from the company's organs; and/or
- seek approval from the authorized agency in accordance with the provisions of legislative regulations.

These restrictions on share transfers are widely regarded as simply examples of share transfer restriction, and a variety of variations are actually used in Indonesian legal practice.

The further variety of share-transfer restrictions are now explained.

6.1.2.1. ABSOLUTE PROHIBITION OF DISPOSAL

In general, the majority of foreign jurisdictions in industrialized countries deem an absolute prohibition of alienation void and ineffective. In the common law approach in the United States, for example, such a restraint in stock transfer is invalid as against public policy because stocks are treated as personal property, and the same principles governing personal property are applied to stock transactions.[7] However, no leading case in Indonesia is found for the same result.

For example, a form of ownership limitation that requires that the stock be transferred only to Indonesian citizens is valid and effective (Supreme Court No. 1529 K/Pdt/2005).[8]

6.1.2.2. CONSENT REQUIREMENT

A shareholder may be required to obtain advance consent from a company organ to convey his shares (Article 57 Paragraph 1 Item b).[9] In general, not only the sale or transfer of the shares, but also any pledge to do so is limited.

It is uncommon to find absolute recognition of the validity of such a consent requirement in referable foreign jurisdictions. This is because a shareholder's

---

7 For example, a type of ultimate restraint on alienation in real property is called fee tail, a form of ownership which requires that property be passed down in the same family from generation to generation. This has also been widely abolished. Also, under the tax law, 26 U.S. Internal Revenue Code Article 338 stipulates certain stock purchases be treated as asset acquisitions.

8 However, if the foreign owner's maximum shares in the company's business field has been amended to 100 percent, or has opted out of the Negative Investment List, there seems to be considerable room to claim invalidity of such a restraint.

9 Company organs means the general meeting of shareholders, the board of directors, and the board of commissioners (Article 1 Paragraph 2).

right to monetize shares may be indefinitely ignored by others for no good reason. Indonesia, however, explicitly allows such a requirement at Article 57 Paragraph 1 Item b of the 2007 Company Act, and, further the Court does not place a limitation on this requirement.

In *Yayasan Sandhykara Putra Telkom (YSPT) vs. Tn. Zaenal Abdi* (No.2507K/ Pdt/2013), PT. Sandy Putra Makmur's articles of association and bylaws required the written consent from the board of directors and the board of commissioners for the transfer of any rights over shares. However, the stocks of shareholder (Ny Tri Ekorini Prasetio) in PT. Sandy Putra Makmur were sold to a third party (Tuan Gunanda) without satisfying this requirement. The court decided the share sales and purchase contract in this case were void in the absence of the consent in accordance to the articles of association on the basis of the specific item of the 2007 Company Act. The court did not consider whether the third party was a *bona fide* purchaser, or whether an indefinite consent requirement remained valid.

A case that rendered the sale of stocks invalid and ineffective due to not satisfying a consent requirement written in articles of association (No. 85/ PDT.G/2013/PN.Jkt.Pst)

In this case, PT. Indotruba Tengah ("IT") had the following shareholders:

- Yayasan Kartika Ekapaksi as the holder of 6,200 shares
- PT Minamas Gemilang as the holder of 3,100 shares
- PT Anugerah Sumber Makmur as the holder of 3,100 shares

Yayasan Kartika Ekapaksi desired to sell its all stocks in IT to an outsider, PT Mulia Agro Persada, and made a written shareholders' resolution as if consent from other shareholders had been obtained. The court viewed this sale of stocks void because the shareholders' resolution did not fulfill "consent from all the shareholders" in the articles of association of PT. Indotruba Tengah, nor Article 91 of the 2007 Company Act.

A noteworthy feature in this case is that the court did not consider whether the share purchaser was a *bona fide* purchaser, and directly invalidated the stock sales without considering compensation for damages.

One advisable point in drafting contracts is considering an exception for a share conveyance among the same group of companies. Generally, it is better to place stock transfers among the same group companies as an exception to mandatory consents. There is no need to equally require consent from other shareholders where a shareholder needs to transfer shares within the same corporate group for reorganization or management purposes. For other shareholders, it would instead be safer to require joint and several liability to the share transferor, because the share transferee's financial capacity may be insufficient to perform the preexisting contract as a mere special purpose company (SPC) or substantially smaller company.

6.1.2.3.   COMPANY'S BUY-BACK

A company can repurchase issued shares only if it fulfills the following requirements in Article 37 Paragraph 1.

- The repurchase of shares does not cause the net assets of the company to become less than the subscribed capital plus the mandatory reserves set aside.
- The total nominal value of all the shares repurchased by the company, and any pledge of shares or fiduciary security over shares held by the company itself or by some other company whose shares are directly or indirectly owned by the company, does not exceed 10 percent of the total amount of capital subscribed in the company, unless otherwise provided in legislative regulation in the field of capital markets.

A company's buy-back without observance of the above conditions is invalid (Article 37 Paragraph 2), and its board of directors become jointly and severally liable for losses incurred by *bona fide* shareholders (Article 37 Paragraph 3). Also, the shares repurchased by companies may only be possessed by the companies for 3 years or less (Article 37 Paragraph 4).

6.1.2.4.   SHAREHOLDER BUY-BACK

If shareholders duly agree on a buy-back option, any stock sale in defiance of this option is per se void, as a result of which even a *bona fide* purchaser cannot be protected.

Public companies are governed by buy-back regulations in OJK Regulation No. XI. B.2.

The Supreme Court decided in 2014 that shares attached to a buy-back option cannot be transferred to the third party within the buy-back option, and a default in the buy-back constitutes an illegal action (No. 685K/Pdt/2014).

A creditor meeting for PT. Karabha Digdaya ("KD") that was bankrupt was held with its shareholders and the shareholder creditors PT Bank International Indonesia Tbk ("BII") and PT Bank Lippo Tbk ("Lippo"). In this meeting, the attendees decided to suspend KD's repayment and to give other shareholders a buy-back option to purchase BII and Lippo's KD shares in 6 months. When the other shareholders sought to buy shares from BII and Lippo at 6 months, however, BII and Lippo had sold out their shares to the third party (presumably because of concerns that they may be unable to recover). The Supreme Court decided that BII and Lippo's stock sales were illegal against the buy-back option and ordered them to perform as agreed.

Notably, the Supreme Court did not consider whether the purchaser was a *bona fide* purchaser or not, nor did it order any remedy of damages other than performance of contract.

RIGHT OF FIRST OFFER AND RIGHT OF FIRST REFUSAL

Article 58

In the event that the articles of association mandate that selling shareholders must first offer their shares to shareholders with a particular classification or other shareholders, and such shareholders do not make the purchase within 30 days from the offer date, the selling shareholder may offer and sell the shares to third parties.[10]

Both the right of first refusal and the right of first offer are widely used by shareholders among closely held companies.

The right of first offer is commonly triggered when a shareholder elects to make his shares available for purchase. The shareholder must "first offer" to sell the shares to the holder of the right of first offer on terms and conditions predetermined by the shareholders. If the holder of the right of first offer does not exercise its right to purchase the shares in a timely manner, the shareholder may proceed to offer the shares for sale to third parties.

The court views that a share sale to a third party in disregard of other shareholders' right of first offer is valid and effective if such a right of first offer is only written in a shareholders' agreement, but not in a company's articles of association (District Court of Central Jakarta Decision: No. 507/Pdt.G/2013/ PN.Jkt.Pst).

The right of first refusal is triggered when a shareholder receives an acceptable offer to purchase from a third party. Prior to accepting the third party's offer, the shareholder must allow the holder of the right of first refusal to purchase the shares either upon the same terms and conditions contained in the third party's offer, or upon terms otherwise specified in the shareholders' agreement. Unlike a call option, the right of first refusal does not give the holder of the right the ability to force the other party to sell the shares. It generally provides that the holder of the right has the ability to require that the shares be sold to such a holder for the same price and on terms that the owner is willing to accept from a third party, if and when the other party decides to sell the shares to any third party.

The shareholder may proceed to sell to the third party only if the holder of the right of first refusal does not exercise their right to purchase the shares in a timely manner. However, in many cases, a right of first refusal does not set the price for the asset in advance. Therefore, shareholders often resist granting

---

10 *Dalam hal anggaran dasar mengharuskan pemegang saham penjual menawarkan terlebih dahulu sahamnya kepada pemegang saham klasifikasi tertentu atau pemegang saham lain, dan dalam jangka waktu 30 hari terhitung sejak tanggal penawaran dilakukan ternyata pemegang saham tersebut tidak membeli, pemegang saham penjual dapat menawarkan dan menjual sahamnya kepada pihak ketiga.*

rights of first refusal because they have a chilling effect on the marketability of the shares. Brokers and interested parties are reluctant to expend substantial time and money to negotiate a lease or purchase agreement for a deal when they know the stock seller must submit the final deal to the holder of the right of first refusal, who can then elect to purchase the share on the terms presented to him, and thereby take advantage of a fully negotiated deal.

Even if a third-party purchaser begins negotiations with the stock seller, the first refusal may worsen the relationship for investors. For example, the holder of the rights temporarily may not have the funds required to purchase shares. If other shareholders take advantage of that momentary circumstance by offering their shares to the first-refusal holder, the rights holder will be unpleasantly surprised, and have no option but to forego purchasing the shares. The situation would be worse if the terms and conditions were already agreed with an unwanted third party.

It is clear neither of the rights prevents a shareholder from negotiating with a third party in advance. Let us suppose that company's articles of association are in line with Article 58, and shareholder A desires to discuss selling his shares at the highest price with an outsider X before negotiating with the holder of right of first offer shareholder B. Stock seller A will be able to proceed with commercial negotiations with a third party X. It would be safer for A and X to agree on a formal letter of intent which simply states, for example, what would happen if Shareholder A proceeds to negotiate a sale of shares with third party X: "In the event that a shareholder seller A first offering shares to shareholder B, and shareholder B does not purchase within 30 days from the bidding date, shareholder A must sell shares to X."[11]

6.1.2.5. RIGHT OF FIRST NEGOTIATION

The right of first negotiation means the right to engage, in good faith, in exclusive negotiations with the stock seller, which can be triggered before the stock seller offers the stocks to another party. From the stock seller's perspective, the obvious advantage of this right over the right of first refusal, is that the right is triggered before the stock seller has to invest time and money in negotiating a deal with a third party. Also, the seller can avoid the chilling effect on the marketability of the shares, once the right of first negotiation period has lapsed.

Because this right is not defined under any laws or regulations, there are a number of variables. Sophisticated parties use a variety of techniques to give more substance to a right of first negotiation. The parties may predetermine a formula of pre-sale valuation, or mandate that the existing shareholder purchase the shares. To assure that the price demanded by the stock seller is

---

11 *Dalam hal pemegang saham A penjual menawarkan terlebih dahulu sahamnya kepada pemegang saham B, dan dalam jangka waktu 30 hari terhitung sejak tanggal penawaran dilakukan ternyata pemegang saham B tersebut tidak membeli, pemegang saham A harus menjual sahamnya kepada X.*

a fair one, the stock seller may be prohibited from selling the stocks to a third party for a price less than the price last offered by the holder of the first negotiation right, or at a specified percentage of such a price. Additionally, the parties may agree that if the stock seller fails to sell the shares to a third party within a specified time period, then the owner must again give the holder of the right the ability to negotiate exclusively for the sale of the shares for an additional period.

6.1.2.6. TAG-ALONG RIGHT

A tag-along right – or co-sale right – is a minority shareholder's contractual right to join the majority shareholder's share sales to a third-party purchaser. That is, the majority shareholder can sell his shares to an outsider only when the minority shareholder is given the opportunity to also sell his shares to the purchaser or decide not to exercise the right. This can prevent the majority shareholder from leaving a minority shareholder with shares which are then difficult to sell. Since a majority shareholder has a premium for the management right, the minority shareholder can enjoy not only withdrawal from investment, but also any premium in share price.

This sort of exit strategy is heavily dependent on how interested the parties are in the stock sale, and the bargaining power of shareholders. Often the exit strategy established in the first place is rarely used when shareholders are in a position to exit from the company. For example, the majority shareholder may attempt to place some conditions on tag-along rights, such as limiting the right to only a certain percentage of shares. This is because not only minority shareholders, but also the majority shareholder should be entitled to cash in their investment. In turn, minority shareholders may attempt to have the right of first refusal or first offer and, if they choose not to exercise the right, then exercise any tag-along right.

In sum, it is totally up to the bargaining parties at the time of negotiation.

6.1.2.7. DRAG-ALONG RIGHT

A drag-along right is a majority shareholder's right to force a minority shareholder to join in the sale of his shares to a third-party purchaser.

A foreign investor who is not familiar with the Indonesian management environment, or an investor who aims only to seek margins in stock prices without involvement in corporate management, may not like a change of a main shareholder also responsible for management. A drag-along right may be required for these investors so that they must also sell out their shares when the shareholder in charge of management sells its shares.

Further, all investors may desire to sell their shares should the company's industry fade, or the potential for future share earnings become gloomy. They may then prefer an arrangement that all their shares are to be sold out as one package should any shareholder finds a share purchaser.

However, placing all these conditions a contract requires careful consideration, since they can also lead to a circumstance where a shareholder loses any choice over control, or must sell under undesirable terms and conditions.

6.1.2.8. PUT OPTIONS AND CALL OPTIONS

In the share purchase context, a put option is a contractual right to sell a specified amount of stocks at a specified price within a specified time, and a call option is a right to buy an agreed amount of shares during a certain time period for a certain price.

The options may be used in cases where a foreign shareholder suddenly attempts to withdraw from participation in the Indonesian market, or a domestic investor attempts to sell its shares to an unknown third party, or any other unexpected situation.

A common example of such an unexpected situation in Indonesia is a sudden change in the maximum shareholding rate of foreign investment in the Negative Investment List. In this situation, the foreign investor must find a "white knight" who can help him, whether the foreign investor decides to permanently retrieve their investment or not. Generally, from a foreign investor's perspective, this sort of policy change can be suddenly enacted without warning, and finding a domestic share purchaser at fair price within a specified period may be tremendously arduous. To the shareholders of a closely held company, it may be virtually impossible. As a last resort, the foreign investor may seek a nominee who lends his name to the business, despite knowing that such a nominee contract is void under Article 1320 of Civil Law, and Article 33 of the 2007 Capital Investment Act. As an entrepreneur and business leader, the foreign investor may hope to entrust an angel investor with his shares. In an even more desperate situation, he may attempt to lend funds to the volunteer at a very low interest rate to attract the white knight, who would then save the investor from the nightmare by purchasing the shares with the lent money. Even if the purchaser turns out to be a white knight in good faith, the share seller should be concerned about whether the purchaser later suddenly disposes of the shares in his keeping. Thus, the foreign investor hopes to obtain a call option. Of course, the white knight should be able to walk away from the volunteer activity at some point should things not work out in a way that was expected. Thus, the white knight may have a put option.

When drafting a contract, not only including these options but also considering a situation where the other parties fall in default in performance may be helpful. Requiring a penalty interest from exercising the option is an example of a safety clause.

6.1.3. *Validity of contractual restrictions on share transfer*

As discussed, a variety of restrictions other than the kinds specified in Article 57 Paragraph 1 are widely used in Indonesia. Nonetheless, it remains unclear whether the Indonesian Court recognizes the validity of contractual restrictions that veer away from Article 57 Paragraph 1.

Therefore, it is desirable to set forth a liquidated damages clause in a contract. That is, the parties may predetermine the minimum remedies in the case where a party breaches the contract and sells his shares to a third party despite the restriction on share transfers in the contract. By doing so, the parties will have a strong incentive to strictly follow the restrictions on share transfers. Of course, the contract should be drafted in a way that a party in default should remedy the liquidated damages irrespective of the actual damages incurred by the other party.[12] This is particularly so given that the plaintiff, who has a burden of proof about the damages, will have substantial difficulty in showing the exact amount of damages and causation.

Advice on contract drafting concerning share transfer in Indonesia

a. Parent company's shares

The founders of a PMA often use a special purpose company (SPC) in a foreign common law jurisdiction as a parent company. One advisable point in drafting contracts in this case is that the restriction on transfer must be imposed not only on the shares in the PMA, but also to the shares in the SPC. If the shareholders restrict sales or share transfers in the PMA only, the ultimate shareholder may still transfer the shares in the SPC to a third party, successfully avoiding the restriction on alienation.

In addition, the contract should have a clause that the directors must approve a share transfer which has been approved according to the articles of association. If such a share transfer requires a special resolution of the board of directors, the shareholders should be able to dismiss any director who rejects the shareholders' resolution.

b. Equity-linked securities

A variety of types of shares and securities are used in Indonesia, despite the limited kinds specified in the 2007 Company Act. Hence, not only stocks but also equity-linked securities – such as convertible bonds – must be subject to any restriction on transfer. Otherwise, the securities holder could freely sell these to third parties without any encumbrances or approvals.

---

12 Even if such a clause on the restriction of share transfers is rendered voidable and cancelled because it is other than the kinds stated in Article 57 Paragraph 1, the parties may still claim liquidated damages against the party in default, unless such a clause is against morality (*kesusilaan yang baik*) at Article 1254 of the Indonesian Civil Act on the ground that the share seller defaulted on the contract before the clause was cancelled.

Otherwise, upon the third-party purchaser exercising conversion rights or any other similar rights or options, the preexisting minority shareholder's ownership would be diluted.

c. Liquidated damages

Minority shareholders often demand to set forth certain types of material defaults in a contract draft that give themselves the right to terminate the contract without responsibility. However, they often forget to draft the effect of such termination. Basically, a shareholders' agreement is for minority shareholders to limit the sale actions of majority shareholder in general. Liquidated damages to be paid irrespective of the actually incurred damages, would be a good example.

d. Governing law and jurisdiction

This section explains only the cases where contracts are governed by the laws and regulations of Indonesia. The majority of sizable corporate share acquisitions in Indonesia are, nonetheless, based on the law and jurisdiction of common law countries. An Indonesian court's judgment may be unconvincing in large corporate cases for some reason. Even if one prevails in the merit, it may not be the end of case in actual practice. Setting aside this question, another matter is the lack of sufficient cases, and immature previous judgments. In any case, an Indonesian court's judgment may greatly deviate from the converging conclusion of most investor's jurisdictions. Thus, the Singapore International Arbitration Centre (SIAC) is often used for dispute settlement. Choosing SIAC may have some advantages, such as the allowance to choose a non-Indonesian, neutral venue and substantial case data, and some awards from SIAC have been recently recognized and enforced in Indonesia. However, enforcing foreign arbitration awards in Indonesia is still considerably difficult due to the reluctance of the Central Jakarta District Court to issue a writ of execution.

6.2.   *Restriction on transfer of shares by operation of law: treasury stock and cross-shareholding*

Article 36

(1) The company is not allowed to issue shares, either to be owned by the company itself or to be owned by other company, whose shares are directly or indirectly owned by the company.
(2) The prohibition on share ownership referred to in Paragraph (1) shall not be applicable to share ownership obtained based on transfer by operation of law, by grant, or by bequest.

(3) The shares obtained as stated in Paragraph (2) must be transferred to another party who is not prohibited from owning the shares in the company within 1 (one) year after the date of transfer.

Basically, this paragraph bans two things: treasury stocks and cross-shareholding. The prohibition on share ownership of the "company itself" (*dimiliki sendiri*) means that a company should not keep treasury stocks, being its own outstanding stocks issued by itself and retained in its own treasury. The prohibition on owning "shares owned directly or indirectly owned by the Company" (*dimiliki oleh perseroan lain*) is an interdiction against cross-shareholding or circular ownership.

6.2.1. Treasury stocks

Official Elucidation of Article 36 (1)

In principle, share issuance is an attempt to accumulate capital; therefore, the payment obligation for shares should be borne by other parties. For the sake of certainty, this Article determines that a company may not issue shares for its own ownership. . . .

Article 37

(1) The company may buy back shares which have been issued under the following conditions:

  a the buy-back of shares shall not result in the net assets of the company being less than the issued capital plus the statutory reserve that has been set aside; and
  b the total nominal value of all shares bought back by the company, the pledge of shares or the fiduciary security on shares held by the company itself, and/or other company whose shares are directly or indirectly owned by the company, does not exceed 10 percent of the amount of issued capital in the company, except where otherwise regulated in the legislation in the field of capital markets

(2) The buy-back of shares, either directly or indirectly, contrary to Paragraph (1) is deemed void by operation of law.
(3) The Board of Directors shall be jointly and severally liable for the losses resulting from the buy-back suffered by shareholders who have acted in good faith, which is then void by operation of law as referred to in Paragraph (2).
(4) The shares bought back by the Company as stated in Paragraph (1) may only be possessed by the Company for not more than 3 years.

Article 38

(1) The buy-back of shares referred to in Article 37 Paragraph (1), or further transfer, may only be conducted based on approval from a shareholders' meeting, except where otherwise provided in legislation in the field of capital markets.

Article 39

(1) The shareholders' meeting may deliver to the Board of Directors the authority to approve the implementation of the shareholders' meeting resolution as referred to in Article 38 for the period of not more than 1 year.
(2) The authorization granted pursuant to Paragraph (1) may be extended each time for the same period.

A treasury stock is a stock that the issuer purchases back, reducing the amount of outstanding stocks.

While the United States has been comparatively generous in allowing companies to own treasury stocks, the majority of civil law countries have reacted sensitively to the practice in the past. The United States permits treasury stocks with some limitation such as no dividends, no voting rights, and the maximum proportion of total capitalization specified by law. In contrast, civil law countries disallowed treasury stocks, except for some cases specified by law. Since Indonesia has adopted the latter approach, the old trend in civil law jurisdictions has remained solid.

The reasons why the majority of civil law countries prohibited treasury stocks were as follows:

- A company cannot own itself.
- Paying out share subscriptions reduces the company's assets, harming the interest of other shareholders and creditors.
- Paying out share subscriptions only to specified shareholders is virtually the same as giving a refund only to a selected shareholder, thereby endangering shareholder equality and the principle of capital repletion.
- The acquisition and disposition of stocks in this manner is decided by directors who are familiar with the corporate situation, and the result is equal to an undue profit using insider trading, which security law strictly prohibits.
- If the company exercises a voting right attached to treasury stocks, the company is controlled by its directors without contribution.

Whether the same rationales were considered in Indonesia is unclear, however Indonesia prohibits treasury stocks and permits acquisition by succession or by operation of law as exceptions under Article 36 Paragraph 2. The acquisition necessary to dispose odd-lot stocks or the repurchase by shareholder's appraisal rights are thought to be examples of the latter.

One problem is a lack of clarity about whether the share acquisition by bequest (*kepemilikan saham habah wasiat*) includes share repurchases due to merger and acquisitions. The official elucidation states that

> Paragraph (2) Share ownership resulting in the ownership of shares by the Company or a crossholding of share ownership is not prohibited if the share ownership is obtained on the basis of assignment by law, grant, or testament since in such case there is no issuance of shares that require payment from other parties, and thus it does not contravene the provisions on prohibition as intended in Paragraph (1).

However, it is arguable whether having treasury stocks due to a merger does not contravene the provisions on prohibition as intended in Paragraph (1), since there is no issuance of shares that require payment from other parties.

After a merger, can the surviving company acquire treasury stocks to the extent it previously owned shares in the merged company? (Is acquisition of newly issued shares due to merger an exception to the prohibition of treasury stocks?)

There are two different approaches in civil law countries. The first approach permits a company's ownership of treasury stock, the value of which is instead treated as zero. This approach may allow the issuance of new shares of a surviving company to itself. The second approach acknowledges the value of treasury stock, thereby treating a disposal of treasury stock as if it were a regular asset being disposed. Under this approach, a surviving company immediately after merger cannot issue its new shares to itself.

Under the first approach, a company may be necessarily permitted to issue shares to itself because (i) a surviving company previously continued to own shares in a merged company, (ii) if not permitted, a merging company must sell out its shares in any subsidiary immediately before the merger, thereby bringing a chilling effect to the merger and acquisition market, and (iii) a surviving company should literally survive after the merger, and thus it must be differently treated in regard to the merged company's treasury stocks. The opposing view maintains that (i) if permitted, excessive treasury stocks may be made upon the merger, and (ii) there is little advantage in allowing treasury stocks in a merger. Japan has changed its policy to prohibit treasury stocks in a merger, while South Korea allows not only the surviving company to hold treasury stocks after a merger, but also sales of such treasury stocks to a third-party purchaser.

In Indonesia, treasury stock is not permitted in principle, pursuant to Article 36 Paragraph 1, and share acquisition by bequest (*kepemilikan saham habah wasiat*) is permitted only exceptionally. However, whether this exception includes share repurchase due to a merger and acquisition is unclear. Neither corporate tax law nor Indonesian accounting principle sufficiently specifies this issue. Since Article 36 Paragraph 3 permits the sale of treasury stock to a third party, at least the 2007 Company Act seems to choose the first approach in the same manner as South Korea does.

An Indonesian M&A expert has offered an opinion that treasury stock is permitted in mergers on the basis of share repurchase allowed under Article 38. However, this opinion is thought to be wrong, because the matter of a surviving company's treasury stock in a merger is not whether a company can repurchase already outstanding shares, but whether the issuer can issue *new* stocks to itself in the first place at the beginning of the surviving company.

A surviving company's treasury stock ownership as a result of a merger is widely accepted and used in actual practice at Indonesia in the absence of a clear law or a court decision. Nonetheless, this will remain vague and obscure until a new law is drafted or a court's decision clearly states the legal position. Therefore, a shareholders' resolution must be carefully drafted in a way that the parties cannot later claim nullity, invalidity, cancellation, or termination of the agreement, merger, or all related transactions.

Even if allowed as an exception, the ownership of treasury stock cannot be extended for more than 1 year (Article 36 Paragraph 3).

Stock repurchase must be based on approval of a shareholders' meeting or the board of directors, if authorized by shareholders (Article 38 Paragraph 1 and Article 39 Paragraph 1).

Insofar as legitimately obtained, treasury stocks may be transferred or sold to a third party (Article 36 Paragraph 3), or cancelled, pursuant to capital reduction resolved by the shareholders' meeting (Article 47 Paragraph 1).

A company cannot exercise voting rights (Article 40). A minority shareholder's rights, such as appraisal rights or a right of derivative suit, are not applicable due to the nature of each right. Also, Article 40 Paragraph 2 explicitly rejects a dividend rights applying to treasury stocks. Although the 2007 Company Act is silent about preemptive rights or the distribution of assets at liquidation in relation to treasury stocks, they should rightfully be rejected. Surely, a stock split should also be applied to treasury stocks.

The acquisition of its own stock issued by itself in an unpermitted way is *per se* void (Article 37 Paragraph 2). This paragraph is imperative, and a mandatory provision. In the event that a company possesses treasury stock in an unpermitted way, its directors are jointly and individually liable for the losses incurred by *bona fide* shareholders and any third parties.

Cross-shareholding

Official Elucidation of Article 36 (1)

. . . A company is also prohibited from a crossholding ownership, which occurs when a Company owns shares issued by another Company that owns the first Company's shares, either directly or indirectly.

The definition of direct crossholding is when one Company owns shares in a second Company without ownership in one or more "intermediary Companies" and, conversely, the second Company owns shares in the first Company.

The definition of indirect crossholding is when on Company owns shares in a second Company through ownership in one or more "intermediary Companies" and, conversely, the second Company owns shares in the first Company.

Crossholding, or circular ownership, is where shares are held by two or more companies in one another.

Cross-shareholding (or crossholding) structures differ from a pyramid structure in that the voting rights used to control a group remain distributed over the entire group rather than being concentrated in the hands of a single company or shareholder. This may help reinforce and entrench the power of a central controller and closely tie each business to the economic destiny of different corporate entities.

Crossholdings have been long popular in Indonesia, as in many other Asian countries. A well-known example is the Lippo group, controlled by the Riady family.[13]

In the principles of modern company laws, crossholdings in parent–subsidiary relationships and non-parent–subsidiary relationships are generally treated in different fashions. This is because the reason for prohibition of cross-shareholding in parent–subsidiary relationships is different to the rationale for banning cross-shareholding in non-parent–subsidiary relationships.

Crossholdings in parent–subsidiary relationships are prohibited. A subsidiary's ownership of its own parent company's stocks is no different from the parent company's ownership of treasury stocks, and it circumvents the regulation against having treasury stocks. The parent company has the power and authority to order its subsidiary to keep its own shares, and the actual reason for owning a parent company's shares is under the parent company's direction, unless such a subsidiary exceptionally desires to own and control its parent company. South Korea sets forth the same principle at the Corporation Act in 1984, mainly due to strong resistance to further formation of *chaebol*, behemoth conglomerates

---

13 For details, see Lucian Aye Bebchunk, Reinier Kraakman, & George Triantis, *Stock Pyramids, Cross-Ownership, and Dual Class Equity*, Harvard Law School Olin Discussion Paper, 1999, p. 8.

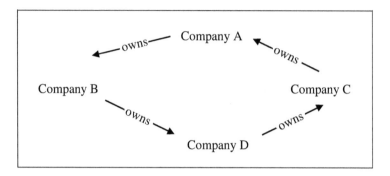

Figure 5.3 Example of crossholding

controlled by a chairman with omnipotent power.[14] However, it is not clear whether Indonesia – whose markets have been governed by conglomerates in a similar fashion – had a similar purpose behind at the time of legislation of the 2007 Company Act. This may have, instead, been simply imported.

Prohibition of crossholdings among non-parent–subsidiary relationships has different rationales: it stagnates the economy, ruins the nature of the company as an independent and separate legal entity, expands economic downturns by preventing reallocation of capital, and hollows out capital.[15] However, some argue that crossholding in a non-parental relationship has persuasive reasons not to be fundamentally prohibited, because it provides some economic advantages such as a defensive tactic against a hostile takeover attempt. Thus, some countries, including the United States and South Korea, do not ban it outright, but instead place limitations on how voting rights are exercised.

However, whether the two types of crossholding should be differently treated in Indonesia may be argued in the absence of a court's specific ruling.

Article 36 Paragraph 1 should be carefully read and interpreted with its elucidation. The Article itself states that companies are "not allowed to *issue* shares to own (*dilarang mengeluarkan saham baik untuk dimiliki*)" instead of "not allowed to *own* shares (*dilarang memiliki saham*)." The official elucidation (*penjelasan*) explains that the prohibition is not only on "issuance," but also against "ownership" itself, and thus stock purchase for crossholding purposes after issuance should also be prohibited.

14 Lee Chul Song, *Advance of Regulations on Cross Shareholding*, KCI,, 1984, Hanyang University, p. 13
15 If two companies subscribe to shares at IDR 1 billion from each other, the actual cash movement between the companies, or the actual financial capacity of the two companies, is not IDR 2 billion. The number in the books is simply fictitious, and deviates from the actual assets that the companies have. Thus, the capital is "hollowed out."

6 Board of directors and board of commissioners

1. Director

A board of directors is a mandatory and necessary company's organ, and it is the group of individuals who are elected to act as representatives of the shareholders for the management and supervision of the company's activities. Board meetings are not called every day, but at any time necessary. The procedures to convene the board are stipulated in the articles of association. Unless provided otherwise in the articles, it is not necessary to inform members of the aim or agenda of a meeting in advance.

A director is a member of the board of directors who has authority to take part in company decision-making and the supervision of affairs. A director is not an organ in himself, but one of a number of members who collectively make up a company organ.

A director has not only a duty of care and loyalty, but also a duty to manage the company (Article 97) and deal with various matters related to a company.[1] In contrast to a shareholders' meeting, proxy voting is not allowed at board meetings. Directors must attend to participate and vote in board meetings and cannot delegate authority to another person at the meeting.

The 2007 Company Act does not require an outside director for a closely held company. An outside director is, however, separately required and regulated by separate regulations concerning financial companies and listed companies.

2. Appointment of directors

The company founders appoint the initial directors by the establishment deed, and a shareholders' resolution appoints the directors for a certain period thereafter (Article 94 Paragraphs 1–3).

---

1 (i) Documentation of the list of shareholders, special list of shareholders, shareholders' resolutions, resolutions of the board of directors, financial statements; (ii) maintenance of material documents such as memorandum of board of commissioners; (iii) obtaining approval from shareholders in the event of transfer, assignment, or mortgage of an aggregate of 50 percent or more value of company's assets, etc.

To qualify for appointment, a candidate should be an individual who can perform a legal action and should not have been, within the preceding 5 years, (i) declared bankrupt, (ii) a director or commissioner adjudicated to have caused the bankruptcy of a company, or (iii) sentenced for a criminal offense that caused financial loss to the state or financial sector (Article 93 Paragraph 1). The company is required to keep documentary proof (a letter from the prospective director confirming he meets the requirements) (Article 93 Paragraph 3). If these qualifications and requirements are not met, the appointment is nullified by operation of law when the other directors and board of commissioners become aware of this (Article 95 Paragraph 1). The important part in the Act seems to be "the acknowledgement of the other members of the board of directors or board of commissioners" of the lack of qualifications, rather than the under-qualification itself. The annulment of the appointment should be announced in a newspaper and the MLHR should be notified.

Unlike modern corporate laws in other countries,[2] the 2007 Company Act does not stipulate a prohibition on directors holding any "side job," or include any non-competition clause. Thus, the appointment of a director will not be automatically cancelled because of his position of unlimited liability in other legal entities, or for conducting other work at any outside entity in the same industry. Unlike the lack of other provisions within the Act, this absence is thought to be actually good considering circumstances peculiar to Indonesia. Indonesia is one of the richest countries in terms of natural resources, yet because companies are required to conduct operations only within a specific administrative region, there is an overwhelming number of resource extraction and export companies.[3] A large natural resource business must inevitably have several subsidiary companies, even if located in the same district (*Kabupaten*), as each company cannot operate in two or more regions at the same time. Thus, the majority of Indonesian natural resources business entities exist as groups of subsidiary companies, with one in charge of each permitted region. If all the directors of these companies were not allowed to also be a director of another subsidiary company in another region, a competent director would be unable to manage the same project or business in the same group. One ramification could be that companies within one group would record the names of merely superficial directors, while keeping an unrecorded "virtual"controller.

Thus, the absence of a non-competition clause in the 2007 Company Act is thought to be better fitted to Indonesian business circumstances. It is particularly so given that a director's conflict of interest can be still redressed under Article

2 *Konkurrenzverbot des Vorstand* clause (Section 88 of AktG) in Germany, Article 397 of Commerce Act in South Korea, Article 356 (1) of Companies Act in Japan.
3 For example, a mining company must be established only in a designated region and obtain a certain permit (*Wilaya Izin Usaha Pertambang*) to operate the business within a mining area (*wilayah pertambangan*) in the designated region. The company cannot operate the business outside of the permitted area.

99 Paragraph 1 Item b, and directors in financial and listed companies are in any case restricted from competing according to separate regulations.

In the meantime, cumulative voting, which allows a minority to concentrate their votes by permitting voters to select more than one candidate, has not been adopted or popular in Indonesia.

The appointment of directors in financial companies – including those operating in banking, insurance, pensions, and credit guarantees – requires OJK's screening in advance.

2.1. *Director nationality and working permits*

Although shareholders of pure domestic PMDN should only be Indonesian citizens, it does not need to appoint only citizens as directors. Hence, forming a board of directors with non-citizens is possible.[4] The practical issues are organizing the work permit, visa, residence, and other practical issues at the time of establishment. One of 19 forbidden roles for foreigners in the regulations of the Ministry of Manpower and Transmigration (*Kementerian Tenaga Kerja dan Transmigrasi No.40 Tahun 2012*) is "Official Executive Head" (*Kepala Eksekutif Kantor*), which can confuse foreigners; despite its literal meaning, it does not mean CEO.

Parenthetically, a foreigner should be registered as a director for several years before seeking to become a citizen of Indonesia.[5] There is no law or regulation stating this requirement, but the authority has long used this tacit rule about when the President should sign the approval for nationality change, and this unwritten policy may from time to time require more qualifications.

Article 37 of Ministry of Manpower Regulation No. 16 of 2015, which was subsequently amended by Regulation No. 35 of 2015 concerning Procedures for Utilization of Expatriates ("Regulation 16"), states that "it is not mandatory to have working permit for board of management domiciled abroad."

Regulation 16 further stipulates that working permit must be issued even for temporary activities such as the following:

- roles for providing guidance and training in the implementation and innovation of industrial technology to increase the quality and design of an industrial product and cooperation related activities for offshore marketing;

---

4 Thus, a foreign business person in Indonesia often must entrust their shares to a native Indonesian, and then appoint himself as a president director. See the details in the section *Capital Investment Act.*

5 To apply for a permanent residential permit (*KITAP*), the immigration requires a title of registered director as a minimum qualification at least a year before the application for change of nationality to Indonesian. If there are two or more registered directors in the articles of association, the applicant must own at least 5 percent or more shares, and will have a smoother process if 25 percent or more shares are owned – Kim Jongsung, Changing Nationalities to Indonesia, *Korean News*, May, 2016, Korean Association in Indonesia.

- roles in the film industry that have received relevant regulatory approval;
- providing speeches;
- attending meetings with the head or branch offices in Indonesia;
- carrying out audits, quality controls or inspections on an Indonesian branch; and
- a role of an expatriate during a probation period.

3.   Termination and suspension of directors

Reasons for the termination of a director are variable:

- A resolution from a shareholders' meeting (Article 94 Paragraph 5 and Article 105 Paragraph 1)
- Either (i) bankruptcy, (ii) adjudication to have caused the bankruptcy of a company, or (iii) a criminal offense which caused financial loss to the state or relating to financial sector, and the acknowledgement of such a fact by other directors or the board of commissioners (Article 93 Paragraph 1 and Article 95 Paragraph 1)
- Termination of term
- A cause for dismissal as determined by the articles of association
- A loss of qualification as determined by the articles of association (Article 94 Paragraph 4)

The termination comes into effect directly upon the occurrence of any reason listed, irrespective of whether such termination has been registered through the MLHR or not. For example, in the event that a director is dismissed due to the reasons listed in the second point above, this should be disclosed through a newspaper and notified to the MLHR (Article 95 Paragraph 2). Still, the termination of director becomes immediately effective upon occurrence of the reasons listed in this point and before such a disclosure or notification to the MLHR is made, since the appointment of the director becomes void by operation of law (Article 95 Paragraph 1).

Because obtaining a resolution at shareholders' resolution takes some time, a director may be immediately suspended by the board of commissioners. A written notice of suspension should be given to the director, and a shareholders' meeting should be convened within 30 days of such a suspension (Article 106). Inasmuch as the director objects to dismissal, he must be given the opportunity to defend himself (Article 105).

Unless the shareholders' resolution explicitly states the date of dismissal, the dismissal by shareholders' resolution is then deemed under Articles 93–95 to have come into effect on the date of the resolution. The dismissal should be notified to the MLHR for registration in the Company Registry within 30 days of the shareholders' meeting (Article 111 Paragraphs 7 and 8).

4. Director's authorities and duties

4.1. Director's authorities

Unless otherwise provided in articles of association, or laws regarding duty of care and fiduciary duty under Articles 99–102, a director represents the company without condition or limitation. A director can participate in a company's decision-making and supervise other directors' performance of duty, and is qualified to become a president director (Article 98).

4.2. Director's duties

Because they have the authority to represent a company, a director has a fiduciary duty to avoid a situation in which they have, or could have, a direct or indirect interest that conflicts with, or might possibly conflict with, the interests of the company (Article 92 Paragraph 1 and Article 99), the duty of care in good faith (Article 97 Paragraph 2), and the duty to manage and supervise the company and attend meetings of the board of directors.

Applying the same level of scrutiny in judging the duty of management and supervision to all the directors as a one-size-fits-all rule is unreasonable. Not every director in every company takes the same range of duties and responsibilities, which depend on divisions, classifications, expected roles, corporate policies and environment, salary, and other factors.

As mentioned, the 2007 Company Act does not codify a duty to refrain from holding an outside position, nor a duty of non-competition. Also, neither the 2007 Company Act nor the Penal Code includes provisions on breaches of trust or misappropriation.[6] Thus, a conflict of interest clause (Article 99) or fraud (Article 399 of Penal Code) is alternatively sought by the vast majority of plaintiffs in cases which would have been covered by these provisions under corporate legislation in other countries.

The OJK regulations (Article 35 Regulation Concerning the Board of Directors and the Board of Commissioners of Issuers or Public Companies – No. 33/POJK.04/2014) require a company's directors and commissioners to formulate and publish guidelines that codify for directors their legal basis, description of duties, responsibilities and authorities, values, working periods, meeting policies – including

---

6 An example of criminal breach of trust clause: Section 405 of Penal Code – Whoever, being in any manner entrusted with property, or with any dominion over property, dishonestly misappropriates or converts to his own use that property, or dishonestly uses or disposes of that property in violation of any direction of law prescribing the mode in which such trust is to be discharged, or of any legal contract, express or implied, which he has made touching the discharge of such trust, or willfully suffers any other person to do so, commits "criminal breach of trust." Section 406 – Whoever commits criminal breach of trust shall be punished with imprisonment for a term which may extend to 7 years, or with a fine, or with both.

attendance in the meetings and minutes of meetings – and reporting and account-ability. Directors and commissioners must also prepare a code of ethics that contains principles and professional behaviors for conducting the duties of board of directors and board of commissioners, employees, and staff.

5.   Director's responsibilities

5.1.   *Responsibilities as to the company and third parties*

The board of directors shall be jointly and severally responsible for any direc-tor's act in defiance of his duty or against articles of association or law.

Because a director makes any corporate decision as a member of the board of directors, the influence and significance of his position and actions is enor-mous. Thus, the law expands the company's responsibility to include every decision-maker's individual actions to protect other stakeholders in the event that such decisions damage a company or third person should a director not fulfill an obligation.

The term *joint and several liabilities* means that responsibility lies not only with the director who actually committed a crime or breached his duty, but also with the directors who agreed to the decision in a board meeting. It is unclear whether a director should provide written opposition to such any reso-lution he thinks is wrongful, or whether remaining silent through abstaining from any vote is enough to be free from this responsibility. At least when it comes to the annual report, being silent by refraining from signing the report is not enough. Unless a director who does not sign an annual report specifies the reasons in writing, it is deemed that he has in fact approved the annual report (Article 67 Paragraph 3). For matters other than the report, a plaintiff seeking a remedy from a director who did not vote in the meeting, or did not sign a resolution, may argue, for example, "the director should be liable unless he specified the reasons in writing because the 2007 Company Act must be uniformly interpreted and, thus, Article 67 Paragraph 3 must be applied *mutandis mutandis*." The defendant director could counter-argue, for example, "burden-ing a defendant by adding a condition that does not even exist in the law is cruel to the defendant (*nulla poena sine lege*)." To date, the stance of Indonesian courts is unclear.

To be free from liability for the loss incurred by a company or third person, the director must prove that

- Such a loss is not caused through his fault or negligence.
- He has performed his management of the company in good faith and prudently for the interests of the company and in the pursuit of its purposes and objectives.
- That there is no conflict of interest, either directly or indirectly, in manage-ment decisions that results in the loss.

- He has taken precautionary measures to avoid the loss (Article 97 Paragraph 5).

Thus, directors are essentially required to ensure appropriate oversight of divisions and workers and to provide policies or systems to monitor and prevent avoidable losses. If directors can prove they took action to prevent continuing damage or loss once detected, they cannot be held accountable for those losses.[7] Also, any director or commissioner causing a loss to the company by acting – or approving an act – against the company's articles of association is subject to criminal prosecution (Article 398 of Penal Code). The details are explained in the following section.

5.2.   Causes of responsibilities

5.2.1.   Director's act against law or articles of association

Any act against the imperative provisions of the 2017 Company Act is void, and directors should be held responsible for the result of such acts. However, any director's act in breach of any provisions in the articles of association is not automatically nullified, but the director should be held personally liable for any consequences.

A case that rejected the directors' responsibilities to remedy damages incurred by a third party due to the observance of laws and company's bylaws is *Pe. A. Tjong v. Bank Persatuan Dagang Indonesia* (Supreme Court No. 367 K/Sip/1972)
When Mak Kim Goan, director of the defendant bank, directly issued a check to Pe. A. Tjong, the bank to pay the check was another bank, Bank Negara Unit I. Subsequently, the check was rejected due to insufficient account balance, and the plaintiff filed a claim to seek the stated amount and interest. The Supreme Court stated "the director's personal responsibility is a matter of the bank's internal procedures" (*Tanggung jawab pribadi Direktur tersebut, merupakan prosedur intern bank*) and determined that the director's responsibility in this case was based on whether the check was legally issued in accordance with law and the company's bylaws. The court affirmed that the director, Mak Kim Goan, had no responsibility because the bank issued the check pursuant to the Checks Act and internal policy.

---

7 "*Angota Direksi tidak dapat dipertanggungjawabkan atas kerugian . . . apabila dapat membuktikan mengambil tindakan untuk mencegah timbul atau berlanjutnya kerugian tersebut.*" Article 97 Paragraph 5 Item d.

> A case that affirms a director's responsibility due to non-compliance with procedural requirements is *PT Greatstar Perdana Indonesia vs. PT Indosurya Mega Finance.* (No. 030 K/N/2000)
>
> Since Budi Handoko, director of PT. Greatstar Perdana Indonesia, issued a check to PT. Indosurya Mega Finance without obtaining approval from the board of commissioners, the check issuer did not pay the check to PT. Indosurya Mega Finance until the due date stated on it. Then, PT. Indosurya Mega Finance filed a petition in bankruptcy over PT. Greatstar Perdana Indonesia, because of the default in payment obligation of the check. The Supreme Court rejected the petition and determined that the issuing bank had no responsibility and the director who had not obtained the advance approval from the board of commissioners should be personally responsible.

In addition to civil liability, a director who causes damage to a company through an act, or approval of act, in defiance of the articles of association could face a prison sentence of up to 1 year 4 months (Article 398 of Penal Code).

5.2.2.   Director's breach of duty

5.2.2.1.   LOSS TO A THIRD PARTY

A director who has not performed with a duty of care in good faith is liable for damages incurred by a third party as a result (Article 97 Paragraphs 2 to 4). A default in repayment alone does not provide a presumption of the director's breach of duty.

The trend in Indonesia is that the loss to the third party is limited to the direct loss. Thus, the direct consequences between the breach of duty and the loss incurred to the third party must be proven.

5.2.2.2.   LOSS TO A COMPANY

In the event that a loss is incurred by a company due to a director's breach of duty of care or fiduciary duty (Article 99), the director is responsible for the damages. However, the director's work in another company in the same field, or the director's unlimited liability for another entity alone does not automatically prove the breach of duty, as explained earlier.

To be relieved from the responsibility for breach of duty, the director should show that he reported any potential conflict to other members of the board of directors or the board of commissioners, obtained assistance from relevant professionals, and observed the procedures required by law, the articles of association, and any bylaws.

5.2.2.3.   CONFLICT OF INTEREST DETRIMENTAL TO THE COMPANY

Although a director has a responsibility to refrain from pursuing an interest detrimental to the company (Article 99), the existence of conflict of interest between a company and the director itself does not immediately mean a breach of duty.

Instead, it means that the director cannot represent the company in such a case where he has a direct or indirect interest detrimental to the company.

Majority shareholders, directors, and commissioners in public companies must disclose and obtain advance approval from a shareholders' meeting if their private economic interests will be in conflict with the company's economic interests, and the company may as a result incur losses (OJK Regulation No.IX.E.1). However, this clause is simply lacking sufficient details, whereby it can be easily circumvented. Firstly, opportunity cost is not regarded as a loss, and thus this clause is helpless to seek a responsibility from a director who took a personal interest using information obtained from his position and work. Since the conflict of interest occurs when the majority shareholder, director, or commissioner's economic interests are detrimental to a company according to this clause, it is unclear whether this clause applies *mutatis mutandis* to interests of any family member that were detrimental to the company or, even if applied, to how many family members it could be applied. What if a friend of director took the interest?

5.3. Director's responsibilities in bankruptcy

If a company is insolvent due to excessive debt, and such insolvency is due to directors' actions or negligence, each member of the board of directors is jointly and severally liable for all liabilities which are not repaid from the insolvent estate (*setiap anggota Direksi secara tanggung renteng bertanggung jawab atas seluruh kewajiban yang tidak terlunasi dari harta pailit tersebut*) (Article 104 Paragraph 2). According to its literal meaning, for example, if a board is composed of 10 directors and one director intentionally incurs losses and as a result the company becomes insolvent, all 10 directors must take responsibility for the entire loss, whether they were aware of the problem or not. Reasonably, responsibility should be limited to those directors who were either intentionally involved or negligent. That is, "each member of the board of directors" should be interpreted instead as "each member of the board of directors (who were intentionally involved or negligent)." At present, the Article suggests "each member of the board of directors (regardless whether they have acted wrongfully or not)." So far, the Supreme Court's interpretation of this clause has not been clear.

The Bankruptcy Act (Article 3 Paragraph 1 of Law No. 37 of 2004 concerning Bankruptcy and Suspension of Obligation for Payment of Debts) states "a decision on a bankruptcy petition and other related issues as intended by this Act shall be rendered by the Court having jurisdiction over the region in which the domicile of the debtor is located." While "other related issues" in this article are thought to include a director's responsibilities, the Bankruptcy Act does not specify any particular issues that fall under this catch-all phrase.

5.4. Director's responsibilities in tax law

According to Law No. 16 of 2009 concerning general provisions and procedures of tax (the Tax Act), a director has responsibilities to (i) obtain a tax registration number (NPWP), (ii) correctly write a notice letter and submit it to the tax authority,[8] and (iii) procure the company's scrupulous payment of tax. If a company does not faithfully pay tax, the tax authority can impose the tax amount to the director (Article 32 Paragraph 2 of Tax Act).

What if a director resigns after his company fails to pay tax scrupulously? In a tax claim in litigation seeking withdrawal of tax enforcement against an individual director,[9] the court stated

> even if the director was incumbent at the time when [the] tax occurs, the tax authority cannot impose the company's delayed tax to the director who had . . . already resigned at the time of the tax authority's disposition.

5.5. *Director's responsibilities in criminal law*

Article 374 of Criminal Act

Embezzlement committed by a person in charge of bailment because of a work relationship, as a means of livelihood, or compensation shall be subject to imprisonment for a maximum of 5 years.

Article 398 of Criminal Act

Any director or commissioner of a company, Indonesian stock company (*Maskapai Andil*) or Cooperative (*Koperasi*) which has been determined to be bankrupt, or on which the judicial settlement has been ordered, shall be punished by a maximum imprisonment of 1 year and 4 months:

1   If he participated in or has given a permission to an act in contrary to the articles of association which results in loss incurred by the company, Indonesian stock company, or Cooperative, and such a loss caused the bankruptcy or order of judicial settlement;
2   If he has participated in or has given permission to borrow money under hardship with an intent to delay the bankruptcy or the judicial settlement of the company, Indonesian stock company, or Cooperative, knowing that the bankruptcy or the judicial settlement could not be avoided thereby; or . . .

8 Article 1 Section 13 Indonesian Tax Law: "The Notice Letter shall mean the letter used by the taxpayer to report its tax calculation and payment, tax object, and/or not tax object, and/or asset and liabilities in according to the prevailing tax regulation."
9 No. 102/G/2010/PTUN-JKT. Many foreign countries have a separate Tax Tribunal to examine cases involved in unreasonable taxation. In Indonesia, however, Administrative Court also determines tax cases.

Article 399 of Criminal Act

Any director or commissioner of a company, Indonesian stock company, or Cooperative which has been determined as bankrupt or of which a judicial settlement has been ordered, shall be punished by a maximum imprisonment of 7 years, if he does any of the acts below in order to fraudulently curtail the rights of the creditors of the company or Cooperative

1   Act to cash out which does not exist and not journalize any income or matter on credit account in the books
2   Dispose of any property for nothing or at apparent undervalue
3   Benefit a creditor in bankruptcy or judicial settlement, or when he knew that such a bankruptcy or settlement could be avoided; or . . .

As explained earlier, there is no penal code provision concerning breach of trust in Indonesia. Hence, an injured person normally seeks a director's criminal responsibility using the fraud provision under Article 399 of Criminal Act. This article seems to be widely applied in public, private, and commercial relationships, and its application is also often drastic and decisive.[10]

Therefore, there is a converging opinion from Indonesian lawyers that in the event a commercial dispute arises, prosecuting a director of the defaulting company is, practically, the most effective approach. In other words, filing a criminal complaint against a director for any misrepresentation, deceitful behavior, or other violation in license, permit, tax, or other regulations, and then settling on satisfying conditions is widely regarded as the most effective method to seek redress.

Nevertheless, it appears difficult to equally apply this article against those crimes that other countries could punish under misappropriation or breach of trust. This is mainly because of the elements written in Items 1–4 of Article 399.

---

10 The development of applying the law of criminal fraud in Indonesia seems similar to the development in the application of the Mail Fraud clause (18 U.S.C. §1341) and Wire Fraud clause (18 U.S.C. §1348) in the United States, which were initially legislated in contemplation of fraudulent crimes against many unknown victims using mail or wire. However, a condition of using mail or wire later became degraded simply to a condition for federal jurisdiction in the 1980s, where any fraud without using mail or wire could be applied by these clauses. These clauses have been used from the 1980s to prosecute those crimes which other countries would prosecute as a breach of trust. For details, see Peter J. Henning, Maybe It Should Just Be Called Federal Fraud: The Changing Nature of the Mail Fraud Statute, *Boston College Law Review*, 1995; Lisa Casey, Twenty-Eight Words: Enforcing Corporate Fiduciary Duties through Criminal Prosecution of Honest Services Fraud, *Scholarly Works, Paper 777*, 2010; John C. Coffee, Jr., Modern Mail Fraud: The Restoration of the Public/Private Distinction, *American Criminal Law Review*, 1998; Craig M. Bradley, Forward: Mail Fraud after McNally and Carpenter: The Essence of Fraud, *Journal of Criminal Law and Criminology*, 1988; Jed S. Rakoff, The Federal Mail Fraud Statute, *Duquesne Law Review* Vol. 18, 1980.

For example, a president director providing a corporate guarantee for another beneficiary without any compensation could be punished under breach of trust provisions in many countries.[11] However, it is hard to apply Article 399 to such an act, because giving a corporate guarantee does not immediately constitute a disposal of any property for "nothing or at apparent undervalue" as under Item 2 until the company is actually foreclosed. Insofar as the Indonesian Crime Act does not codify the criminal breach of trust, that Article 399 is comparatively clear, and that the courts do not arbitrarily interpret the law, it seems hard to apply Article 399 to all the acts that could constitute a criminal breach of trust if such breaches occurred in other countries.

Note

Are the responsibilities of directors in Indonesian companies excessive compared with those of other countries?

There is an old Korean saying: "One who wants to wear the crown, should bear the crown." A director's great authority and heavy responsibilities illustrate exactly the meaning of the saying.

When those ambitious, conscientious, and brilliant people – deadly in high school, university, law school, or their MBA – hit 30, they rocket to the top position. What do they find when they get there? An 80-hour work week. Many people seem to have totally misguided image that people running things are sitting in a black-leather chair smoking a big cigar, telling subordinates what to do. They see a billionaire on the cover of a Monopoly game. The truth is that such executives work all the time: they work from the second they wake up to the second they go to sleep. They do not casually work. Somebody goes to library for 6 hours, and later says: "I studied in the library for 6 hours." The truth is no, he did not. He studied for only half an hour simply because he can't keep up the workload. Six-hour study with full concentration is never easy job for many people. So, while

---

11 Furthermore, in some countries, no one can guarantee that a criminal breach of trust would not punish a director who provides a corporate guarantee for another company after obtaining approval from all shareholders and the board of directors: "The breach of trust always works. . . . The very nature of criminal breach of trust is a betrayal. And a betrayal is an ethical matter, which should be resolved by civil methods [rather] than criminal proceedings. However, because separating an unethical act and criminal behavior is so obscure that forecasting what act would be subject to breach of trust is very difficult in reality. Thus, the likelihood of acquittal judgment against proceeding on breach of trust is statically 5 times higher than against proceeding on other crimes. Even if [there is] no personal benefit or actual loss, breach of trust can be formed with only a risk of loss because the elements of breach of trust are too much comprehensive." Choi Jun Seon, *The Problems in Criminal Breach of Trust in Commercial Act and Its Solutions*, KERI Insight, 13–06, 2012, Korean Economic Research Institute.

of course there are corrupt people among the vast number of people running corporate operations, most built themselves up to be so efficient and
smart that one finds it hard to believe. And they work 80 hours a week.
The vast majority of directors in billion dollar companies, or partners in
top-tier law firms, are conservative, are very low on agreeableness, and very
high in conscientiousness. And, surely, low on openness as well. They want
to win and dominate. The "brass knuckles" competition drives these sorts
of things. People often have no idea of the amount of responsibility that
comes along with such roles. To run a million-dollar company, a director
needs to know that there are enemies who want to take him down all the
time, while he checks all the balances of complicated finance, handles a
number of concurrent lawsuits, stays on the top of changing and emerging
technologies, constantly interacts with major customers, travels frequently
to maintain corporate relationships, regulates politics inside of business,
and yet, that's merely touching on the complexity that a director actually
deals with. It is no picnic. Only a man insane enough to occupy this position truly occupies the position.

Then, the proper question at this point would be: "Is the *crown* in Indonesia heavier than one in other countries?" The answer is both yes and no.

Recent authoritative comparative company law research among six core
jurisdictions of France, Germany, Italy, Japan, the United Kingdom, and
the United States[12] shows that the standard employed for directorial liability to creditors in the United States has the lowest intensity, as it shifts a
directors' duty of loyalty in relation to insolvent firms to the corporation,
rather than to individual creditors. In the meantime, enforcement is most
intensive in the United Kingdom, where a state-funded investigation into
possible misconduct must be launched for every corporate bankruptcy,
with a view to initiating possible disqualification proceedings. As a consequence, in the United Kingdom, disqualification is approximately 100
times more common than is a judgment in a private suit against directors
of an insolvent company.

In Indonesia, the average tenure of Indonesian directors is 11 years,[13]
which is considerably longer than the 1-year contracts or actual average tenure of 2–3 years in developed countries. Indonesia does not have a claw-back
provision which forces a director to return a paid bonus or payment depending on managerial performance, such as the one contained in the U.S. Sar-
banes–Oxley Act. Nor does it have an independent public institution only
for objective investigation against a director's wrongful behavior, such as in

---

12 See Reinier Kraakman et al., *The Anatomy of Corporate Law: A Comparative and Functional Approach*, 2nd ed., Oxford University Press, 2009, pp. 134–137.
13 Marleen Dieleman & Maythil Aishwarya, *Indonesia Boardroom Diversity Report 2012*, October 2012, Centre for Governance, Institutions & Organisations NUS Business School, p. 13.

the United Kingdom. The harsh parts of being a director in Indonesia take other forms. A director of Indonesian company who made his best efforts in good faith and yet could not successfully defend against insolvency will still bear the risk to be arbitrarily determined as personally liable, if the judicial system fails to successfully roots out corruption with strong will. For details, see later section *Moral hazard*. Also, due to the erroneous drafting of Article 104 Paragraph 2 of the 2007 Company Act, given frequent insufficient proof of mature decisions and the lack of a database of systematic analysis, even a director who objects to other directors' wrongful decision can still be placed under the shadow of personal responsibility.

In particular, the preposterously harsh criminal sanctions applying to directors accused of breaching their responsibilities underlie the abuse of investigation, prosecution, and judicial power of the authorities. Squeezing out directors is even aggressive, due to Indonesia's tendency to harshly and strictly investigate and sentence a foreigner's alleged corruption, violation of the Negative Investment List or antitrust laws, often much more for other crimes.

In many cases, foreign directors of international companies may not actually be high profile at all from the perspective of the foreign company's head office. Yet even if their treatment and compensation is merely as a senior manager, or even as a regular employee, their civil and criminal responsibilities are equal to those of a representative director.

6. Shareholders' supervision of directors' illegal acts

6.1. *Proactive measures: preliminary injunction and investigation right*

A preliminary injunction is a court's order to prevent a person from doing something, or from not doing something, before a full hearing can take place. In Indonesia, there is no separate and particular injunction against a company director who is potentially involved in wrongful conduct. Although there is a provisional injunction (*Putusan Provisi*) available, obtaining an actually effective and speedy provisional injunction is difficult in practice. Instead, the 2007 Company Act provides an "investigation right" for a minority shareholder who owns 10 percent or more of the outstanding shares. This is explained in the section *Investigation Rights.*

6.2. Ex post *measure 1: derivative suit*

Article 97

(3) Each member of the board of directors shall be fully and personally responsible for the losses suffered by the company if the concerned member has made mistakes and been negligent in carrying out his or her duties . . .

(4) In the event that the board of directors consists of 2 or more members, the responsibility as referred to in Paragraph (3) shall be jointly and severally borne by each member of the board of directors.

(5) Members of the board of directors shall not be required to be responsible for losses as intended in Paragraph (3) if they can prove that

    a the losses are not caused by their mistakes or negligence;

    b they have managed in good faith and prudently for the interest and in accordance with the purposes and objectives of the company;

    c there are no conflicts of interest either directly or indirectly in their management acts causing the losses; and

    d they have taken action to prevent the said losses from occurring and continuing.

(6) On behalf of the company, the shareholders representing at least 1/10 of the total voting shares may file a claim through the district court against members of the board of directors who have caused losses to the company due to their mistakes and negligence.

Article 1365 of Civil Act

Every unlawful action which causes a loss to another person obliges the person who caused the loss to pay for the loss.

A derivative suit is a lawsuit brought by a shareholder on behalf of a company against a director who engaged in wrongful conduct or negligence (*"Gugatan Yang Diajukan Oleh Pemegang Saham Terhadap Anggota Direksi Yang Melakukan Kesalahan Atau Kelalaian"*: Article 97 Paragraph 6). Indonesia also adopted a derivative suit to allow a minority shareholder to claim when it cannot expect his company to call the directors to account.

6.2.1. Standing

An initial complaint can be made by a shareholder (or shareholders) of more than 10 percent of total voting right shares at the time of filing a suit (Article 97 Paragraph 6).[14] These shareholders must be registered in the list of shareholders

---

14 If the minimum shareholding rate is too low, a derivative suit may be abused, and if it is too high, a minority shareholder cannot be protected from a director's tyranny. In South Korea, the minimum shareholding rate for a derivative suit is 1/100 of total outstanding shares, which is considerably lower than that in Indonesia. However, South Korea instead further requires continuous ownership of such shares for at least 6 months so as to prevent abuse of the derivative suit process. In the United States, even a single shareholder can file a derivative suit. However, it also requires a shareholder owning less than 5 percent shares to deposit securities to the court to prevent abuse from these suits.

at the time of filing a suit.[15] The plaintiff files the claim as a representative organ of the company for the sake of company's interest. A director or commissioner can also file a claim (Article 97 Paragraph 7). The commissioner's authority to file a claim is not limited to only where all the members of board of directors have a conflict of interest.

Even if written in the list of shareholders, a shareholder who already exercised an appraisal right is thought to be unable to file a derivative suit, because he cannot be essentially seen as a shareholder. A mere stock option holder would not have a standing, because he is not yet a shareholder.[16]

A creditor to company also cannot have a standing, even if he has interests in the company's losses. Given the drafting of Article 97 Paragraph 6, a convertible-bonds holder is also deemed to not have standing.[17]

A defendant is limited to a director or a former director (Article 97 Paragraph 6), and a commissioner or a former commissioner (Article 114 Paragraph 6).[18] Since a derivative suit is based on the third party's standing, a court judgment obtained by shareholders binds the company, and other shareholders cannot file the same claim (Indonesian Civil Procedures Article 23.1 and followings).

---

15 Although Indonesia takes this as granted, shareholder status does not necessarily depend only on the list of shareholders from a global perspective. In a minority of U.S. states (e.g. Iowa, Massachusetts, and Washington) regulate that only record-owners in a list of shareholders can file a derivative suit, while the majority of U.S. codified law, including New York BCL§626(a) and case law (*Rosenthal v. Burry Biscuit Corp.*, 60 A.2d 106, Del. Ch. 1948) provide that a shareholder can file a derivative claim with successful establishment of legitimate and actual share ownership, even if not registered on a list of shareholders.

16 This is same in the United States. See *Simons v. Cogan*, 549 A. 2d 300 (Del. 1988).

17 In the United States, there is a case for a convertible bonds holder's derivative suit due to the convertibility to shares (*Hoff v. Sprayregan*, 52 F.R.D. 243, S.D.N.Y., 1971), and a case rejecting a convertible bond holder's standing for derivative suit before such a holder actually converted the bonds to stocks (*Kusner v. First Pennsylvania Corp.*, 395 F.Supp. 276, D.C. Pa. 1975). The American Law Institute's *Principles of Corporate Governance* also acknowledges a convertible bond holder's standing. (ALI PCG §7.02).

18 The current Indonesian derivative suit is similar to a very old type of U.S. derivative suit from the beginning of the nineteenth century. In the United States, since the famous case of *Dodge v. Woolsey*, 59 U.S. 331, 1855 WL 8235 (U.W., 1855), the derivative suit has been used to file a claim against the third party as well. In this case, the directors rejected the request of shareholders to file a tax claim against a tax imposition based on unconstitutional law. The shareholders consequently filed a claim against the bank using a derivative suit, and the court recognized the shareholders' derivative suit against the tax authority. Nowadays, a derivative suit in the United States means not only (i) a suit against a director who defaults in a duty of care or fiduciary duty, but also (ii) a suit to seek rescission of sales from an assignee of corporate assets (*Bassett v. Battle*, 253 A.D. 893, 1 N.Y.S.2d 869, N.Y.A.D. 2 Dept. 1938), (iii) a suit to seek company's compensatory damages against the third party (*Green v. Victor Talking Mach. Co.*, 24 F.2d 378, ed Cir. 1928), (iv) a suit based on *ultra vires* doctrine (*Lee Moving & Storage, Inc. v. Bourgeois*, 343 So.2d 1192, La. App. 1977), and (v) a suit based on a contract between a company and a third party (*Boothe v. Baker Industries, Inc.*, 262 F.Supp. 168, D.C. Del. 1966). In Indonesia, the types of derivative suits from (ii) to (v) are not available.

6.2.2. Procedures

The procedures and requirements are comparatively simple.

To prevent abuse from a derivative suit, many jurisdictions outside Indonesia stipulate several other requirements as well as a minimum shareholding. The examples of such requirements for shareholders include:

- Posting a bond for defendant's costs[19]
- Making a demand that company directors must counter-sue should the case prove futile[20]
- Retaining share ownership for a certain period[21]
- Obtaining no proper action from a related director, even after requesting him to make redress or corrective action
- Obtaining a pre-review from a commissioner in advance

In Indonesia, except for the 10 percent minimum shareholding rate, no such additional requirements are stated. That is, a commissioner's pre-review, requests to the director, or posting bonds is not required.

The current legislation is regarded as adequate to encourage a derivative suit in Indonesian practice. First, a commissioner is a merely an employee, and thus the independence of commissioners is not secured in reality. In other words, inasmuch as a commissioner has no discretion to file a claim, a commissioner's ability to pre-review should not exist. In some states in the United States, shareholders must follow the resolution of board of directors to refrain from filing a claim unless they can prove the directors' abuse of discretion.[22] Considering that the aim of a derivative suit is to protect minority shareholders, such legislation is deemed not proper for Indonesia, since it weakens the protection of minority shareholders' rights.

Although not required in law, it would be reasonable that a plaintiff should own a share of the company at the time of director's misconduct.[23] This would not be a decisive obstacle, since a claimant could search for a shareholder holding stock at the time of director's misconduct. The problem is whether the successor who inherits the shares of a shareholder who dies without filing a derivative suit has standing (*alis waris*) by operation of law

---

19 In New York, this requirement is waived if a shareholder owns 5 percent or more of the shares, or his shares are worth more than US$50,000.

20 In the state of New York, futility means that (i) a majority of board is interested or under the control of interested directors, (ii) the board does not inform itself of the transaction to the extent reasonable under the circumstances, (iii) the transaction is so egregious on its face that it could not be the result of sound business judgment.

21 In South Korea, the required ownership period is 6 months.

22 Harry G. Henn & John R. Alexander, *Law of Corporation and Other Business Enterprises*, 4th ed., 1983, West Publishing Company, p. 1070.

23 Same with the U.S. Federal Rules of Civil Procedure Rule 23.1

(*karena hukum*) via bequeath (*warisan lewat surat wasiat*) or intestate succession (*warisan tanpa surat wasiat*). No particular case is found concerning this matter. In Indonesia, an ancestor's assets immediately belong to the joint assets of his spouse and direct descendants upon his death. Hence, a foreign investor may be involved in a dispute upon the death of an Indonesian shareholder who joined the ownership solely because of the Negative Investment List. For example, any person amongst the spouse and descendants may request monetary compensation from the company using share repurchase or any other method and, if rejected, file a derivative suit against the director appointed by the foreign shareholder. Since it is unclear whether he has a standing as a plaintiff, there is a difficulty in drafting a motion to dismiss (*ekpsepsi*).

6.2.3. Strategy in an Indonesian derivative suit

A sophisticated plaintiff often requests the company provide data and information to collect evidence before filing a suit, and the shareholder can in any case immediately exercise investigation rights through a court should such a request be rejected (Article 138). Because investigation rights require $1/10$ share ownership – equal to the requirement for exercising the right to file a derivative suit – this requirement is already met by shareholders who have decided to file a derivative suit.

If such investigation is deemed legitimate and reasonable, the court will appoint a maximum of three independent experts, free from any conflict of interest, for the investigation pursuant to Article 139 Paragraph 3. The cost and expenses for the experts' work is not proportionally allocated, but simply borne by the parties according to the court's discretionary decision pursuant to Article 141 Paragraphs 2 and 3. Once the full data and information is received, the shareholder can claim a derivative suit against a director (Article 97 Paragraph 6) or commissioner (Article 114 Paragraph 6) armed with the evidence in full.

A director's act subject to complaint may give rise to two or more separate and distinct offenses. If a director's act damaging a company by breach of his duty also constitutes a tortious act in civil law (Article 1365 and 1366 of Civil Act), a shareholder has multiple bases of claim. A tortious act means "not only breach of law but also any act breaching the actor's legal duty and obligation or infringing other person's property and any trust socially recognized" (*Hoge Raad* decision on 31 January 1919). Although this was a Dutch judicial judgment in Indonesia's colonial period, today's judgments in tort cases stand on this decision.

As foreign investors often create a joint venture company because of the Negative Investment List, a conflict arising between Indonesian and foreign investors may cause the Indonesian investor to file a derivative suit against a director appointed by a foreign shareholder, using the authority's unfavorable attitude against foreigners.

6.2.4. Business judgment rule

Article 97

(5) A member of the Board of Directors shall not be liable for the loss as referred to in Paragraph (3) if it is proven that:

    a Such loss has not resulted from its fault or negligence;

    b It has performed the management of the Company with good faith and prudence for the interest of the Company in the pursuit of its purposes and objectives;

    c There is no conflict of interest, either directly or indirectly over the management that results in the loss; and

    d It has taken a precautionary measure to avoid the loss.

The business judgment rule is a case law – derived doctrine in the United States rooted in the principle that the

> directors of a corporation . . . are clothed with [the] presumption, which the law accords to them, of being [motivated] in their conduct by a *bona fide* regard for the interest of the corporation whose affairs the stockholders have committed to their charge.[24]

In most states of the United States, a court refrains from retrospectively judging a director's business decisions, because a judge has no professional experience or knowledge about extremely complex business,[25] but also such because retrospective judgment may ultimately harm investors' interests.[26] Not only that, a U.S. court has defined the business judgment rule as "a rule of judicial restraint which holds that courts will not inquire into the business judgment of directors who are acting without self-interest and in good faith."[27]

Although the doctrine stems from common law jurisdictions, there are substantial variations in how it is applied in many countries. For example, while the business judgment rule is used as a defense at the motion-to-dismiss stage, and the so-called entire fairness test then kicks in on the merits in the United States, the business judgment rule can be adopted at any stage in

---

24 *Gimbel v. Signal Cos.*, 316 A.2d 599, 608 (Del. Ch. 1974).
25 *Mills v. Esmark*, 544 F.Supp. 1275, 1282 n.3 (N.D. Ill. 1982); Robert N. Leavall, Corporate Social-Reform, the Business Judgment Rule and Other Considerations, *Georgia Law Review* Vol. 20, 1986, pp. 565, 603; Henry G. Manne, Our Two Corporation System: Law and Economics, *Virginia Law Review* Vol. 53, 1967, pp. 259, 270.
26 *In re Caremark International Inc. Derivative Litigation*, 698 A.2d 959, 967 (Del.Ch. 1996).
27 *Minstar Acquiring Corp. v. AMF Inc.*, 621 F.Supp. 1252 (S.D.N.Y. 1985).

Indonesian courts. Also, Indonesian lawyers often use the business judgment rule as a defense in criminal case against a director, despite a lack of a well-founded rule.[28]

A defendant director in a derivative suit can successfully prove the facts required by Article 97 Paragraph 5 if he can show that he (i) reported the issue to the board of commissioners or the board of directors, (ii) obtained assistance and advice from experts both in and out of company, and (iii) strictly followed the procedures required by law, the articles of association and any bylaws. Therefore, a director must document all these processes to protect himself, particularly when making a bold investment or daring judgment.

6.3. Ex post *measure 2: a claim for damages*

Article 61

(1) Each shareholder is entitled to file a claim against the Company at the District Court if the shareholder suffers losses caused by the Company's actions that are considered unfair and unreasonable under the resolution of either a General Meeting of Shareholders, the Board of Directors, or Board of Commissioners.

Elucidation:

Paragraph (1) The lawsuit basically contains a request to the Company to discontinue the detrimental actions and take certain steps to remedy the consequences from those actions and to prevent similar actions in the future.

(2) A claim intended in Paragraph (1) shall be filed to the District Court whose jurisdiction covers the Company's domicile.

6.4. *Effect of unlawful representative act*

A director's actions as a representative of a company is valid and lawful as far as these actions follow the articles of association and remain within the company's capacity. In *Pe. A. Tjong v. Bank Persatuan Dagang Indonesia*, the Supreme Court determined that the validity and lawfulness of a director's act depends on whether the director has followed the law and company's articles of

---

28 "This doctrine is still new, therefore, in criminal law enforcement in Indonesia is still unclear. . . . Criminal law enforcement in Indonesia has not fully implemented the doctrine to assess whether losses incurred from a business decision is a criminal element." Dr. (cand). S. E. Parameshwara, Implementation of Business Judgment Rule Doctrine in Indonesia, *IOSR Journal of Humanities and Social Science (IOSR-JHSS)* Vol. 21, No. 8, ver. 12, 2016, p. 17.

association and bylaws. Therefore, the effect of a director's act would be a problem only where a director does not follow certain internal procedures, bylaws, the articles of association or the law, where he acts beyond his authorization or the company's capacity, or where such an act is made solely for his own interest or a third party's benefit.

6.4.1. Should a company be responsible for a contract that an unauthorized representative formed under the company's name?

In the event that a contract clearly requires obtaining a shareholders' resolution or approval from the board of directors in advance, the other party to the contract is not protected even if formation of the contract is a result of the representative or director's acts.

Then, could the company still be free of liability even if it actually contributed to the formation of the contract that an unauthorized representative or director signed? For example, let us suppose that a majority of the board of directors knowingly left the unauthorized representative to incite a third party and form a contract using the company's name. Alternatively, let us suppose that the company's employee even partially assisted in the formation of the contract. Is the company still not liable for the contract under the 2007 Company Act? Unfortunately, it will not be liable if we rely only on the 2007 Company Act. This is because the theory of *apparent authority* or *ostensible authority doctrine* is not well recognized in Indonesia.

In the context of corporate law, apparent authority theory is that a company should be bound by its legal representative's actions, even if the representative had no actual authority, whether express or implied. In the United States, the United Kingdom, Canada, and South Africa, this doctrine is recognized under the context of law of agency. That is, a director or representative is an agent of company and, thus, the company is estopped as a principal. In other words, the third party is given an assurance upon which he relies, and it would be inequitable for the principal to deny the authority thus given. In sum, *apparent* authority can legally be found, even if *actual* authority has not been given. Not only common law countries, but also civil law countries such as South Korea and Germany have the same or similar doctrines.[29] Basically, all modern jurisdictions protect a third party who has trusted and relied on the person who actually had no such authority to form a contract, by making the company directly responsible for the contract insofar as the company has somehow attributed such trust and reliance on the unauthorized person. Unfortunately, this is not

---

29 The similar doctrine has been developed and adopted by the courts as a principle of trust (*Prinzipien der Vertrauenshaftung systematisiert hat*) in Germany, and as a theory of externally shown rights (*Gwonli Wegwan Ilon*) in South Korea.

the case in Indonesia.[30] Only an individual director becomes liable for the result, albeit most individual directors cannot afford to pay a corporate-level debt.

6.4.2.   *Director's act after annulment of appointment*

Article 95

(1) Appointment of members of Boards of Directors who do not fulfill the requirements contemplated in Article 92 shall be void by operation of law from the time when the other members of the Board of Directors or the Board of Commissioners notice that the requirements were not fulfilled.

(1) A legal action performed for and on behalf of the Company by a member of the Board of Directors contemplated in Paragraph (1) before his or her appointment becomes annulled shall remain binding on the Company and the Company shall be liable for such a legal action.

(2) A legal action performed for and on behalf of the Company by a member of the Board of Directors in Paragraph (1) after his or her appointment becomes annulled shall be void and that former member of the Board of Directors shall be personally liable for such a legal action.

Article 95 Paragraph 3 is not an adoption of apparent authority theory, because while it protects a *bona fide* party who trusted a shown authority, it also protects a party who was aware that the authority was untrustworthy. Because the court does not interpret it differently, this Article allows an unqualified director to form a contract with an informed party. An important point in Article 95 Paragraph 1 is that the contract will be voided "from the time when the other directors or the board of commissioners notice that the requirements were not fulfilled." Probably, this Article is aimed at protecting a *bona fide* third party who formed a contract with a company without knowledge that the signatory had a reason to be immediately dismissed for any of the reasons under Article 92 Paragraph 1 (viz. the director had been actually bankrupt, been a director of commissioners declared to cause a company to become bankrupt, or has been sentenced for crimes which caused losses to the state or were related to finance sector). This is because there is no good reason to protect a third party who

---

30 "[T]he Indonesian Company Law and the articles of association of an Indonesian company normally stipulate certain requirements to obtain a corporate power (approval) from the organs of the company, i.e., board of commissioners' approval and/or shareholders' approval. Lack of corporate approval would legally affect the validity of the corporate guarantee and cause the board of directors to be held liable against any loss in relation to such provision of corporate guarantee/security." Theodoor Bakker & Ayik Candrawulan Gunadi, *Indonesia Lending and Secured Finance 2016, 2.3: Is Lack of Corporate Power an Issue?*, ICLG.

deliberately forms a contract with a company despite knowing earlier than other members of the company that the company's signatory should have been already dismissed. This Article should have been drafted in a way that protects only a *bona fide* party.

7. Board of commissioners

A board of commissioners is a mandatory and necessary company organ which has the authority to supervise directors' activities and financial books (Article 108).

Listed companies, companies related to operations of public funds, or debt collection companies should have at least two or more commissioners. For a regular, closely held company, one commissioner is sufficient, irrespective of its size.

Members of a board of commissioners are appointed by a shareholders' meeting (Article 111). Eligibility for appointment is the same as for directors – within the previous 5 years, a candidate should not have been declared bankrupt, have been a director or commissioner adjudicated to have caused the bankruptcy of a company, or have been sentenced for a criminal offense which caused financial loss to the state or was related to financial sector. Proof of compliance with this eligibility should be kept by the company (Article 110). Also, payments to commissioner must be determined by a shareholders' meeting.

A commissioner has a duty of care in good faith (Article 114 Paragraph 2), a duty to write minutes (Article 116), and duty to state opinions concerning a shareholders' meeting (Article 116 Item c). Also, a commissioner has full authority to supervise directors' activities, internally audit financial statements, and carry out management of a specific matter during a certain period if shareholders so resolve (Article 118), in which case the relevant articles about a board of directors apply *mutandis mutandi* to the board of commissioners.

A board of commissioners can suspend a certain director with reasonable grounds and inform shareholders of such suspension. Because it takes some time for a shareholders' final resolution to dismiss a director, a board of commissioners can immediately suspend the director's status. In turn, the director should be notified of such suspension in writing, and a shareholders' meeting should be convened to determine whether to dismiss him within 30 days of such a suspension notice (Article 106). Should as a suspended director oppose the suspension, he must be given an opportunity object in writing before the shareholders' resolution (Article 105). In addition, if the shareholders' meeting has not determined the date to dismiss the director, the effective date of dismissal will be presumptively the date when such a shareholders' meeting is closed.

In the event that a commissioner is negligent in his duty, all commissioners are jointly and severally liable for the consequential loss incurred by a company (Article 114 Paragraphs 3 and 4). Also, if a commissioner deliberately or through gross negligence breaches his duties and thereby damages a third party, all commissioners must hold joint and individual liability to directly remedy such damage incurred by the third person (in application of *mutandis mutandi* of the same article). To seek a remedy from a commissioner through a derivative suit, a shareholder must have at least 1/10 ownership, in the same manner as lodging a derivative suit against a director (Article 114 Paragraph 6).

Nevertheless, a commissioner is not liable for the loss if he can prove that

- He has performed the supervisory duty with good faith and prudent principles in the interest of the company and in accordance with its purpose and objectives.
- He has no personal interest to the board of directors' decision which caused a loss to company.
- He has provided advice to the board of directors to prevent such a loss (Article 114 Paragraph 5).

If the liability is sought in bankruptcy, the commissioner should also prove that the loss to the company is not a result of his fault or negligence (Article 115 Paragraph 3).

Indonesia has a unique company organ, a Sharia Supervisory Board (*Dewan Pengawas Syariah*). A company following Islamic Sharia law must have this separate board composed of one or more Sharia experts appointed by shareholders from the Indonesian Ulema Council. Sharia, or *syaria*, is a religious legal system derived from several Islamic texts and laws including the Quran, Sunnah, Hadith, Fiqh, and Kalam. Notably, Indonesia has kept Islamic banks implementing the Sharia financial system, offering Sharia financial products and services, and managed under Islamic philosophy and regulations. Although there was a time when it was contentious whether Sharia law could help successfully manage a company, that is no longer an issue, even in this largest of Muslim-majority countries.[31]

---

31 "Despite its status as the world's largest Muslim-majority country, Indonesians still favor conventional banks over those that adhere to Islamic principles. The market share of Islamic banks in the country has remained below 5 percent over recent years, despite the existence of sharia banking in the country since the early 1990s. Perhaps the main reason lies in human nature, as consumers are attracted to products that offer good benefits and reliable services." Grace D. Aminanti, Sharia Bank Struggling to Grow, *The Jakarta Post*, July 22, 2016.

7 Operation of the company

1. Change of articles of association

There are two types of changes that can be made to a company's articles of association.

The first type is the change which becomes valid with approval from the MLHR. In other words, the effective date of this change is the MLHR's approval date. An amendment is required when any of the following company details are changed (Article 21):

- Name
- Place of domicile
- Terms of incorporation
- Purposes and objectives
- Main business activities
- Amount of authorized capital
- Any reduction in the issued and paid-up capital
- Change in status from private to public company, or vice versa

The other type are the changes that only require notification to the MLHR, that is, any change of articles of association other than those listed above or otherwise needed to be approved by the MLHR. The effective date is the date when the MLHR receives the notification of changes to the articles of association.

Even if articles of association do not change, any occurrence or alteration of the following matters must be notified to the MLHR:[1]

- Changes in shareholders and total number of shares
- Changes in members of board of directors or board of commissioners

---

1 Peraturan Menteri Nomor M-01. HT.01–10 Tahun 2007 tentang Tata Cara Pengajuan Permohonan Pengesahan Badan Hukum Dan Persetujuan Perubahan Anggaran Dasar, Penyampaian Pemberitahun Perubahan Anggaran Dasar Dan Perubahan Data Perseroan.

- Changes of address of the company
- Dissolution of the company
- Termination of the legal entity by acquisition, merger, or separation
- Completion of dissolution

Any change of articles of association must be written in Indonesian in a notarial deed, and then registered (*Daftar Perseroan*). If shareholders resolve any matter requiring a change of articles of association, it must be recorded in a notarized deed within 30 days of the resolution. A change of articles of association recorded after 30 days cannot be submitted to the MLHR.

To issue an approval or receipt of notification regarding any change to articles of association, the MLHR must make a public notification to the *TBN RI* state gazette within 14 days of either approval or receipt of notification.[2] Although a company has no responsibility to keep the MLHR approval (or receipt of notification) in the office, it would be better to store it as an evidence of a valid change to the articles of association to later avoid the type of red-tape obsession predominant in Indonesian legal practice.

Registration of a company is governed by the Company Registration Act No. 3 of 1982 (*Undang-undang Nomor 3 Tahun 1982 tentang Wajib Daftar Perusahaan*: UU-WDP), and not by the 2007 Company Act.[3] Conversely, UU-WDP is irrelevant to matters stipulated under the 2007 Company Act, such as

---

2 For details about public notification, see Peraturan Menteri Nomor M.02.HT.01.10 Tahun 2007.
3 Because those matters to register pursuant to UU-WDP were not commonly registered at the regional office of commerce in actual practice, the 1995 Company Act was enacted in a way that it could directly govern the company registry. As the registration practice had become more stable since then, the 2007 Company Act was legislated so that UU-WDP is restated to govern the company registry again. According to UU-WDP, a company should register the following matters:

- Company's name, main place of business, purpose of establishment, business field, and term of existence
- Current address in Indonesian territory
- A date and number of both Deed of Establishment and the MLHR's approval of legal status
- The number of amended Articles of Association about fundamental matters, and the number and date of MLHR's approval of the amendments
- The number of amended Articles of Association about other matters, and the number and date of MLHR's receipt of notification
- The name and location of the public notary who made the Deed of Establishment and/ or amended the Articles of Association
- The names and addresses of shareholders, members of the Board of Directors and Board of Commissioners
- The date and number of Articles of Association for company's dissolution, and a date and number of the court's decision of dissolution reported to the MLHR
- Loss of legal status
- Financial status

the MLHR's approval or receipt of notification regarding amendment of articles of association, or conferment of a legal entity status. A company's obligation under UU-WDP is specified in detail under *Peraturan Menteri Perdagangan Republik Indonesia Nomor 37/M-DAG/PER/9/2007 tentang Penylenggaraan Pendaftaran Perusahaan*. This regulation stipulates the company's obligations related to the situation when the company desires to change the notification already submitted to the MLHR.

2. Financial accounts

Since a company is an organization with capital seeking to make a profit, it needs to clarify how to calculate profit and loss, or to treat assets.

An Indonesian company is required to follow the Indonesian accounting standard, *Pernyataan Standar Akutansi* (PSAK). A PMA may choose International Financial Reporting Standards (IFRS) for the sake of foreign shareholders, with additional costs in practice.

The accounts of the company should also observe tax laws. Since the calculation of accounts in tax mainly aims to calculate taxable income, it is different from the accounting under the PSAK. A company should pay a tax calculated according to tax laws.

2.1. Accounting reports

2.1.1. Financial statements

According to the 2007 Company Act, a financial statement refers to accounting documents approved by resolution of an annual shareholders' meeting. These are approved after the board of directors prepares the draft statements for each accounting period and obtains confirmation of the statements from the board of commissioners. The statements must include a balance sheet, profit and loss statement, statement of cash flows, and statement of stockholder's equity, pursuant to Article 66 Paragraph 2.

A balance sheet (*neraca*) is a financial statement of the assets, liabilities, and capital of a company at a particular point in time, detailing the balance of income and expenditure over the preceding period, which generally shows what the company owns and owes, as well as the amount invested by shareholders.

A profit and loss statement, or income statement (*laporan laba rugi*) is a financial statement that summarizes the revenues, costs, and expenses incurred over a specific period of time (usually a fiscal quarter or year) and provides information about how the company generates profit through increasing revenue and reducing costs.

A statement of cash flows (*laporan arus kas*) is a financial statement that shows how changes in balance sheet accounts and income affect cash and cash equivalents, and breaks the analysis down to operating, investing, and financing activities.

A statement of stockholder's equity (*laporan perubahan ekuitas*) is a financial statement that highlights the changes in value to a stockholders' equity or ownership interest in a company over a given accounting period.

A statement of appropriation of retained earnings is not a mandatory requirement under the 2007 Company Act. Appropriated retained earnings are separately accounted from the standard retained earnings account and show external users the amount of money shareholders will need to contribute from the main account in order to properly fund a special activity.

2.1.2. Annual report

An annual report is a comprehensive report on a company's activities throughout the preceding year and is intended to give shareholders and other interested persons information about the company's activities and financial performance.

An annual report must contain the following (Article 66 Paragraph 2):

- Financial statement
- Report on the company's activities
- Report on the implementation of social and environmental responsibility
- Details on issues which occurred during the accounting year affecting the company's activities
- Report on supervisory duties performed by the board of commissioners during the previous accounting year
- Names of the members of the board of directors and board of commissioners
- Salary and compensation for the members of board of directors, and salary or honorarium and compensation for the members of the board of commissioners for the previous year

Any director or commissioner who has not signed an annual report must specify the reasons in writing. Otherwise, the director or commissioner is deemed to have approved the annual report (Article 67 Paragraph 3).

2.1.3. Effect of submission and approval

2.1.3.1. APPROVAL OF ANNUAL REPORT

An annual report must be signed by all members of the board of directors and board of commissioners in the relevant accounting year and kept at the company's office from the date of notice of a shareholders' meeting to examine the report (Article 67 Paragraph 1). As explained earlier, any director or commissioner who has not signed an annual report must specify the reasons in writing, because the absence of a reason gives a presumption of approval regarding the annual report.

The final approvals of financial statements and audit reports must be obtained from a shareholders' meeting, and this process must be included in the articles of association.

2.1.3.2. AUDIT

According to Article 68 Paragraph 1, a board of directors must submit the annual report of its company for audit by a public accountant if:

- The activity of the company is to collect and/or to manage a community fund.
- The company issues a debt acknowledgement letter to the public.
- The company is a public company.
- The company is owned by a state.
- The company owns assets and/or business with the minimum value of IDR 50 billion.

A small, closely held company that does not fall under Article 68 Paragraph 1 generally has very limited interest-based relationships to certain shareholders, and few creditors or employees, thus the absence of audit report seems not to be a problem.[4]

A board of directors must submit the audit report to shareholders and make an announcement of balance sheet and profit and loss statements no later than 7 days from ratification at shareholders' meeting.

2.1.3.3. AUDITOR'S INQUIRY OF A CLIENT'S LAWYERS CONCERNING LITIGATION, CLAIMS, AND ASSESSMENTS

An in-house counsel or outside lawyer has no legal obligation to provide all details regarding any pending litigation and disputes. From corporate management perspective, it would be wise not to leak confidential information.

It is not an auditor but the company that has the obligation to disclose any contingent liabilities which could turn into to established debts. If such a disclosure is improper, or not made, the auditor may provide a qualified opinion, adverse opinion, or disclaimer to the financial statements. In the end, therefore, lawyers should cooperate with the client's auditors.

Although the level of Indonesian audit standards is not comparable to the depth seen in the United States for instance, the same general practices have been imported and are widely used in Indonesia, particularly by large audit firms. An example of such an imported practice is AU337, which states that

---

4 There is no particular sanction against a small-sized closely held company in relevant laws and regulations including the 2007 Company Act, Keputusan Menteri Perdagangan 121/2001, Peraturan Pemerintah 64/1999, and Ketentuan Penyampaian Laporan Keuangan Tahunan Perusahan.

with respect to litigation, claims, and assessments, the independent auditor should obtain audit evidence relevant to the following factors:

- The existence of any condition, situation, or set of circumstances indicating an uncertainty as to the possible loss to an entity arising from litigation, claims, and assessments.
- The period in which the underlying cause for legal action occurred
- The degree of probability of an unfavorable outcome
- The amount or range of potential loss

In order to retain the above evidence, the auditor should question management about the existence of contingent liabilities, and the client subsequently must send a letter to its lawyers describing all of the contingent liabilities (litigation, claims, and assessments), including any unasserted claims. More often, the letter requests that the lawyers either furnish the following information, or comment on those matters where their views may differ from those stated by management, as appropriate:

- A description of the nature of the matter, the progress of the case to date, and the action the company intends to take (for example, to contest the matter vigorously or to seek an out-of-court settlement).
- An evaluation of the likelihood of an unfavorable outcome and an estimate, if one can be made, of the amount or range of potential loss.
- With respect to a list prepared by management, an identification of the omission of any pending or threatened litigation, claims, and assessments, or a statement that the list of such matters is complete.

The underlying assumption is that an auditor ordinarily does not possess the legal skills required to make legal judgments concerning information coming to his attention. Thus, the letter should request that the lawyer confirm the correctness of the client's understanding regarding these claims (reflected in the letter of audit inquiry) and provide confirmation that the lawyer will advise the client when unasserted claims require disclosure.

The above letter of audit inquiry to the client's lawyer is the auditor's primary means of obtaining corroboration of the information furnished by management concerning litigation, claims, and assessments. A passionate auditor often encloses a self-addressed envelope for reply when sending the above letter. The reason why an auditor obstinately sends the letter to lawyers is the principle that evidence obtained from an outsider is more trustworthy than that of self-interested company leaders. Of course, the lawyer need not to undertake a full reconsideration of all matters upon which he was consulted during the period under audit – most will be aware of the current state of these matters.

Although these processes should be particularly relevant and applicable for public companies and financial companies due to their strict disclosure liabilities, the Indonesian practice – a love of formality and a risk-averse approach – seems to apply the same or tougher strictness to closely held companies.[5]

From the perspective of practice, if any important litigation or dispute is pending, there may be tension between the client, law firm, and audit firm regarding what level of exposure to legal action should be disclosed, and on who will take responsibility for determining whether to disclose, and the degree of disclosure. Since invoices from legal firms, internal resolutions, contracts and certification of payment, and payment guarantees are all examined, any misinformation can be easily revealed. Therefore, it is always wise to keep quiet should a leakage of information be a problem.

Although there are many ways to refuse to reply for an auditor's letter on these matters, such as an inherent uncertainty which makes it difficult for a lawyer to form conclusions regarding pending litigation, the most widely used reason for limited answers from lawyers are so-called substantial attention limitation and confidential information. Substantial attention limitation means that a lawyer may limit his responses to only those matters to which he has devoted substantial attention. Confidential information is used as a reason where the lawyer is not able to disclose information because any leakage of such information may affect the pending case, or bring about a lawsuit against the client. An auditor cannot include "the lawyer did not provide information based on confidentiality" in the financial statement.

2.1.3.4. EFFECT OF APPROVAL

Upon approval from a shareholder's meeting, the financial statements and the profit or loss statements are firmly declared. All the directors and commissioners are jointly and individually liable for any losses incurred due to incorrect financial statements. Only a director or commissioner who successfully proves he has no fault (*kesalahan*) in the incorrect statements can be free from this liability.

Examples of such faults are events such as a director selling his real property to the company at an exorbitant price, or making speculative investment in stocks rather than conducting the company's main business, or making a false representation for approval. To establish a lack of fault, the director or commissioner should be able to prove that he did not contribute to such a circumstance, or that he had no knowledge at the time of approval about the illegal actions of another director.

2.2. *Reserve funds*

A reserve fund (*cadangan*) is a savings account set aside by the company to meet future costs of upkeep and any unexpected costs that may arise. If a company distributes all assets in excess of capital as dividends, both the company

---

5 From a business perspective, accounting firms have incentives to strictly apply the audit process to small clients and close their eyes to issues with giant clients. A reader may be reminded how big firms tend to remain standing strong after large scandals.

and its shareholders and creditors may be heading for a fall should problems requiring expenditures occur in the future. Thus, for purposes of sound development of the company and the protection of interest holders, a certain portion of profits should be put back into the business so to help should it face a "rainy day."

A reserve can be placed in any fund, and it does not require a formal approach to use a certain type of fund. In accounting, this is an account with a credit balance in the entity's equity on the balance sheet.

A reserve may be largely divided into a legal reserve mandatorily required by law, and a voluntary reserve that the company autonomously saves pursuant to its articles of association or a shareholder resolution. Also, the reserve can be divided into an earned surplus reserve and capital surplus. Earned surplus reserve – or profit surplus – is a percentage of profits earned through the company's sound management. A capital surplus reserve is accumulated from equity which cannot otherwise be classified as capital, or from retained earnings because the nature of this amount is irrelevant to profit distribution to shareholders. A stock issued at a premium over par value is an example of creation of capital surplus. Thus, there cannot be a limitation over the reserve.

Although the functions of a depreciation account, an allowance for bad debts, or a reserve for fluctuation are similar to those of a reserve account, these are not reserves in its original sense.

The 2007 Company Act lumps all the different reserve account types together under a reserve (Article 70 Paragraph 1). In a literal interpretation of this Article, and in practice of Indonesian accounting firms, however, this reserve in the 2007 Company Act means only a profit surplus reserve.

If a company has generated profit in any year, it must contribute to the reserve fund from its net profit until it amounts to at least 20 percent of its issued and paid-up capital (Article 70 Paragraph 3). Any reserve fund holding less than 20 percent of the issued and paid-up capital may only be utilized to cover any loss that cannot be covered by other reserves.

2.3.   Engagement letter

An accountant's scope of responsibilities to its clients is quite limited, because when "creative accounting" becomes an issue, the company cannot be free from the primary and ultimate responsibility of collecting and providing financial data. Most importantly, the responsibilities regarding detection of a material distortion other than a trivial amount presumptively lies in the decision of the management of the company.

Even if the likelihood of detecting irregularities (such as a frequent change of internal accounting policy, commissioners, or a scope of supervision) is very high at the time of audit planning, the auditor's responsibility is only to audit the accounts. Should the auditor receive written confirmation from management and employees that all internal documentation has been duly tendered, and there is no additional material information, yet fail to detect misconduct or a dishonest act, it is almost impossible for the client to place responsibility on the auditor unless the auditor commits an intentionally planned crime.

Furthermore, unlike misunderstandings pervasive in practice, drafting a financial statement or note should not be requested to auditors. In principle, the final version of the note is the object of an audit, not an auditor's drafts or proofreading.

Therefore, in general practice, an engagement letter or other types of contract for an audit or accounting consultation merely stipulates the object and period of audit, payment and submission processes, and requests for various documents. Such a letter also warns the client by adding statements such as, for example, "financial statements are management's liability (*laporan-laporan keuangan adalah pertanggungjawaban manajemen perusahaan*)." The letter may also include a statement such as:

> Standards require that we obtain reasonable, rather than absolute, assurance that the financial statements are free of material misstatement, whether caused by error or fraud. Accordingly, a material misstatement may remain undetected. Also, an audit is not designed to detect error or fraud that is immaterial to the financial statements; therefore, the audit will not necessarily detect misstatements less than this materiality level that might exist due to error, fraudulent financial reporting or misappropriation of assets. (*Standar tersebut mewajibkan agar kami mencapai secara layak, daripada kemutlakan, jaminan bahwa laporan-laporan keuangan bebas dari kesalahan laporan yang penting, baik yang disebabkan oleh kesalahan atau kecurangan. Sesuai dengan itu, suatu kesalahan laporan yang penting mungkin tetap tidak terdeteksi. Demikian pula, suatu audit tidak didesain untuk mendeteksi kesalahan atau kecurangan yang tidak penting bagi laporan keuangan; oleh karena itu, audit tidak perlu mendeteksi kesalahan laporan yang kurang dari tingkat kepentingan ini yang mungkin ada karena kesalahan, kecurangan pelaporan keuangan atau penyalahgunaan aset-aset.*)

Because this sort of statement does not provide immunity for an auditor's intentional tort liability or criminal responsibility, this does not need to be revised.

3. Dividends

3.1. Annual distribution of profit

A dividend is a distribution of a portion of a company's profits to its shareholders on a regular basis. The distribution of profit should be based on the number of shares that each shareholder owns. If a company has issued two or more classes of shares having different rights in dividends (i.e. preferred stocks) in accordance with its articles of association, dividends may be distributed on that basis.

The requirements for annual distribution of profit are as follows:

- A relevant provision in articles of association:

  The procedure for the use of profits and allocation of dividends is a mandatory item to include in articles of association (Article 15 Paragraph 1).

- Resolution of shareholders' meeting (Article 71 Paragraph 1):

  Shareholders can claim dividends only after the shareholders approve the company's financial statements. The dividend profit is also only recognized when both the right to claim a dividend, and the amount of dividend, are specifically decided under Indonesian accounting principles. Particularly, the right to claim dividends on preferred stocks automatically arises at the time the accounting period closes, inasmuch as annual reported earnings exist. Because this right is an independent receivable, the shareholder can transfer it separately from share ownership. However, a shareholder cannot claim a distribution of profits, or transfer this right to a third person, without shareholders first making a resolution to approve the financial statements. In the event that a company delays the distribution even after shareholders approve the financial statements, the shareholder may consider either a penalty, remedy, or other compensation. This is because dividend payments are such an important issue for shareholders that paying no dividend without a specific reason may infringe their rights.

- Positive profit balance to distribute (Article 71 Paragraph 3):

  All net profits after any deduction for reserve funds should be distributed to shareholders as dividends, except otherwise resolved in the shareholder meeting (Article 71 Paragraph 2). As elucidation, the shareholders in this Paragraph mean the shareholders recorded in list of shareholders in the relevant accounting period. *All net profits* means the total net profits for the relevant financial year after deducting any accumulated losses from the company's previous financial year. In the event the company's net profits in the relevant financial year cannot completely cover the company's accumulated losses from the previous year, the company cannot distribute dividends because it will have recorded a negative net profit balance.

Dividends unclaimed after 5 years from the stipulated date are retained in a special reserve fund, and affected shareholders should follow the procedures to claim such a dividend. If the dividends remain unclaimed for 10 years, they become the company's asset (Article 73).

3.2. *Interim dividend*

An interim dividend is a dividend which a company distributes to listed shareholders before the end of the relevant accounting period, pursuant to relevant provisions in articles of association (Article 72 Paragraph 1). According to *Yahya Harahap* doctrine, an interim dividend is "a temporary dividend that is declared and paid before the annual profits of company is set by shareholders' meeting."

An interim dividend can promote good investment practices in pursuing dividend incomes rather than chasing short margins by selling shares. Such a dividend can ease a company's temporary monetary pressure and raise general people's interests in stock investment.

The requirements of declaring and issuing an interim dividend are as follows:

- A provision about interim dividends must exist in the articles of association (Article 72 Paragraph 1). While "no contrary provision in the articles of association" is sufficient in some foreign countries, an explicit provision must be set forth at article of association in Indonesia.
- The amount of the company's net assets must not be less than issued and paid-up capital plus reserve funds. (Article 72 Paragraph 2)
- Any interim distribution must not cause the company to be unable to fulfill its obligation to creditors or disrupt the activities of the company. (Article 72 Paragraph 3)
- The distribution must be agreed by the board of directors after seeking approval from the board of commissioners. (Article 72 Paragraph 4)

On the one hand, some argue that interim dividends must be a distribution of the profit at the beginning of an accounting period and based on the carried forward profit at the end of previous period. On the other hand, others argue that it must be a distribution of the profit which will be calculated at the end of the same accounting period in which it is paid. According to Indonesian experts, the view of public authorities zigzag. The conservative and safer view would be that, in order to distribute an interim dividend, profits at the end of the previous period should exist, and a profit at the end of the current period must also be highly expected. Article 72 Paragraph 5 states that in the event the company instead suffers a loss at the end of the accounting year, the distributed interim dividends must be returned by the shareholders. This is thought to be because the 2007 Company Act seeks conservatism in this fashion. Any interim dividends distributed over the amount of retained earnings are, of course, then deemed to be a refund of paid-in capital. As a result, such an interim dividend becomes void, and the directors and commissioners become jointly and severally liable for the loss incurred by company and any third party (Article 72 Paragraph 6). Of course, the company's creditors can also claim unjust enrichment.

3.3. *Protection of minority shareholders from a majority shareholder's continued decision to reserve the profits*

In the event a controlling shareholder continually reserves total profits through majority votes in annual shareholder meetings despite steady profits every year and opposing votes from minority shareholders, the issue is what protection the minority shareholder can seek. More specifically, the issue is whether minority shareholders can force the company to distribute the reserved profits, even if the shareholders' right to claim the dividend receivable can only arise upon a shareholders' resolution on the specific amounts to distribute. The protection of minority shareholders is required because it is generally very hard to sell minority shares of a closely held company that does not distribute its profits.

Unfortunately, no particular case applicable to this issue has been seen. Most Indonesian legal experts in interviews for this book gave a negative opinion about whether minority shareholders can be protected without a contrary provision in articles of association. This appears be the result of strong formalism in general legal practice and a lack of explicit provisions in the 2007 Company Act, rather than because of justice or righteousness.

4.   Bonds

4.1.   Introduction

A shareholder has the right to participate in a decision about how to improve a company's activities and the right to improve his own direct economic interests. The examples of the former are voting rights, the right to claim a derivative suit and inspection rights, while the latter includes dividend rights, preemptive rights, the right to claim a distribution at liquidation, and appraisal rights.

The Negative Investment List derived from the 2007 Capital Investment Act mainly considers the former. That is, foreign ownership restrictions are concerned principally with voting rights, not economic benefit. For example, while an agreement for a foreign investor's use of an Indonesian nominee to exercise a voting right is null and void per se,[6] dividend distributions to foreign shareholders is generally not limited. Indonesia does not place massive restrictions on variable bonds. Besides, a loan advanced to a company is not heavily regulated, and thus offshore loans are widely used. Because an exchangeable bond or convertible bond is also deemed to be debt, or a payable, until exchanged or converted, it may enjoy the advantages of avoiding both the Negative Investment List and any high risk of heavy regulation in Indonesia. Accordingly, a

---

6 "The application of foreign investment rules to public companies is a grey area. Prior to Qatar Telecommunications' acquisition of Indosat in 2008, it was widely assumed that foreign ownership rules did not apply to listed companies. . . . [T]he current Negative List assumes that the Foreign Investment Law applies to listed companies, but contains an exemption for 'portfolio' investments, through the capital markets. Perhaps unsurprisingly, no definition is provided of what constitutes at the time said that they would apply the Negative List to 'controlling' stakes in [a] listed company." Joel Hogarth, Structuring Indonesian M&A Transactions, *International Financial Law Review*, 2012: http://www.iflr.com/Article/3121466/Structuring-Indonesian-M-A-transactions.html, accessed on 19 March 2018.

convertible bond structure in a closely held company, or in fields in which foreign investment is strictly regulated, is very common in Indonesia.

4.2. No explicit rule

The 2007 Company Act not only does not stipulate the requirements to issue convertible bonds or bonds with warrants, it also fails to stipulate the requirements to issue a regular bond. Thus, the bond holder should guard himself by specifically agreeing to every relevant factor.

The typical conditions to create a debt covenant are as follows (the holder needs to constantly supervise whether the company observes these or not):

A   Positive Covenant
The positive covenant specifies what the borrower must do in consideration of the debt investment, and typically includes such requirements to
- provide audited financial statements each year,
- maintain certain minimum financial ratios, and
- maintain life insurance on key employees.

B   Negative Covenant
The negative covenant specifies the actions the borrower cannot take, such as restrictions on
- the sale of certain assets,
- the incurrence of additional debt,
- the payment of dividends, and
- the compensation of top management.

4.3. Convertible bond

4.3.1. Definition

A convertible bond is a type of bond that the holder can convert into a specified number of shares of common stock in the issuing company.

The most widely used type are "vanilla" convertible bonds, which grant the holder the right to convert the bond into a specified number of shares with a specific conversion price agreed in advance. Mandatory convertibles, which force the holder to convert into shares at maturity, are relatively rare in the Indonesian market, because the reason to issue a different bond is to encourage third parties to invest their money and force the holder to lose the right to withdraw their cash is against an investor's interest. Some option or warrant may be additionally attached to convertible bonds, depending on the parties' agreement. In any case, by giving additional rights, potential investors can be incentivized to inject their cash into the bond-issuing company.

The nature of convertible bonds is, thus, a hybrid security that is a debt security before converting to shares, but then becomes an equity security upon exercising the right. In practice, however, people regard convertible bonds as equity securities upon issuance for the better protection of all interest holders.

4.3.2.   Issuance to a third person

Issuing a hybrid security to a third party may infringe shareholders' preemptive rights, because it is essentially equal to issuance of stock. Also, when a controlling shareholder causes the company to issue convertible bonds to associates for control defense against an outsider, it drags down other shareholders' ownership percentage, an unfair result. Furthermore, if the controlling shareholder causes the company to issue bonds and converts them to shares for the purpose of an expedient gift, the preexisting shareholders' value per share decreases. In other words, the share value becomes diluted.

If the holder converts convertible bonds issued after advance agreement from shareholders, the shareholders' preemptive rights are not applicable (Article 43 Paragraph 3.b). However, if the holder converts convertible bonds issued without agreement from shareholders, the shareholders' preemptive rights become a major problem. Hence, the company must fully explain the specific facts of any bond issue to the shareholders in advance so as to prevent any dispute.

4.3.3.   No explicit rule

As discussed earlier, the 2007 Company Act does not stipulate requirements for issuing regular bonds, let alone any for convertible bonds. Therefore, if specific terms and conditions concerning convertible bonds are not written in the articles of association or decided by a shareholder resolution, the board of directors can decide these. However, in the event that the total amount of bonds for one or more related transactions is more than 50 percent of the issuing company's net assets, the board of directors should receive approval from a shareholders' meeting (Article 102 Paragraph 1).

Even though issuing convertible bonds is virtually equal to issuing new stock, whether provisions in the articles of association about stock issuance can be applied *mutatis mutandis* to the issuance of convertible bonds is unclear, due to the lack of explicit legislative or regulatory stipulation, or any referable case. Whether shareholders have a right to receive the convertible bonds in proportion to their shareholding rate is also obscure.

Not surprisingly, there is no specific rule in the 2007 Company Act about decisions by the board of directors concerning issuance of convertible bonds. Thus, the contract with the holder of convertible bonds should be able to guard himself by first deciding – in as detailed a manner as possible – a range of matters, and then obtain subsequent approval from the board of directors and existing shareholders. These matters are

- The total amount of convertible bonds
- A specific grant of the subscription right of convertible bonds and the subscribed amount of convertible bonds
- The amount of convertible bonds for the specific holder
- The terms and conditions of conversion

- What stocks are to be issued at conversion
- The period that the holder can exercise the conversion right
- Whether existing shareholders have subscribed to the convertible bonds

The above details do not need to be written in any announcement or notice for calling the meeting. Practically, it would instead be better if they were recorded in a bond register as specifically as possible, regardless of the fact the law does not require this. Upon the holder's payment, the company should immediately issue the bonds.

4.3.4. Request for conversion

The holder can request conversion at any time unless agreed otherwise. If the company did not obtain the agreement from its shareholders required by Article 43 Paragraph 3, the company should immediately inform shareholders upon the holder's request for conversion.

New shares issuing upon the holder exercising conversion rights should not increase outstanding shares beyond the authorized capital, and any stock issued or converted in excess of the authorized capital registered by the MLHR is per se null and void. Thus, shares to be converted can be withheld until the authorized capital has duly increased. It is better for the convertible bond subscriber to demand sufficient authorized capital in the first place.

4.3.5. Effect of conversion

When new stocks are issued upon a request for conversion, the value of newly issued stock is generally adjusted to match the total value of the convertible bonds. In other words, the number of new stock issued is the quotient equal to the total value of bonds divided by the conversion rate. Upon the conversion, the number of total outstanding stocks increases, and the number of bonds decreases.

If the stock value is less than the conversion price, conversion of the bonds is rendered meaningless as it will be virtually no different to a debt–equity swap.[7]

Let us assume that a company issues convertible bonds or bonds with a warrant and then issues new stocks at a low price, transfers reserves to capital, or

---

7 A debt–equity swap by converting convertible bonds to stocks is different from a debt–equity swap swapping payables to stocks. The right to convert in convertible bonds is an option where the conversion price, period, and other conditions are already agreed, while there is no such prearrangement in a general debt–equity swap with payables. As allowed without prearrangement, a general debt–equity swap with payables is made when the company is suffering hardship. Naturally, any profit is extremely uncertain as it relies on the company's hopeful future normalization. In the meantime, the conversion of bonds is generally elected when the company's value has sufficiently increased.

distributes stock dividends. The first expected result is dilution of the value of stocks and a decrease in the market price of shares. Then, the agreed price to convert the bonds to stock in such a case becomes higher than the actual market price at the time of conversion. In other words, issuing new stock after issuing bonds, the transfer reserves to capital, distribution of stock dividends, or any similar transactions which can affect the stock price, may result in unfair treatment to the bond holder or shareholders. In practice in Indonesia, parties thus should guard themselves by specifically agreeing on a certain formula to adjust or decrease the conversion price in the event of any stock issuance, stock dividends, or transfer of reserves to capital. Although parties may agree on these specific conditions in practice, the lack of rules concerning the adjustment of conversion price or dilution of stock price in 2007 Company Act should be rectified.

4.4. *Convertible note*

See the later section "Warnings against the Attempts to End Run Regulations in Direct Inbound Investment."

5.   Inspection of the company

Articles 138 to 141 stipulate an inspection of a company may take place if there is suspicion of any illegal act by either the company or a director or commissioner. These articles of law appear to be far more creative and innovative than needed, because these are procedures that should be detailed in procedural laws, and not substantive matters to place in company law, given the nature of the provisions.

Indonesian legal practice generally regards these illegal acts as having the same meaning of illegal acts in Articles 1401 and 1402 of the Dutch Civil Code, as defined by Dutch Supreme Court (Lindenbaum/Cohen case of 31 January 1919): "An act of omission, either of which infringes another's rights or failure of perpetrator's lawful duty in written law, morality or against the duty of care which fits in the society in respect to other person or property."[8] In other words, an illegal act of either the company, directors, or commissioners that includes not only breach of codified law, but also of unwritten legal duties such as breach of contractual provisions or tort liability.

To be specific, it does not legally make sense that a foreign court's interpretation of foreign law is legally binding in a domestic court's interpretation of a totally different law. Thus, the view in Indonesian legal practice that the term "illegal act" in a civil case should be understood simply to generally include all tortious acts.

---

8 In the Netherlands, this judgment has been later codified in Article 6: 162 BW.

5.1. Inspection process

The rightful person to submit the application for inspection is a shareholder (or shareholders) who represents at least 1/10 of the total number of shares with voting rights, or other parties who have been given the authority to submit the application for inspection under either law or by the company's articles of association,[9] or a prosecutor's office for public interest (Article 138 Paragraph 3).

If such a rightful person has a reasonable suspicion that a company, director, or commissioner has committed an illegal act that may harm shareholders or a third party's rights, he may submit a request at shareholders' meeting that the company provide relevant data and information. Should the company not provide the requested data or information, the person then can submit a letter of application for inspection to a district court, with written reasons (Article 138 Paragraph 4).

If the court accepts the application, the court appoints three experts to conduct the inspection, and issues an order of inspection. These experts have full power to inspect all documents, assets, or information of the company, and the company and its constituents must provide all requested data (Article 139 Paragraph 5). The experts then report the result of inspection to the court within 90 days of their appointment, and the court then sends this report to the company within a further 14 days (Article 140).

The costs and expenses for such inspection are borne by the company, although in exceptional instances the court may shift this burden to the individual applicant, director, or commissioner (Article 141 Paragraph 3).

5.2. Problems with this provision

It is clear the inspection may function as a good device to protect the interests of minority shareholders. However, as explained in the section *Minority Stockholder and Single-Stock Owner Rights*, there are numerous cases where this right has been abused by a domestic minority shareholder, or his successors or heirs. In short, a minority holder who is granted an opportunity to participate in ownership merely because of the minimum requirement of domestic shareholding required by the Negative Investment List may later change his mind and demand compensation, thus abusing this right. The demand of money by the domestic minority shareholder or heirs, combined with a threat of exercising this right is both importunate and irksome because, first, even an honest company applying appropriate due diligence may get into trouble because of a trifling administration issue. Further, the court may grant the inspection order to an applicant pointing to a trifling matter, even in the absence of convincing evidence regarding any illegal act. The inspection process itself is a substantial burden for the company, even if the company is actually not involved in any illegal act,

---

9 Notably, there is no other party specifically given this authority by laws and regulations.

and a final burden is that negative public opinion may be formed against the company under investigation for the alleged illegal act.

6.   Corporate social responsibility

6.1.   *Indonesia's unique features that strengthen CSR as a legal obligation*

Although some foreign countries also started imposing corporate social responsibility (CSR) requirements recently, for several reasons Indonesia distinctively applies CSR requirements, through numerous laws and regulations. Why Indonesia mandates CSR so strongly should be understood through historical, geographical, philosophical, and economic contexts.

In terms of its geographical and social anthropological setting, one of the main differences of Indonesia from other modern countries is its variety of indigenous societies spread over roughly 18,000 islands. Indonesia is centrally located along ancient trading routes and has a complex cultural mixture, very different from other original indigenous societies. In modern history, no similar country could join the league of advanced economies. Unsurprisingly, a fundamental question has remained as to how a country can harmonize indigenous societies with modern culture, even though many modern companies have been already conducting business for the collection, refining, trade, and export of natural resources in these regions for more than a half century.

For example, is the application of modern laws to indigenous societies correct? Is it correct for a government to suddenly come in and divide the ownership of aboriginal regions in a jungle where the concept of private individual ownership of real property has never existed?[10]

Let us suppose that the government has intentionally left one aboriginal community alone, fully respecting the customary law of indigenous people there. In the meantime, there is a now a modern company who comes, industrializes, and develops the economy of a nearby region only a kilometer away from the aboriginal community. How can the government attract a company to develop the regional economy while leaving a nearby aboriginal region unattached to modern culture? This is not just a supposition, but an actual dilemma that Indonesia has been facing.[11]

---

10 Because of this problem, Indonesia created a legal concept of "customary forest" for indigenous people. However, it was difficult to determine which forest was customary forest and which was not. Moreover, it was difficult to determine who legally owns the customary forest. The Indonesian Constitutional Court determined in No.35/PUU-X/2012 that Article Paragraph 6 of 1999 Forestry Law No. 41 is unconstitutional and must change to delete the word "state" from the sentence: "Customary forests are state forests located in indigenous peoples' territories."

11 A member of the Adat community made a speech in the U.N. "Before the plantation came in, our lifestyle was prosperous. If we needed fruits, we just went to the forest. It was the

Under this setting, it is easy to "pass the buck" for the government to the company, particularly when it has a short of funds to redress all the regional issues. An example of such passing is found in a dispute over regional land. If a state government issues a permit or license to a company for business on state-owned land, such a permit should mean that the government certifies and guarantees that the land is owned by the issuing state and, thus, not impeded by a third person's rights. This is partially because state-owned land is defined as "land existing on the land not impeded by another's land rights" (Article 1 Paragraph 1 of No. 41 Year 1999 Forest Act), but more precisely because, from the license holder's perspective, the fundamental reason to obtain such a permit is to be protected and secured by holding it. From the context of investment and company management, Indonesian legal scholars and the Constitutional Court have the same understanding.[12] Nevertheless, the face of this land permit has an explicit clause, normally on the last page, stating "the issuer shall not be liable if the land is later found [to be] privately owned or if an individual has a right on it."

Naturally, even if the state wrongfully issued a permit resulting in someone's loss, the responsibility to remedy the loss is shifted on to the permit holder. The Indonesian Constitutional Court recognizes this problem as well.[13] Some believe that this is justified by the Indonesian Constitution, which gives priority to national interests, in the Benefit Principle that the responsibilities at the end of the day must be borne by the company who enjoys earnings by using the land.[14] In this case, anyway, if the company does not remedy the loss to the

---

same if we needed medicines, we just went to the forest. But since this company came in and burned our forest, everything has gone. Our life became difficult. The forest fire has been a disaster for us." Ahsan Ullah, *Globalization and the Health of Indigenous Peoples*, Routledge, 2016, p. 7.

12 "These rights are of little value if the guarantee from the government is weak. Aaron Barzel also maintained that the guarantee of land rights be in the form of regulations and be an apparatus for consistent implementation and fair trial or arbitration. (*Hak-hak ini tidak banyak artinya kalau kurang adanya jaminan dari Permerintah. Aaron Barzel mengatakan jaminan atas hak-hak atas tanah ini dalam bentuk peraturan, aparatur pelaksana yang konsisten dan penyelesaian senketa yang adil di pengadilan atau arbitrase.*)" Mahkamah Konstitusi RI, Risah Sidang Perkara Nomor 21/PUU-V/2007 Peihal Pengujian UU RI No.25 Tahun 2007 tentang Penanaman Modal Terhadap UUD 1945, Acara Mengengar Keterangan Ahli Dari Pemohon dan Pemerintah (IV), p. 68; See Suparji, *Penanaman Modal Asing Di Indonesia Insentif v. Pembatasan*, Universitas Al Azhar Indonesia, 2008, p. 265.

13 "I would like to say, I wrote in my dissertation that land rights in Indonesia are less secured than [the actual stipulation of] laws governing the rights to land. (*saya ingin menyampaikan, saya menulis dalam disertasi saya bahwah hak atas tanah di Indonesia kurang dijamin di dalam undang-undang yang mengatur menenai hak atas tanah.*)" Id. Mahkamah Konstitusi RI.

14 Such a passing of the buck is not just made to private companies. Once a hard-to-solve dispute arises, the central, regional, and communal governments impute the blame and burden to one another. Article 33 Paragraph 33 of the Indonesian Constitution declares

local people, it violates a corporate social responsibility, which the official elucidation of Article 15 Item b of the 2007 Capital Investment Act defines as the obligation to "keep balance and suitable to the local community's neighborhood, values, norms and culture."

Second, as a world treasure trove of natural wildlife, Indonesia also has a history of ineffectively regulating corporations, bringing up substantial external diseconomies, particularly environmental exploitation, pollution, and negative impacts on indigenous people.[15] Due to the geographic and physiographic setting of Indonesia, the importance of environmental protection, particularly against damage caused by companies, has become an issue that cannot be emphasized enough.

The 2007 Capital Investment Act sets forth the principle of environmentally sound investment (Article 3 Paragraph 1 Subsection h). The 2007 Company Act mandates that a company conducting business related to natural resources must implement social and environmental responsibility policies under Article 74.

Lastly, the historical catastrophes affecting the national economy in 1997 and 1998 have a significant impact on development of CSR in Indonesia. The financial and economic crisis threatened national survival. Indonesia had the lowest foreign inbound investment among ASEAN countries after the Asian economic crisis of 1997–1998, collapsing from its previous rank of 5th.[16] This was the only net outflow among ASEAN countries.[17] Employees who did not receive their full retirement allowance violently protested, and by cutting off work to Indonesian companies, foreign project holders triggered a series of harsh demonstrations by Indonesian laborers. The notorious May 1998 riots of Indonesia, known as the 1998 Tragedy, brought on the resignation of President Suharto and the fall of the New Order government. The social

---

the state "controls lands, waters, and natural riches," while Article 3 of the 1960 Agrarian Law undercuts traditional communal property rights by stating "the implementation of communal property of *Adat* communities and rights similar to that of an *Adat* community, in so far as they exist, shall be adjusted as such as to fit to the national and state's interest based on the unity of the nation." Similarly, the 1967 Forest Act and its 1970 amendment give priority national interest over customary rights. Nevertheless, the 2016 Regulation (Procedures to Decide Communal Rights on Land of Customary Laws and Communities in Specific Area) again officially excluded a central government's direct control to determine regional issues, by absolutely leaving communal rights to the customs and rights of the community. Not surprisingly, all these laws do not state how far a regional customary law can be tolerated. In academia, many argue the inappropriateness of this buck passing, and even cast a doubt on regional customary law itself.

15 See O. P. Dwivedi, *Environmental Policies in The Third World: A Comparative Analysis*, 1995, Greenwood Press, pp. 91–104; and Ronnie D. Lipschutz & Judith Mayer, *Global Civil Society and Global Environmental Governance*, 1996, SUNY Press, pp. 179–181.

16 See United Nations Conference on Trade and Development, *World Investment Report*, 2003, p. 251.

17 See Thee Kian Wie, *Policies for Private Sector Development in Indonesia*, ADB Institute Discussion Paper No. 46, March 2006, p. 21.

climate heavily blamed transnational companies and foreign investors rather than reflecting upon its national failure. Indigenous movements targeting multinational companies also appeared in the beginning of 2000s. They denounced transnational companies vehemently and demanded they take responsibilities in Indonesia.[18]

This phenomenon in Indonesia also coincided with the trend of progressive corporate law in Western world. After the fall of Enron in 2002 and the collapse of Lehman Brothers in 2008 with subsequent global recession, the power of neoliberalism has heavily declined, and the global academic world of corporate law has ruminated over the role of corporation in society. At the same time, the idea of CSR has risen to prominence to become, in the words of *The Economist*, "an industry in itself, with full-time staff, newsletters, professional associations and massed armies of consultants."[19] A study describes this period as

> embraced by corporations, touted by academics, and advanced by non-governmental organizations (NGOs) and policy makers as a potential mechanism for achieving social policy objectives and furthering economic development, CSR has become one of the flavors and hopes of the new Millennium.[20]

The United Kingdom responded this social climate with its Companies Act 2006 requiring directors to have regard to community and environmental issues when considering their duty to promote the success of their company and the disclosure to be included in the Business Review.

The global discourse on CSR and voluntary initiatives, largely Western-led, strongly inspired and animated Indonesia to mandate CSR. While management scholars have focused on the financial gains for the firm through CSR, the controversial issues in the legal context was how to regulate CSR. Should it be a legal norm, ethical norm, or something else? The question was further elaborated in Indonesia: should Indonesia regulate CSR in a voluntary way or as an obligation to companies?

Although it had not reached any notable social consensus regard to the concept of CSR, the social climate and public demands made a substantial pressure to implement CSR anyhow. Under this mood, the UN issued a foresighted

---

18 "Indonesia has its own indigenous movement that targets transnational corporations. The Urban Christian Mission, for example, has provided a focus for labor education and foreign networking. This has largely been ignored by the foreign activists concerned with issues of corporate responsibility in Indonesia. This might perhaps reflect the propensity of CSR to stimulate a form of industrial colonialism." Melody Kemp, *Corporate Social Responsibility in Indonesia: Quixotic Dream or Confident Expectation?*, Technology, Business and Society Programme Paper No. 6, United Nations Research Institute for Social Development, December, 2001, p. 33.

19 Two-Faced Capitalism, *The Economist*, January 24, 2004, p. 53.

20 Paddy Irel & Renginee G. Pillay, Corporate Social Responsibility in a Neoliberal Age, *Corporate Social Responsibility and Regulatory Governance*, UNRISD, 2010, p. 77.

research paper about adaptation of CSR in Indonesia.[21] This insightful study written by Melody Kemp concludes as follows:

> It is hard to consider something as abstract as CSR. . . . At this point in Indonesian history, CSR itself can only remain an image projected onto a screen – an outline with little depth. While concepts such as governance and CSR are fashionable, generating a new language and teams of experts, Indonesia's difficulties are perhaps more basic and to do with simple national survival. . . . CSR only makes a difference to those few corporations targeted by consumers or who are already thinking ethically and responsibly. . . . Indonesia may be able to benefit from CSR, but it cannot rely on CSR to solve issues of exploitation, environmental devastation and poor labor standards. . . . At this juncture in its development, Indonesia can indeed accommodate the tenets of Western CSR, as it has accommodated the tenets of human rights. But in reality, the inherent conflicts between CSR and, in particular, political culture may ensure that in Indonesia implementation of CSR is merely cosmetic. Indonesia's recent history is littered with examples of agencies advocating the latest trend and congratulating Indonesia for illusory change. It is pertinent to ask whether CSR has anything more to offer Indonesia at this time than what could be offered by overall structural reform. . . . I contend that any effective implementation of CSR requires the machinery of an effective democratic government and civil society.

Although the above study foresaw that CSR would only make a difference to those few corporations targeted by consumers or who are already thinking ethically and responsibly, they turned out to not just be a few. Nor were they just corporations targeted by consumers. A research on CSR activities of top 50 Indonesian Listed Corporations from 2003–2007 revealed that Indonesian companies had been already aware of the increasing demands and provided CSR to stakeholders in the emerging economy prior to establishment of legislation concerning CSR.[22]

Still, it was evident that Indonesia could not simply rely on CSR for national survival. The country needed an overall structural reform in national level

21 Melody Kemp, Corporate Social Responsibility in Indonesia: Quixotic Dream or Confident Expectation?, Technology, Business and Society Programme Paper No. 6, United Nations Research Institute for Social Development, December, 2001, p. 33.

22 See details at Juanita Oeyono, Martin Samy, and Roberta Bampton, An Examination of Corporate Social Responsibility and Financial Performance: A Study of the Top 50 Indonesian Listed Corporations, *Journal of Global Responsibility, Emerald Group Publishing Limited*, Vol. 2, No. 1., 2010, p. 11. The study measured as per GRI indicates that five out of 45 companies (11 %) completed a maximum of six Global Reporting Initiative (GRI) indicators, 10 companies (22 %) fulfilled five indicators and 16 companies (36 %) complied with four indicators.

and some effective machinery of a mature civil society because its difficulties were more basic. Indonesia desperately needed to revive its economy and bitterly perceived the need for encouraging foreign investment as a more stable source of foreign capital than regular short-term financial investment.[23] Naturally, this scathing historical lesson resulted in a political climate that stressed foreign direct investment in the private sector. As a part of the overall structural reforms for national survival and to satisfy the rapid changes of the social climate and public mood, the 2007 Capital Investment Act bill was proposed to Parliament.[24] And, of course, it did not forget to include CSR provisions under Article 15. At the same time, the Indonesian government proposed the 2007 Company Act bill to Parliament on 12 October 2005, which included Chapter V – Corporate Social and Environmental Responsibilities.

To implement mandatory provisions obliging CSR to private companies irrespective of its size was extremely rare from global perspective at that juncture. India often proudly calls itself as the first country to mandate CSR with its Companies Act 2013.[25] This is not true, albeit its CSR requirements are certainly much specific, sophisticated, and more stringent than the CSR provisions in Indonesia. Anyhow, with 2007 Company Act and 2007 Capital Investment Act, Indonesia officially chose the untraditional view for a model of stakeholders and became a leading example of triumph of progressive corporate law against proponents of the traditional shareholder-centric view.

Then, has this triumph of progressivism brought some meaningful results from legal perspective? In other words, is this implementation of CSR something other than as Melody Kemp prophesizes: "At this point in Indonesian history, CSR itself can only remain an image projected onto a screen – an outline with little depth. . . . But in reality, . . . in Indonesia implementation of CSR is merely cosmetic."

23 After this sharp history lesson, Indonesia declared 2003 as the "Indonesia Investment Year," with a number of favorable policy changes to promote foreign direct investment and increase investor confidence. United Nations Conference on Trade and Development, 2003, p. 48. See also Je Seong Jeon, The Changing Relation between Indonesian State and Foreign Capital: Focusing on the Formation of the International Business Chamber after Democratization, *Korean Association of Southeast Asian Studies, the Southeast Asian Review*, 2010, Vol. 20, No. 1, p. 267; Thee Kian Wie, *supra* note 17, pp. 22–26.
24 The 2007 Capital Investment Act directly mentions that its legal authority is the Decree of the People's Consultative Assembly concerning Economic Policy in the Context of Economic Democracy, which was legislated in 1998 as a result of these events.
25 India has recently enforced the Companies Act 2013 to mandate CSR at a very detailed level. It requires that one-third of a company's board comprise independent directors; at least one board member be a woman; and the companies to disclose executive salaries as a ratio to the average employee's salary. The striking requirement is "2 percent rule": the board committee must ensure that the company spends at least 2 percent of the average net profits of the company made during the 3 immediately preceding financial years.

6.2. The current regulatory frame of CSR in Indonesia and its problems

6.2.1. The 2007 Company Act and 2007 Capital Investment Act

The 2007 Capital Investment Act obligates every company to implement a corporate social responsibility policy as follows:

Article 15 of the 2007 capital investment act

Every investor has an obligation . . . to implement corporate social responsibility.

Elucidation of article 15 item b

"Corporate social responsibility" means a responsibility mounted in every investment company to keep creating relationship which is in harmony, in balance, and suitable to the local community's neighborhood, values, norms, and culture.

These provisions remain vaporous and indefinite without either concrete obligation or sanction. Unsurprisingly, this lack of any practical utility is nothing different from other abstract principles or general statements stipulated in a dominant part of the 2007 Company Act. Not only this provision, but also most of the provisions in the 2007 Company Act are covered in a rather brief and descriptive manner, being unsuccessful in bringing out any practical utility from each challenging subject.

Unlike the 2007 Capital Investment Act, adoption of the 2007 Company Act has invited strong reactions from various actors. The controversial CSR provisions of the 2007 Company Act are as follows:

Article 1 of the 2007 Company Act

Social and Environmental Responsibility means the commitment from a Company to participate in the sustainable economic development in order to increase the quality of life and the environment, which will be valuable for the company itself, the local community, and society in general.

Article 74 of the 2007 Company Act

(1) The Company having its business activities in the field of and/or related to natural resources shall perform its Social and Environmental Responsibility.

(2) Social and Environmental Responsibility as referred to in Paragraph (1) shall constitute the obligation of the company which is budgeted and calculated as a cost of the company. Social and Environmental Responsibility shall be implemented with due observance of fairness and appropriateness.

(3) A company which fails to perform its obligation stipulated in Paragraph (1) shall be imposed with sanctions in accordance with the provision of regulations.

(4) Social and Environmental Responsibility shall be further specified by Government Regulation.

A few scholars welcome the adoption of this mandatory provisions, either those who criticized its vagueness[26] or those who thought the stipulation is neither excessive nor unsuitable.[27] Nonetheless, business interests represented by the Indonesian Chamber of Commerce (*Kamar Dagang dan Industri*: KADIN) and several companies instituted an unconstitutionality suit before the Constitutional Court. The applicants claimed that Article 74 of the 2007 Company Act is unconstitutional because (i) forcing CSR as a legal obligation comes into a head-on collision against the CSR movement's voluntary emphasis and thus is against the principle of legal certainty in Article 28 D (1); (ii) the different treatment between the companies in natural resource industry and others is discriminative, against Article 28 I (2); and (iii) it harms efficiency of economic justice, against Article 33 (4).[28]

The Constitutional Court ruled that Article 74 is correct, non-discriminative, and just, therefore not unconstitutional. In the Court's deliberations, the concept of CSR is flexible depending on country, and thus mandatory nature of CSR in Article 74 is compatible with the current social, economic, and legal circumstances in Indonesia and gives legal certainty given Indonesia's weak law enforcement. The Court also determined that Article 74 is based on the potential risks posed by companies' behavior to natural resources particularly and thus is not discriminative against certain companies.

---

26 Patricia Rinwigati Waagstein, The Mandatory Corporate Social Responsibility in Indonesia: Problems and Implications, *Journal of Business Ethics* Vol. 98, No. 3, 2011, pp. 455–466.

27 Yu Un Oppusunggu, Mandatory Corporate Social and Environmental Responsibilities in the New Indonesian Limited Liability Law, *Indonesia Law Review*, Vol. 1, 2013.

28 Decision No.53/PUU-VI/2008. (*Mahkamah Konstitusi, Putusan No 53/PUU-VI/2008, Perkara Permohonan Pengujian UU No. 40 Tahun 2007 tentang Perseroan Terbatas, terhadap UUD 1945. Tanggal 15 April 2009*).

Despite this determination, some scholars still denounce its concept of CSR.[29] They assert that this mandatory provision clearly and substantially deviates from the voluntary nature of CSR, although it may meet the validity test under the Constitution. Their research concludes that this provision will have only unwanted side effects. It is certainly logical that the mandatory CSR burdens can reduce the total voluntary CSR activities. Also, if a company must bear unwelcome costs in a recession, it may attempt to compensate for them even in the recovery period. In other words, a mandatory nature of CSR can aggravate corporate ethics, frustrating the intent to mandate CSR. The vaguer the CSR laws and regulations are, the more CSR activities become biased and purely perfunctory as the following:[30]

a   Camouflage: companies may carry out CSR simply to cover up unethical business practices.
b   Generic: CSR programs may be too general without necessary rigor because such programs are forced by others.
c   Directive: CSR policies and programs may be formulated through a top-down process based on interest of company or shareholders only.
d   Lip service: CSR may not be a part of the corporate strategy and policy.
e   Kiss and run: CSR programs may be just ad-hoc and unsustainable.

This opinion contradicts others holding a view in favor of mandatory nature.[31] At least, the mandatory nature of this provision still remains controversial.

Although the Constitution Court has determined its legal certainty, the provision is not user friendly, as it apparently lacks any specificity and practicality. For instance, it alone cannot answer several practical questions: how much must be budgeted and calculated as a cost of the company? What if a start-up company is only two university students developing smartphone applications with very small capital? Should it still budget for CSR as much as other large companies do? What if a large company is currently suffering from significant financial difficulties and does not have sufficient funds to budget for CSR? What if it is a small retail shop in financial difficulties?

This unclear provision without any practical guidelines was harshly criticized by scholars and the media.[32] Some argue that the mandatory nature is even

---

29 Made Arjaya, Moch Bakri Sihabudin, & Bambang Winarno, Deviation Concept of CSR Regulation in Indonesia (Article 74 of Law 40 of the 2007 on Limited Liability Company), *Journal of Law, Policy and Globalization*, Vol. 23, 2014.
30 Victor Imanuel Nalle, The Corporate Constitutionalism Approach in the Formulation of CSR, *Indonesia Law Review*, Vol. 5, No. 1, 2015, p. 6.
31 Umar Hasan, Kewajiban Corporate Social Responsibility Dilihat Dari Perspektif Hukum, *Forum Akademika*, Vol. 25, No. 1, 2014.
32 B. Sujayadi & F. Kurniawan, *Mapping on Indonesian Company Law*, Mapping Paper, Sustainable Companies Project, 2011.
    Armand Maris, *Compulsory CSR: Indonesia Takes a Tough Stance But Clarity on Definitions Is Lacking*, The International Public Relations Association, May 22, 2014.

problematic in practice, as it not only requires a precise concept of interpretation of CSR and identification of the duty bearer and beneficiaries, but also an effective implementation mechanism and a means of verifying the impact.[33] It further notes that to not seriously jeopardize the efficacy of this mandatory component, Article 74 requires much more detailed consideration.

So far, Melody Kemp's prophecies seem to have come true: "At this point in Indonesian history, CSR itself can only remain an image projected onto a screen – an outline with little depth" and "In reality, . . . in Indonesia implementation of CSR *is merely cosmetic.*"

These cosmetic outlines with little depth have been further elaborated in two ways: (i) direct CSR regulations mandated by central or local governments; and (ii) other laws and regulations obligating companies to perform some public functions.

6.2.2. *Direct regulations on CSR by central or local government*

As Article 74 (4) of the 2007 Company Act entrusts further specification to the Government Regulations, the Indonesian Government issued the specific Government Regulation No. 47 Year 2012 concerning Corporate Social and Environmental Responsibility (2012 CSER Regulation).[34] The point of this regulation is surprisingly straightforward and simple. The board of directors in any company that utilizes or impact natural resources must consider the appropriateness and reasonableness in preparing and setting action plans and budgets. If a company conducting business in the field of or relating to natural resources does not carry out its social and environmental responsibilities, it will be penalized. If it does, it may be given an award by the authority.

This 2012 CSER Regulation merely gives burdens to individual directors without successfully specifying any criteria about what is appropriate or reasonable. In other worlds, this so-called specification of CSR miserably fails to answer the questions initially raised about the vague provisions of Article 74 of the 2007 Company Act: How much is "appropriate and reasonable" for the budget? How much is reasonable for a start-up company? What if a company has earned 1 billion rupiah and yet has a very high risk of losing 10 billion rupiah?

The 2012 CSER Regulation also seem to fail to further specify the concept of CSR: who are the precise stakeholders that a company should protect? What is the interest of stakeholder to which a company must contribute? One scholar claims that lack of these concrete specification made the 2012 CSER Regulation

---

33 Patricia Rinwigati Waagstein, The Mandatory Corporate Social Responsibility in Indonesia: Problems and Implications, Journal of Business Ethics Vol. 98, No. 3, 2011, pp. 455–466; and Eny Suastuti, Beberapa Kendala Dalam Penerapan CSR (Analisis Pasal 74 UUPT), *Journal Hukum* Vol. 9, No. 2, 2014.
34 *Peraturan Pemerintah Nomor 47 Tahun 2012 tentang Tanggung Jawab Sosial dan Lingkungan Perseroan Terbatas.*

as "not synchronized with corporate paradigm."[35] He indicates that its CSR implementation model be biased and purely perfunctory as "camouflage," "generic," "directive," "lip services," and "kiss and run."

Several local governments also raced to issue their own local regulations. A study in 2014 describes 13 local regulations about CSR, for example, the 2011 East Java Provincial Regulation No. 4 regarding Corporate Social Responsibility,[36] and the Regulation of the Governor of East Java, Regional Regulations in Malang.[37]

These regulations commonly do not distinguish different sizes or business field of the applicable company. For instance, the 2012 No. 5 Local Regulation of Tulungagung concerning Corporate Social Responsibility mandates CSR to every company in goods or services of production activities with an aim to earn profits.[38]

While some scholars argue that local regulations in Kota Malang are compatible with the CSR as stated in Article 74 (4) of the 2007 Company Act,[39] some scholars maintain that these Provincial Regulations and Governor Regulation destroy the system of regulating CSR.[40] According to this argument, Article 74 (4) of the 2007 Company Act entrusts further specification about CSR to the

---

35 Victor Imanuel Nalle, The Corporate Constitutionalism Approach in the Formulation of CSR, Indonesia Law Review, Vol. 5, No. 1, 2015, p. 6.
36 Peraturan Daerah Provinsi Jawa Timur tentang Tanggung Jawab Sosial Perusahaan. Perda Jawa Timur No. 4 Tahun 2011, Ld No.4 Tahun 2011 Seri D.
37 Riana Susmayanti, Kosep Tanggung Jawab Sosial Dalam Peraturan Perundang-Undangan di Indonesia, *Arena Hukum* Vol. 7, No. 3, 2014, pp. 363–387. This study seems to miss 2012 No. 5 Local Regulation of Tulungagung concerning CSR.
38 *Pemerintah Kabupaten Tulungagung. Peraturan Daerah Kabupaten Tulungagung No. 5 Th.2012 tentang Tangungjawab Sosial Perusahaan.*

   Article 1 (5) Corporate Social Responsibility, hereinafter abbreviated as CSR, is the responsibility attached to "every" company to keep creating harmonious and balanced relationships in accordance with the environment, values, norms and culture of local communities. (*Pasal 1. Ayat (5) Tanggung Jawab Sosial Perusahaan yang selanjutnya disingkat TSP adalah tanggung jawab yang melekat pada setiap perusahaan untuk tetap menciptakan hubungan yang serasi, seimbang dan sesuai dengan lingkungan, nilai, norma dan budaya masyarakat setempat.*)

   Article 1 (6) a business actor, hereinafter referred to as a Company, is an organization or individual that is incorporated as a legal entity or non-legal entity conducting business activities by "collecting capital, engaging in goods and/or services of production activities with an aim to obtain profits." (*Pasal 1. Ayat (6) pelaku usaha yang selanjutnya disebut Perusahaan adalah organisasi atau perorangan bauk yang berbadan hukum atau tidak berbadan hukum yang melakukan kegiatan usaha dengan menghimpun modal, bergerak dalam kegiatan produksi barang dan/atau jasa serta bertujuan memperoleh keuntungan.*)

39 One claims that the regulations in Kota Malang are at least compatible with CSR principal adopted by 2007 Company Act. Riana Susmayanti, Kosep Tanggung Jawab Sosial Dalam Peraturan Perundang-Undangan di Indonesia, Arena Hukum Vol. 7, No. 3, 2014, pp. 363–387.
40 "Regulating CSR in Provincial Regulations and Governor Regulation actually destroys the systematics of regulating CSR. Based on the Limited Liability Company Law, the delegation of regulating CSR intended only in Government Regulation. While the Government Regulation on Environmental and Social Responsibility of Limited Liability Company does not further delegate the regulating of CSR into the Provincial Regulation." Victor, *supra* note 35, p. 11.

Central Government regulations only and that the Central Government has never empowered any local government to further regulate CSR. In this view, these regional regulations are also oblivious of the purpose of CSR as not successfully protecting the interest of stakeholders as it made the involvement of stakeholder in this local area fell into merely an option, not a requirement.

Lastly, the Ministry of Environment issued the Guideline of CSR on Environment.[41] It provides guidelines how to implement CSR on environment such as

a   identifying the negative impact of environment of business operational plan,
b   identifying the potential impact on natural resources and environment of the community around business operational area,
c   identifying the needs and aspiration from community towards the business operation, and
d   drafting a corporate social and environmental activities plan.

This procedure without strong binding effects needs the substance about CSR on environment, which should be regulated under central government regulations. Victor Imanuel Nalle asserts that the absence of any such regulation "shows that the government has no desire to regulate the orientation of CSR to stakeholders."[42]

6.2.3.   CSR in other laws and regulations

There are additional layers in the CSR regulatory framework laid by other laws and regulations in various industries and fields. The examples are as follows:

*   Article 58 Paragraphs 1 and 2 of Law No. 39 Year 2014 concerning plantations, which mandates any companies in plantation business to develop its surrounding community by at least 20 percent of the company's own plantation.
*   Article 15 Paragraph (1) of Ministry Regulation No. 98 Year 2013 states that a company applying for a plantation business for an area of 250 hectares or more must facilitate the local community's development by providing the local community with a plantation area of at least 20 percent of the total area given to the company.
*   Article 15 of Ministry Regulation No. 26 2007 concerning licensing guidance for plantation businesses requires applicants for plantation business licenses to prove their commitment to building plantations for communities and promote relationships.

41 Tim Penyusun Pedoman CSR Bidang Lingkungan, *Pedoman CSR Bidang Lingkungan,* Jakarta: Kementerian Lingkungan Hidup, 2011.
42 Victor, *supra* note 134, p. 11.

- Mining Law No. 4 Year 2009 specifically requires CSR and calls for a standard percentage of company's profits to be contributed to community welfare, although the amount of the percentage is not clarified.
- Article 88 of Law No. 19/2003 State-Owned Company Law requires allocation of funding of the net profits of the state-owned company for developing small- and medium-sized enterprises, cooperatives, and the social environment.
- Ministerial Regulations No. Kep.236/MBU/2003 concerning partnership and development program of state-owned companies with small- and medium-sized enterprises, cooperative, and the local communities

Local customary laws in favor of local community that are not stipulated in a written form place an additional layer over these regulations. Although many of these regulations do not explicitly use the term CSR, the nature of these stipulations is apparently to enforce companies to perform social and public functions.

In addition, systematic "buck passing" often obliges companies to perform public function as discussed earlier. The Government land permit over state-owned land with stipulation that "the issuer shall not be liable if the land is later found [to be] privately owned or if an individual has a right on it" is an example. Even if the state wrongfully issues a permit to a company resulting in a loss to someone or some entity, the responsibility to remedy the loss is shifted onto the permit holder.

These CSR regulations spread over all different levels (i.e. the local, regional, and national), and different Ministries with different substantive rules are heavily confusing in practice. Some further blame the systematic complexity that there are four coordinating Ministries and plenty of additional Ministries, each of which has its own CSR budget and regulations.[43] According to this opinion, these budgets highly differ per Ministry, as does their power to exercise authority, and this systematic inefficiency makes a general policy on CSR extremely difficult. It explains the background as these regulations are created to pool CSR funds for government-led programs, and legislative and executive bodies are dominated by politicians who want to use CSR funds as political resources.[44]

6.3. Have these CSR laws and regulations saved Indonesia?

Could we still confidently say that adopting CSR with so many regulatory layers has actually paved the way for a new era for prosperity? I contend that it has not.

Although Indonesia started using the term CSR in 1990s and forming its regulatory framework in the 2000s, actual CSR activities in Indonesia have been

43 MVO Nederland, Country Scan CSR in Indonesia, *CSR Netherlands*, July 12, 2016, p. 14.
44 MVO Nederland, *supra* note 43, p. 9.

practiced, nurtured, and developed by Indonesian people since the 1970s.[45] A majority of the initial activities seem to focus on either developing local community where the company was located or giving a monetary charity to the local residents and small- and medium-sized enterprises.[46] Absent mandatory regulations, these voluntary CSR movements root within the Indonesian socio-cultural tradition, which emphasizes the importance of moral value of collective life, such as unity, sustainability, public interest, and social function.[47] From the managers' perspective, on the other hands, it is simply difficult or even impossible to operate in remote and rural areas without hospitality from the local community.[48]

In 2000s prior to the legislation of CSR as a mandatory legal obligation, the CSR activities of 50 listed companies were already active and showed their deep understanding of CSR.[49] Even unlisted companies appear to have already begun the social activities prior to the mandatory regulations.[50] A survey of 375 Jakarta companies in 2005 showed that 209 of the 375 companies or 55.75 percent

---

45 "*Konsep CSR di Indonesia sebenarnya bukan hal yang baru karena CSR sudah dikenal dan dipraktekan di Indonesia sekitar tahun 1970an. Dalam pengertiannya yang klasik CSR masih dipersepsikan sebagai ideology yang bersifat amal (charity) dari pihak pengusaha kepada masyarakat di sekitar tempat beroperasinya perusahaan. Disamping itu masih banyak pihak yang mengidentikkan CSR dengan Community Development.*" Dani Amran Hakim, Urgency of Implementation of Corporate Social Responsibility as an Effort to Ensure the Rights of Labor, *Fiat Justisia, Lampung University* Vol. 10, No. 4, 2016.

46 For instance, Unilever Indonesia has incorporated the social contribution policies of developing local community into their strategic plans as early as the 1970s and 1980s. Regarding the details, see Sri Urip, *CSR Strategies Corporate Social Responsibility for a Competitive Edge in Emerging Markets*, John Wiley & Sons, 2010, pp. 30–40. In the meantime, some state-owned companies such as PT Krakatau Steel, PT Pertamina, and PT Telekomunikasi Indonesia began charity for the community than strategic philanthropic activities. Nursahid, Fajar. Praktik Kedermawaan Sosial BUMN: Analisis Terhadap Kedermaan PT. Krakatau Steel, PT. Pertamina dan PT. Telekomunikasi Indonesia, *Jurnal Galang* Vol. 1, No. 2, 2006, p. 5.

47 Tineke Lambooy, *CSR in Indonesia: Legislative Developments and Case Studies*, Constitute Press, pp. 14–20.

48 "Trust is the main thing. If there is no trust between the company and local people, nothing good will come out. In the practice, CSR should make a resource measurably in 'trust' based on the impact of CSR program, and conduct a procedural fairness in CSR program. Actually, the impact of CSR programs positively is the most important to get 'trust' from the local community." Andi Erwin Syarif & Tsuyoshi Hatori, Corporate Social Responsibility for Regional Sustainability after Mine Closure: A Case Study of Mining Company in Indonesia, *IOP Conference Series: Earth and Environmental. Science*, 2017, p. 11; empirical research by interviewing a number of managers in Indonesia indicates the same. See Simon Hendeberg & Lindgren Fredrik, *CSR in Indonesia: A Qualitative Study from a Managerial Perspective Regarding Views and Other Important Aspects of CSR in Indonesia*, BA thesis, Högskolan Gotland, Sweden, 2009, p. 40.

49 Samy, *supra* note 22.

50 Hendeberg, *supra* note 48, pp. 40–41. Also, see CSR Activities disclosed by Korindo Group. At www.korindo.co.id/sustainability/?lang=id.

were performing CSR activities in the form of kinship activities (116 companies), donations to religious institutions (50 companies), donations to social institutions (39 companies) and community development (4 companies).[51]

Evidentially, Indonesian companies have already contributed to their societies in a variety of forms, even when there was no mandatory legal obligations to do so. Has adoption of the laws and regulations of CSR then incentivized and encouraged companies to contribute to society more than before? It is seriously doubtful.

As discussed earlier, local companies in the natural resources industry are particularly required to perform CSR activities, by the numerous layers of laws and regulations such as 2007 Company Act, 2007 Capital Investment Act, 2012 CSER Regulation, Provincial Regulation, Ministry Regulations, laws for the industry and customary laws. Nonetheless, there is no convincing evidence that these layers help development of the local community more than the companies had previously done voluntarily. On the contrary, there is overwhelming data showing that these regulations are ambiguous, conflicting with one another, legislated with misguided attempts to use CSR funds, confuse good-faith practitioners, discourage voluntary CSR activities, have no effective enforcement, and do not help monitor the companies.

The stipulations about CSR in 2007 Company Act and 2012 CSER Regulation remain "as an image projected onto a screen – an outline with little depth": they lack justification to impose mandatory costs irrelevant to size or profit of companies as well as fail to define appropriateness and reasonability. The implementation of CSR spread over all different levels with different substance is "merely cosmetic," as the incoherent regulations fail to bring out practical utility out of a challenging theme. Systematic inefficiency with a number of Ministries having different powers complicates the problems. Poor monitoring capacity and legal enforcement system is a bigger challenge.[52] This challenge is Indonesia's never-ending quest.[53]

Under the totality of circumstances, it is extremely difficult to expect that laws and regulations can be satisfactorily applied to relevant parties in an

---

51 Suprapto & Siti Adipringadi Adiwoso, Pola Tanggung Jawab Sosial Perusahaan Lokal di Jakarta, *Majalah Galang* Vol. 1, No. 2, 2006.

52 "As a form of corporate responsibility in the case of coal mining is implemented through a program known as Corporate Social Responsibility (CSR). This program is constrained by the lack of supervision and activities within the CSR program. . . . Only a small number of companies implementing CSR programs." H. Joni, Corporate Responsibility for Impacts of Mining Coal in Kalimantan, *Journal of Law, Policy and Globalization* Vol. 67, 2017.

53 De Soto, a Peruvian economist, comments: "When you step into an airplane in New York to fly to Jakarta, what you are leaving behind is not the high-tech world of fax machines and ice makers, televisions and antibiotics; many people in the Third World also have those. What you are leaving behind is the world of enforceable legal representation." Why Capitalism Works in the West but Not Elsewhere, *International Herald Tribune*, January 5, 2001.

effective way as a national system must work. All these had been already fore-known before adopting them. Melody Kemp (2001) indicates that it was premature to speak of CSR in Indonesia when the tools of civil society were structurally and legislatively weak. Probably the current tools are structurally much better than the ones in 2001, and yet they are not as satisfactory as they should be.

Let us take an example one of the top CSR-performing companies. The following are excerpts from CSR Activities disclosed by Korindo Group, an Indonesian unlisted companies group, who won the Best CSR Award from the Ministry of Environment and Forest in 2013, the Investment Coordinating Board (BKPM) in 2015, and Governor of Pupa Province in 2015 and 2016.[54]

- Supports the construction of 28 schools with 208 teachers at remote areas in Indonesia and provided and operate 36 school buses
- Scholarship for 8,115 students from primary to secondary school and 677 students from university
- Support and operate 10 vocational schools, practice facilities and employment for local high school graduates
- Built and operate 19 clinics for free medical checks and medication for local community
- One polyclinic is under construction in Papua (total capacity of 115 beds with 85 medics and paramedics)
- Conduct mobile doctor services to remote areas to reach over 1,800 indigenous people who are isolated in remote Central Kalimantan and Papua every year
- Provided healthy supplements for 4,680 children 5 years and under in 72 child medical centers
- Provided 1,000 medicine package for flood victims in Jakarta
- Supported the families of 300 fruit farmers in Wonogiri, Central Java
- Built and support the operation of breeding farms for local community with capacity of 7,000 chickens, 100 cows, 50 pigs, and 10,000 fish.
- Planted 221,600 productive trees in Bogor, West Java, Wonogiri, Central Java, Boven Digoel, Papua, and Timor Leste
- Removed 12 tons of garbage from rivers and cleaned the surrounding areas
- Built and maintained 551 km road and 80 bridges in East & Central Kalimantan, Maluku and Papua
- Built over 200 housing units for land owners and tribal chiefs
- Provided 8 MW of electricity and clean water to 13,350 people in Central Kalimantan and Papua
- Supported the construction of 66 religious buildings (mosques, church, etc.)

54 See Korindo Group, *supra* note 50.

- Built and operate 20 clinics with 85 medics and paramedics and ambulances
- Supported the building of 30 village offices and meeting halls
- Built 10 markets and 200 stores and supermarkets for local community
- Built and operate three sport halls and over 30 soccer fields, badminton, and volley fields with their sports teams

The Korindo Group has been operating a separate office at headquarters to systematically plan and manage the CSR system and activities. They are organized by a spontaneous and voluntary way, as none of these activities are mandatorily required for a company by laws or regulations. Simply, there is no such laws or regulation obligating a company to build a market, school, hospital, medical center, or soccer field. Nor does any local regulation or guidance mandate a company to constantly provide electricity, clean water, public transportation, educational support, etc. In other words, these activities are not direct products of the laws and regulations, and the best CSR-performing companies appear not to have been created simply by the laws and regulations.

That is not different with other regular companies. The followings are excerpts from the CSR activities of PT. Blora Patra Energi and PT. Banyubang Blora Energi.[55]

- 2013: Donation to Orphanage (Rp. 1,000,000); Purchase of animal for Deso Kedinding (Rp. 2,000,000); and establishment of a water reservoir for Deso Kedinding (Rp. 30,000,000)
- 2014: Construction of a mosque (Rp. 20,000,000); lighting of street lights (Rp. 100,000,000); installation of electricity for water reservoir (Rp. 1,700,000); cleaning water (Rp. 10,000,000)
- 2015: CSR for disabled, forum care, discussion activities, etc. (Rp. 2,645,000)
- 2016: CSR for Maulid Nabi, Harlah PMII, scholarship for outstanding students, etc. (Rp. 1,350,000)

The same as CSR activities of Korindo Group, these are not the products of the laws and regulations. Seeing these and other data, the research concludes that major companies engaged in the oil and gas sector in Central Java do not correctly understand the meaning of CSR as law requires and the actual CSR program is still running in the form of giving and generosity.[56] In other words, launching numerous laws and regulations itself does not significantly incentivize the CSR activities to these companies.

55 Monica Puspa Dewi, FX Adji Samekto, & Yusriyadi, Testing the Implementation of Corporate Responsibility in Realizing Social Justice (A Case Study in Central Java, Indonesia), *International Journal of Business, Economics and Law*, Vol. 13, 2017, pp. 116–117.
56 Dewi, Samekto, & Yusriyadi, *supra* note 55.

Then, why do they practice CSR irrespective of effective regulations? Is it because these companies are targeted by consumers or those who are thinking ethically and responsibly as Melody Kemp predicted? Some may say yes.[57]

Some may say that it is because of Indonesian socio-cultural tradition, which emphasizes the value of social function, public interest, and surrounding communities as mentioned earlier. Certainly, a number of scholars maintain that cultural characters affect CSR implementation.[58]

The more conclusive reason may be because managing and operating business in remote areas is significantly difficult without credibility from the local community.[59] Indonesia's unique geographical and anthropological setting composed of indigenous societies spread over roughly 18,000 islands accounts for this explanation. A survey on 87 practitioners in Indonesia concludes that CSR in Indonesia is to gain social reputation as part of public relationship.[60]

It may be partially because CSR has a significant effect toward the company's financial performance – stock price.[61] This may not be entirely true for all the companies. A research conducted with 40 manufacturing companies listed on the Indonesia Stock Exchange in 2008 to 2010 shows that lucrative companies with high profits are resistant against openly disclosing their CSR activities despite their high level of social contribution. This tendency is explained as the directors may try to report their earning as much as possible by not disclosing

---

57 "CSR in Indonesia also represents the consumers' needs to provide properly and accurately information about its products to its customers; respecting consumer rights beyond the legal requirements; focusing on Ethical consumerism, namely to raise consumers' concern on environment and ethical issues." Rachmat Kriyantono, Public Relations and Corporate Social Responsibility in Mandatory Approach Era in Indonesia, *Procedia-Social and Behavioral Science, Elsevier and Global Conference on Business & Social Sciences*, 17–18 September, Denpasar, Bali, p. 324.

58 Sarah Ashton Morrow, *Guanxi and Legitimacy: Understanding Corporate Social Responsibility and Public Relations in China and the U.S.*, The University of Alabama Tuscaloosa, Alabama, 2014; Judy Muthuri & Victoria Gilbert, An Institutional Analysis of Corporate Social Responsibility in Kenya, *Journal of Business Ethics* Vol. 98, 2011, pp. 467–483; Nunung Prajarto, *CSR Indonesia: Sinergi pemerintah, perusahaan, dan publik*, CSR: Indonesia: Synergy of Government, Company and Public, Yogyakarta: Fakultas Ilmu Sosial dan Ilmu Politik Unitersitas Gadjah Mada, 2012; and Loong Wong, Corporate Social Responsibility in China: Between the Market and the Search for a Sustainable Growth Development, *Asian Business & Management* Vol. 2, No. 8, 2009, pp. 129–148.

59 See Erwin et al., *supra* note 48, and Hendeberg et al., *supra* note 48.

60 "This research proved that the majority of companies assume that CSR is public relations concern. Therefore, CSR is seen as a part of communication management between organization and its public to create goodwill, to serve public interest, and to maintain good morals and manners (Cutlip, Center, & Brown, 2006; Grunig & Hunt, 1984; L'Etang, 1994; Lattimore, Baskin, Heiman, & Toth, 2007). It is not surprising because based on these functions, it can be said that public relations practitioners have proper knowledge to plan and direct CSR programs to be appropriate action to ensure mutually beneficial relationships and to gain social legitimacy." Rachmat, *supra* note 57.

61 Saffana Afiff & Samuel P. D. Anantadjaya, CSR & Performance: Any Evidence from Indonesian LQ45? *Review of Integrative Business & Economics Research* Vol. 2, No. 1, 2013.

their costs incurred for CSR activities, and the company also may not feel a necessity to disclose information that can potentially disturb itself under the regulations.[62] In other words, it is not always wise to reveal their activities openly as part of public relationship.

Either likely because of socio-cultural traditions, managerial utility, public relationships, financial performance, or a combination of any of these factors, an effective legal frame and enforcement is not forthcoming.

---

62 Istianingsih, Impact of Firm Characteristics on CSR Disclosure: Evidence from Indonesia Stock Exchange, *IJABEL* Vol. 13, No. 6, 2015.

8 Material changes of company

1. Overview of consolidation, merger, and acquisition

1.1. Definition

The use of various terms and jargon in regular business often do not match their accurate definition in law, tax, or accounting. Rather, many terms are misused, or the wrong terms used in many cases. For example, official Indonesian legal documents translated into English use *acquisition*, *consolidation*, and *merger* as meaning different things where in commercial business many use simply *M&A*, *SPA* (share purchase agreement), or other jargon to describe share-transfer transactions.

According to Article 1 of the 2007 Company Act, the definitions of acquisition, merger, and consolidation are as follows:

- **Acquisition** (*pengambilalihan*): A legal entity or individual person's legal action to acquire shares in a company, resulting in transfer of control from of the company.
- **Merger** (*penggabungan*): Legal action by one or more companies to merge with another existing company that results in the merging companies' assets and liabilities passing to the surviving company by operation of law, and thereafter the original merging companies' status as legal entities ceases by operation of law.
- **Consolidation** (*peleburan*): Legal action by two or more companies to consolidate themselves by establishing a new company which obtains the consolidating companies' assets and liabilities by operation of law, and thereafter the original consolidating companies' status as legal entities ceases by operation of law.

Because the definition and articles following Article 112 do not mandatorily require cash contributions for the above actions, the consideration for any acquisition, merger, and consolidation may be securities such as bonds, stocks, and other assets. Nonetheless, the vast majority of transactions in Indonesian commercial business are based on cash for stock, irrespective of the size of the deal.

Mergers by way of asset acquisitions and other type of transactions are not legally regarded as a corporate merger. Hence, those transactions that appear to be mergers and acquisitions, such as the sale of substantially all the assets of a company, are explained in the later section "Types of takeover."

For listed companies, the decision in BAPEPAM No.IX.H.1, 2011's amendment of BAPEPAM-LK97, defines merger as "an act to directly or indirectly change control of a company." Here, the "act" includes a voluntary public bid, and yet many in regular practice regard an act as a transfer of control by share acquisition. The 2011 amendment defines control as holding 50 percent or more ownership. Because the previous 2008 amendment deleted the proviso "that it is not control if the acquirer proves that he does not have control," the investor no longer bears the burden of proof to show that he does not have control to avoid the relevant regulations.

For financial companies, OJK's regulations should be read together in any M&A context. OJK, the Indonesian financial supervisory authority having a specific division of capital market regulations, checks the control issue to determine whether clients of financial companies are related companies (*pihak terkait*) or group companies (*kelompok debitur*). However, the definition is quite obscure.[1]

This book does not explain antitrust or competition context related to M&A, as the related laws and regulations are currently on the verge of amendment.

1.2. *The biggest and most common problems of mergers and acquisitions in Indonesia*

The difficulties and risks in the Indonesian M&A market particularly faced by experienced foreign investors are as follows.

1.2.1. *Moral hazard*

In the Corruption Perception Index prepared by Transparency International with input from a number of financial institutions including the World Bank,

---

1 The OJK definition of "control (*Pengendali*)" uses "control (*Pengendali*)" again:

> Pasal 39. 2. a: *Badan usaha yang merupakan Pengendali Perusahaan Pembiayaan.*
> *Pengendali* (Pasal 1. 21. a. 2): *badan hukum yang memiliki saham kurang dari 25% dari jumlah saham yang dikeluarkan dan mempunyai hak suara namun yang bersangkutan dapat dibuktikan telah melakukan pengendalian perusahaan baik secara langsung maupun tidak langsung.*

Therefore, in obscure and unclear situation, it is always safer to think that one has control because of the possibility of being subject to OJK's sanction. This is particularly so given that counterarguments such as an "unclear definition of control in law," "control weakened because of diluted voting rights," or the fact that "voting rights have never been exercised" are not always acceptable.

Indonesia recorded 96th among 176 countries (with first place being the nation perceived as least corrupt) as of 2018.[2]

Foreign investors or workers are exposed to this risk.[3] The corruption dramatically escalates before a national holiday season, such as Ramadan, or year-end period, or around elections in and out of an M&A context.[4] Since a vast majority of foreign investors are required to work with a regional partner due to the Negative Investment List and take responsibility for dealing with Indonesian officers, legal costs and risks increase dramatically.[5]

2 "'Indonesia's judicial system is susceptible to corruption as a result of ineffective regulatory mechanisms and conflicting legislation' (CSG 2014). 'The outcome of judicial proceedings – including criminal investigations and court verdicts and appeals – can be influenced through bribes' (BTI 2014). 'Corruption has deprived the judicial system of professionalism and objectivity. . . . Dispute settlement mechanisms are inefficient and remain an area of concern for foreign companies' (CSG 2014). 'In 2013, a Constitutional Court Chief Justice, Akil Mochtar, was charged with accepting a US$260,000 bribe in exchange for fixing a court ruling. Mochtar was found guilty and received a life sentence for corruption' (Deutsche Welle, June 2014)." GAN Business Anti-Corruption Portal, Indonesia Corruption Report, July 2015.

3 "For investors, projects can be stopped by requests for bribes coming from many people, even when they don't necessarily get things done." Neil Chatterjee, Graft Busters Target 'Big Fish' as Indonesian Polls Near, Bloomberg, Feb. 13, 2014. "For example, it is estimated that to obtain KITAS (work visas) for foreign workers, between 10 and 14 facilitation payments will be expected to be paid in cash to officials in the Department of Immigration at central and provincial levels, at a cost of anywhere between US$600 and $5,000 per application (depending on the job function and location of employment). Control Risks' research indicates that these payments, which are usually made through third-party agents, are a key source of supplementary income for officials, with tiered amounts from payments being distributed within departments in line with seniority." Corene Crossin, Martin Brown, & Steve Norris, *Anti-Corruption in Indonesia*, Control Risks, 2013. Despite a comparatively small number of foreign companies, a vast majority of significant fines or penalties are imposed against foreign companies. In 2016, LG International Corp., who had acquired PT. Binsar Natorang Energi, was imposed the highest fine for late filing in Indonesian M&A history, which reached IDR 8 billion (approximately US$600,000, or €550,000) due to being 20 working days date. On the surface, this is due to Law No. 5 of 1999, and Government Regulation No. 57 of 2010, that an acquirer satisfying certain conditions must notify the authority within 30 days, and if this fails, an IDR 1 billion penalty is imposed per day (to a maximum of IDR 25 billion). Here the imposed amount is significantly disproportional to the delayed dates. In the same year, KPPU proportionally imposed a fine of IDR 5 billion to Toray Advanced Materials Korea Inc. who acquired 56.21 percent of Woongjin Chemical Co., for 5-day delay in notice.

4 "Corruption usually escalates around elections as officials take advantage of their posts by trading favors and candidates seek to fund campaigns, Adnan Pandu Praja, vice chairman at the Corruption Eradication Commission, or KPK, said in an interview in Jakarta yesterday." Chatterjee, *supra* note 3.

5 "With 70% of entrepreneurs believing that corruption increased recently in Indonesia . . . foreign companies need local business partners for joint ventures. But they risk prosecution at home, under laws such as the United States' Foreign Corrupt Practices Act and the United Kingdom's Bribery Act, when their local partners engage in corruption. They also risk debarment by multilateral financial institutions such as the Asian Development Bank.

In general, the laws and regulations of Indonesia are often obscure, and authorities not only have discretion to interpret these as they want, but also the power to mandate a company or person must follow an "unwritten law" or internal policy. If there is a gap in understanding or opinion between the authority and applicant, the authority may not discuss how to objectively interpret the relevant law or regulation, but instead may attempt to make a deal.[6] Not surprisingly, a lawyer unexpectedly encountering such an authority's forced interpretation is regarded as either naïve or unprofessional by his client. Sadly, the poor lawyer has no option but to take an approach to ease the regulation by "coaxing" the relevant officer.

As a side note, despite these observations, I have a personal view that Indonesia has a strong will to fix this problem and has been showing substantial progress. Indonesia actually improved its Corruption Perception Index moving up from 143th in 2007 to 90th in 2016. Although some say that the current anti-corruption system alone is not enough,[7] it is still true that the government empowers increasingly significant power to the anti-corruption body KPK, the most trusted public institution in Indonesia.[8] Recently, Indonesia tapped highly respected former KPK spokesperson Johan Budi to serve as the new presidential spokesperson. Many interviewers for this book also mentioned that taking advantage of bribery is no longer a regular course of business. If such a corrupt

---

Foreign companies are increasingly obliged to conduct costly third-party due diligence to assess local partners' anti-corruption compliance measures." OECD, *Indonesia Policy Brief*, October, 2016; "General Cable Corporation, the Kentucky-based wire and cable manufacturer, paid more than $75 million to resolve SEC and Justice Department cases related to improper payment to win business in Indonesia." *SEC Enforcement Actions: Foreign Corrupt Practice Act Cases*, U.S. Securities and Exchange Commission, December 29, 2016.

6 "Extensive bribery in Indonesia's public service is a reason for foreign investors: . . . public officials often exploit ambiguous legislation to extort informal payments and bribes from companies in the process of registering a business, filing tax reports, or obtaining permits and licenses. . . . The anti-corruption legal framework is deficient and does not address facilitation payments." *Indonesia Corruption Report*, July, 2015, GAN Business Anti-Corruption; "One international company interviewed said it had spent months searching for an official schedule of tariffs or fees for permit applications – without success. Another extractive industry company told Control Risks it faces persistent problems with requests for per diems from government officials carrying out site inspections. While Ministry of Finance Regulation number 113/PMK.05/2012 stipulates that officials carrying out government duties on company sites are entitled to per diems, there is no guidance under the law regarding whether the government or the company is responsible for paying. . . . At Indonesia's ports, corruption is often hidden under the guise of processing hold ups for discrepancies in customs documentation – particularly for imported goods." Crossin et al., *supra* note 3, p. 5.

7 "The KPK (Indonesian Anti-Corruption Commission) will, as a result, become a steadily less formidable prosecutorial machine . . . the Tipikor (KPK's designated courts) courts system lost its 100% conviction rate, and acquittals have grown in number since." Crossin et al., *supra* note 3, p. 3

8 Nithin Coca, Indonesia's Anti-Corruption Fight, the Diplomat, *The Diplomat*, February 8, 2016.

deal with public worker is detected, and both the courts and anti-corruption bodies object, the sanctions and punishment will be extremely harsh. I am highly convinced that Indonesia will show a great success in redressing this issue, and the investors will witness significant progress in the near future.

1.2.2. Following correct procedures is important

Because procedures and administrative processes quite often take substantial time, investors and companies should expect considerable cost and allow ample time in early estimations.[9] If, for example, the person in charge of a company is changed during early stages of a transaction, the whole transaction may have to start again from the beginning, despite the cost and time already invested.

For example, an agreement for a joint venture, merger, acquisition, or consolidation commonly requires obtaining a range of relevant permits to operate a business in a certain field, or licenses for the import and export of certain merchandises, tax permits, employment requirements for certain employees, etc. However, these variable licenses and permits often take a much longer time to obtain than may be initially expected. Since the laws and regulations in terms of import, export, customs, and tax are heavily interwoven, a stranger needs considerable time and costs to properly understand them. Should these procedures take too long, the terms of the contract may expire. Thus, safety measures must be well prepared when drafting a contract.

Many successful business people in Indonesia stress the significance of a network with supportive people and acceptance of a commission culture to resolve any inefficiencies. A well-known saying among foreign business people is, "In Indonesia, nothing is possible, but nothing is impossible."

1.2.3. Abrupt changes in the negative investment list

It is not rare to see an abrupt, even drastic, change in the minimum domestic share rate. A change in the Negative Investment List may suddenly require 100 percent domestic ownership of a particular industry or business type. This is not uncommon in Indonesia.

If this occurs, the foreign shareholder should undertake a very rigorous search for a domestic "white knight" willing to purchase the shares. To find a potential share purchaser within the limited time allowed by Indonesian authorities, the foreign shareholder must accept there will be both cost and risk. Even if a voluntary share purchaser is found who is willing to save his desperate and

---

9 "The hassle of long-winded bureaucracy with the nearly 300 permits remains a major bane to investors wishing to funnel investment . . . those of us who operation-shore have to deal with so many permits and it makes the process difficult. We hope the bureaucracy can be more efficient as that will allow a longer time of production." Fedina S. Sundaryani, Red Tape Continues to Block Investment, *The Jakarta Post*, March 31, 2017.

miserable friend – perhaps even not requiring a premium or fee – the lucky foreign shareholder still has many barriers to overcome. For example, the desperate share seller may advance a loan at the lowest interest rate to the domestic share purchaser to buy the stock.[10] Even when transferred to the white knight, the share seller may still not wish the purchaser to join in management decisions, in which case a legal risk kicks in, because a restraint on the domestic shareholder's voting rights would virtually neutralize the aim of the Negative Investment List. Even if everything eventually works fine, he should still focus on good coordination with BKPM or other relevant authorities to prevent any problems.

Sudden and drastic changes do not only occur for the Negative Investment List, but are also a regular phenomenon in other laws and regulations.

1.2.4.   Drastically different laws and legal practice

Still, many laws legislated under the colonial period are effective. The Civil Code of 1847 is still effective and binding despite the nineteenth-century-style stipulations and the lack of a good analytical collection of court judgments to help develop an interpretation and application of law. Many laws and regulations conflict with one another, and these conflicts are difficult to resolve, even through the courts. According to foreign researchers and articles,[11] Indonesian court's judgments are often influenced by corruption among the judiciary and law enforcement.

To resolve these legal risks and costs, many foreign investors design an offshore strategy by establishing a company in a common law jurisdiction, structuring capital with different class shares, and choosing a specific foreign law as its governing law. Although this strategy may give some psychological relief to the parties, it cannot fundamentally resolve the legal risks in the end. For example, if Indonesian property is provided as a security, the governing law and jurisdiction must be Indonesian for execution, since a similar principle of *in rem* jurisdiction applies. Most importantly, Indonesian courts are very reluctant to recognize an international award from a foreign commercial arbitration center, including SIAC, even though in theory, an international commercial arbitration decision should be properly recognized in Indonesia.[12]

---

10 The seller can advance the loan virtually for free by using the lowest interest rate allowed in his home country and paying the dividends to the share purchaser later.

11 Josua Gantan, Rule of Law Seen as Indonesia's Achilles Heel, *The Jakarta Globe*, April 17, 2014; Simon Butt, *Corruption and Law in Indonesia*, Routledge, 2012; OECD, *OECD Investment Policy Reviews: Indonesia 2010*, 2010. Still, I have a strong opinion that Indonesian judicial system has been dramatically improving its own credibility and will show even faster achievement in near future. Annual Transparency International ranking shows the clear improvement from 143rd in 2007, 126th in 2008, 111th in 2009, 110th in 2010, and 90th in 2016.

12 "The recognition of an international award (such as an award from SIAC), faces more difficulties compared to the recognition of an Indonesian Arbitration award. An international award will only be recognized and may only be enforced in Indonesia after it has obtained

In sum, listening with patience to the advice of experienced Indonesian lawyers to understand Indonesian law and related legal issues is much more valuable than discussing these with a foreign lawyer accustomed only to modernized jurisdictions and with only some superficial experience in Indonesia.

1.2.5. Labor

Generally, the main cost in merger and acquisition is the settlement cost with creditors and retirement packages to employees. A so-called golden parachute (e.g. an expensive premium to directors) is not yet an issue in Indonesia. The premium to employees is a much larger issue.

If a company splits, or if shareholders change merely to observe a suddenly changed regulation, for formality, or for whatever unimportant reason, the actual working conditions remain exactly the same with existing conditions. Still, Indonesian employees generally expect to receive a severance payment package, and the laws and regulations also mandate this. Likewise, Indonesian employees are strongly protected by labor laws.

2. Procedures for consolidation, mergers, and acquisitions

2.1. Introduction

All mergers, consolidations, acquisitions, and joint ventures are complex negotiations combined with thousands of pages of papers, issues, analyses, tricky conditions, and equations. Because there are already a variety of excellent books on the strategy and tactics of negotiating mergers and acquisitions, and the strategies in the Indonesian M&A market are hard to standardize, this book explains only the basic legal procedures, key players, and issues.

To introduce the overall procedure, first, the senior management of constituent companies meet and agree to develop negotiations with some rough terms for a deal. Then, the parties execute a pre-bargaining confidentiality agreement – or non-disclosure agreement – for further negotiation. This typically gives the potential share purchaser exclusive negotiating rights for a certain period of time while the purchaser undertakes legal and financial due diligence.[13]

---

a writ of execution from the Chairman of the Central Jakarta District Court. Recent cases show that foreign parties are experiencing considerable difficulty in enforcing foreign arbitration award in Indonesia, due to the reluctance of the Indonesian Court to issue the writ of execution." PNB Law Firm Jakarta, *International Arbitration through SIAC*, April 2015, at www.indonesia-investments.com/id/business/business-columns/bani-vs-siac-indonesian-or-international-arbitration/item5442.

13 If the target company is a listed company, this agreement is drafted in a way that the exceptions of inside-trading rules in BAPEPAM-LK rule can be applied.

Once this agreement is signed, a series of negotiations kicks in. In this process of negotiation, senior management mostly receives advice from financial experts or accountants in and out of the company. It is not common to seek outside investment bankers or consulting firms for advice in Indonesia,[14] because official information about accounting and management of the company is relatively scarce in the absolute majority of cases in Indonesia, a merging company mostly relies on the information from the target company.

Subsequently, the purchaser begins investigation of the seller's business in depth, known as due diligence. Although the seller also can undertake due diligence in a stock swap, it is very uncommon to see a stock-swap transaction for acquisition purposes in Indonesia, because a vast majority of acquisitions are cash-for-stock. In a due diligence, lawyers and accountants review thousands of pages of financial books and records of the target company, checking the accuracy of factual representations, looking for potential legal and financial problems, and searching for trouble spots. This due diligence may be assisted by other relevant experts in a particular business field, such as real estate appraisers or environmental professionals. If the target company is a listed company, BAPE-PAM-LK's inside-trading regulations lay out an exception to the due diligence. Figuratively speaking, due diligence operates as an antivirus program to search for malware when purchasing a used computer.

After the preliminary investigation, the parties negotiate the details of the terms and conditions including the deal price, structure, period, subject of contribution, etc. If this negotiation progresses productively, the parties may separately or additionally execute a non-binding term sheet, memorandum of understanding (MOU), or a heads of agreement to confirm a range of negotiable terms and conditions. The result of these series of negotiations is the final draft of the agreement. Once each company's board of directors approves the final draft and authorizes senior management to sign the agreement, lawyers prepare notices and disclosures to convene a shareholders' meeting to approve the resolution. Importantly, the companies should notify its employees of the merger at the latest 30 days before the shareholders' meeting and make a public notification through one or more nationally circulated newspapers.

While this process is underway, lawyers prepare a timetable showing various tasks to be concluded by each stage up to the final closing, which generally include the process for shareholders who may find the deal "repugnant" and seek to exercise appraisal rights, the protection of creditors, procedures dealing with a number of government institutions, obtaining licenses and permits, preparation of banking, and the other work required to start a business. Although this time schedule can be drafted after the agreement is signed, it is better to prepare it beforehand because of the time required to notify employees, the 30-day public notification, and the period of creditor protection.

---

14 Meeting with an influential public officer may be much more effective than consulting with professional management consultants or investment bankers.

Even if the agreement is signed by the both parties after approval from shareholders, it takes some months to complete all the tasks for closure to finalize the deal successfully. A proper registration and filing process follows, and ex post public notification is made through one or more newspapers within 30 days. If applicable, the KPPU should be noticed to as well.

Once all these tasks in the closing agenda are completed, and all the conditions in the agreement are met including cash for stock, asset contribution, and so on, a closing statement is executed and signed.

Depending on the type of company and field of business, dealing with Indonesian government agencies such as the MLHR, Bank Indonesia, OJK, and BKPM is important in consummating a transaction.

2.2. Terms and conditions for a potential share purchaser in the early stages

Since underwriters in charge of sales of shares mostly charge a success fee, a share purchaser does not bear much cost if a deal fails to be finalized. Greater costs and expenses are incurred, rather, by a potential investor to examine and study the target company repeatedly through legal due diligence, financial due diligence, regulation research, funds preparation, and other search costs.[15]

Because a share seller wants to sell at the highest price possible, he may search for other investors and put up a "horse race," or secretly negotiate with several candidates at the same time. In turn, a potential investor does not want to run this sort of risk under already uncertain circumstances and thus can require an exclusive right to negotiate, seeking security or liquidated damages so as to become an official negotiator of the highest priority. Since a share seller also needs to provide an incentive to encourage a potential purchaser to come to the negotiation table, he may promise a "lockup" condition, which compensates all relevant search costs incurred by the opponent party in the event that the share sale and purchase deal is frustrated.[16] Alternatively, he may promise a "topping

---

15 Particularly, many foreign investors contact law firms and accounting firms in their home country, who will then contact Indonesian regional firms, substantially increasing costs. This way of business seems particularly common for South Korean and Japanese institutional investors, who need professional assistance in their mother tongue, while U.S. investors tend to directly contact a trustworthy law firm in Indonesia, as the main players have an affiliation relationship with international laicism.

16 In the United States, a lockup condition in the share sale and purchase context refers to (i) setting up a termination fee or liquidation damages; (ii) obtaining an option to purchase treasury stocks or new stocks in better conditions; or (iii) receiving a "crown jewel" option to purchase material assets of the target company in case that the stock seller attempts to abruptly change its sales plan, or sells the stocks to a third party for a better price or conditions. Because a majority shareholder should be able to commonly sell out some or all shares off the market, it is unlikely to obtain a part of shares owned by him as security for the transaction. Thus, it is much more probable to set up a lockup condition in a way of promising a liquidated damage to an investor in case the deal fails. Choong Kee Lee,

fee," a condition which refers to giving the topping-fee right holder a certain portion of the price gap between the highest price of bidding and the lower price that a topping-fee right holder bids. If the share seller pays 90 percent of the price gap upon selling the shares to a third party, it would bring up a lockup effect, since the seller obtains little profit by selling it to another party.

One should be concerned about their economic effect when using these terms and conditions.

2.3. Valuation

One of the great issues in M&A negotiation is the question of valuation. How much does the target cost "as is," and how much will its value increase after it is combined with the share acquirer? Valuation should calculate the synergy that the merger or acquisition will gain, which may become a material issue even in litigation, such as in the damage assessment portion of breach of fiduciary duty cases, or in statutory proceedings.

If the target company is publicly traded in a liquid market and has adequately made public disclosures, the market price of the stock is, in theory, the valuation of the business. In the United States, the merger company typically pays a sizeable premium over the market price of the stock, which often reaches around 25 percent above market price on average.[17] Although it is unclear whether the similar level of premium is applied in the Indonesian market, this important factor remains the same in the Indonesia market too; the size of premium is determined predominantly by what the buyer believes it can do with the target company assets that the target company is not currently doing itself. Because the share purchaser is interested in the income stream that a given target business will produce and historical figures of the target company's income statement are in some way predictive of future performance, in many cases, valuation is handled by multiplying the target's historical earnings by a certain factor.

There a number of earning figures for the valuation purposes, such as EBIT (Earnings Before Income Tax) or EBITDA (Earnings Before Interest, Taxes, Depreciation, and Amortization), the latter of which is most commonly used in informal discussions, because it accurately reflects the actual cash flow of the target. In either case, a merging company should principally reply on the target company's information in Indonesia, because there are few other reliable sources of material information about the target company. This is particularly the case, given that either in a hostile or non-hostile takeover, the target company has reason not to be open and cooperative regarding their tactical choices. Even if

---

Special Feature Enterprise and Law: Justification and Limitation of Devices Inducing, Compensating and Releasing from M&A Negotiations in the Context of Sales of Control Block, *The Law Research Institute of Hongik University* Vol. 13, No. 4, 2012, pp. 1–39.

17 Dale A. Oesterle, *The Law of Mergers and Acquisitions*, 3rd ed., West, 2005, p. 14.

the share purchaser has highly trustworthy information and uses sophisticated valuation methods using discounted cash flow analysis reflecting the time value of money, managing the risk of currency inflation and the risk of volatility in the projection, the valuation will still remain subjective and inaccurate. This is because even experts have variable and different opinions about the same transaction, and the most sophisticated professionals can still provide only a value range decorated with buzzwords and jargon. Therefore, it is not going too far to say that the final valuation is up to negotiation. Thus, it is an art rather than science.

2.4. Legal due diligence

A legal due diligence checklist is typically standardized for quality control purposes. It is formatted to avoid duplication or omission and efficiently distribute work to the number of lawyers required. The checklist can make it clear which person is responsible for what work and also help a team leader evaluate how efficiently each lawyer is working. However well made the standardized format of the list, due diligence may be greatly complicated, depending on the target company's contracts, potential litigation, licenses, permits, and other circumstances.

This section explains the generalized documents and records required for most of companies in legal due diligence.[18] It should be noted that these items are merely a sample, and additional documents may need to be examined depending on the business field, the company's circumstances, investor interests, and terms and conditions in contracts.

2.4.1. Company structure

The documents and records needed to examine corporate structure are follows:

- Deed of Establishment and MLHR's approval of establishment
- Articles of association and all amendments thereof, with approvals and acknowledgement letters issued by the MLHR in regard to any amendments
- Minutes of meetings of shareholders, board of directors, and board of commissioners, including any resolutions adopted outside a meeting from the date of establishment of the company

---

18 It is rare to include details of legal due diligence in company law guide books. Nonetheless, this book includes some details of the process to show the scope and range of the related work, because foreign investors (or foreign legal representative in charge) tend to underestimate the duration of the timeframe, the scope of workload, the range of documents, and other particulars in Indonesia based on their experience in foreign countries. Because of the gap between practice in foreign countries and Indonesia, and the unique difficulties found in Indonesian practice, foreign investors are recommended to examine the overall process in advance.

- Current effective power of attorney, authorizing a third party, and any proxy documents
- Due diligence reports and financial reports

The following items must be examined with the above documents and records:

- Company's name and address
- Company's purpose
- Company's duration
- Changes in issued and unissued shares, and paid-in and unpaid capital, from the date of establishment
- Changes in types of shares
- Changes in the members of both the board of directors and board of commissioners
- Procedures of appointment and dismissal of members of both the board of directors and board of commissioners
- Dividend procedures and for distribution of remaining assets
- Whether the MLHR has approved the matters from the first four items
- Whether the MLHR has been notified of other matters

Regarding the functions of each document and record, please see the section "Establishment and amendment of articles of association." Notably, the State Gazette is generally required to be examined in standard format. However, it is merely a document that MLHR issues within 14 days of establishment of company, or of any amendment to the articles of association. It does not have any legal effect, nor is the company required to keep it in the office. The important document is MLHR's approval or acknowledgement.

2.4.2. *Capital and shareholders*

The documents and records regarding to company's capital and shareholders are as follows:

- List of shareholders
- Documents related to share transfers, including share sale and purchase agreements, and shareholders' resolutions
- Contracts between the company and shareholders
- Contracts of share pledges and related papers
- All mortgage-related documents (including registration of *Lembaga Fiducia*)

The following items must be examined with the above documents:

- Company's capital structure
- Shareholding rate of each shareholder
- Shareholders' names and addresses

- Terms and conditions in any share transfers, conveyances, or purchase contracts and performance thereof
- Pledgee names and addresses
- Terms and conditions in any share pledge contract, and performance thereof

The special list of shareholders is merely for form's sake. No sanction is imposed on any negligent update of the special list of shareholders, and seeking a remedy for any direct damages based on an incomplete special list of shareholders is far-fetched.

2.4.3. *Board of directors and board of commissioners*

The documents and records required regarding the board of directors and board of commissioners are as follows:

- List of current directors and commissioners, and the minutes of shareholders' meeting regarding appointment thereof
- List of previous directors and commissioners, and the minutes of shareholders' meeting regarding appointment and dismissal thereof
- Any power of attorney appointed by directors
- A copy of the ID of directors and commissioners

The following items must be examined with the above documents:

- List of current directors and commissioners
- Qualifications of members of the board of directors and board of commissioners
- The quorum of directors required to resolve the acquisition of shares, any sales of assets, corporate activities, and other important issues
- Whether the company has made any external appearance to outside parties for authority or representative power

2.4.4. *License and permits*

All registrations, consents, approvals, permits, licenses, and exemptions required or obtained by the company in connection with the operation of its business must be examined including, among others, the following:

- Company registration certificate (*Tanda Daftar Perusahaan*)
- Letter of domicile (*Surat Keterangan Domisili Perusahaan: SKDP*)
- Tax registration certificate (*Surat Keterangan Terdaftar: SKT*)
- Any permit or licenses for management of company such as a nuisance permit (*HO*)
- Taxpayer registration number (*Nomor Pokok Wajib Pajak: NPWP*)
- Value-added tax (VAT) number (*Pengusaha Kena Pajak: PKP*)

- Business place permit (*Surat Ijin Tempat Usaha: SITU*)
- Approval for foreign investment (or investment registration letter) from BKPM (*Surat Persetujuan Penanaman Modal Asing:* "BKPM Approval") and amendments thereof
- Registration of Capital Investment
- Approval of business from BKPM (*Izin Usaha*)
- Capital investment activity report (*Laporan Kegiatan Penanaman Modal: LKPM*)
- Other operational licenses depending on the type of business activities that the company engages in
- Details and copies of all documents relating to any anti-corruption policies and procedures that have been implemented by the company to ensure compliance with Law No. 31 Year 1999 as amended by Law No. 20 Year 2001 regarding Corruption Eradication (if any)

2.4.5. Contracts and legal documents

All the significant factors of important contracts must be examined, including what the subject matter is, whether specific conditions have been satisfied, how parties have performed, whether there are any risk exists, etc.

2.4.6. Company's assets

The documents and records regarding to assets are as follows:

- Equipment list and certificate of ownership of the listed item
- Certificate of ownership of liquid assets
- Any documents that show any encumbrances such as mortgages, charges, pledges, guarantee, claims, hypothecations, legends, defects, exceptions, reservations, limitations, impairments, rights of purchase, deeds of trust, liens, easements, caveats, or other impediments
- List of accounts receivables, prepared on an agreed receivables basis
- Details of all shares currently held by the company in other companies, as evidenced by share certificates or registration of the company on the list of shareholders of other companies (if any)
- List of intellectual property
- List of all other assets
- Related to real estate assets, a schedule of all freehold and leasehold properties owned, occupied, used, or controlled by the company in relation to its business, and all licenses to occupy any such properties (together with copies of the title deeds including all leases, head leases, subleases, and licenses where relevant, and including the following details or documents in respect of each property

  - Short address and description of the property, including the title number
  - Area and site plan

- Rights benefiting the property and third-party rights to which the property is subject
- Current use and value
- Copies of all documents evidencing and/or relating to the company's ownership of any property (e.g. notarial deeds, agreements, certificates, and situation drawings)
- Copies of all documents evidencing the company's rights over land (e.g. land title certificates, notarial deeds, agreements)
- In the case of any leasehold property:
  - Term and commencement date of any lease
  - Annual rent or fee payable
  - Rent review dates
  - Evidence of all past rent reviews
  - Service charge accounts for the last 3 years

2.4.7. Insurance

Every evidential document related to insurance and payment of premiums.

2.4.8. Employees

The documents and records regarding to employees are as follows:

- Registration number, job, titles, and current status of employees.
- Copies of workers' social security program enrollment documents (*Jaminan Sosial Tenaga Kerja: Jamsostek*) and the evidence of payment
- Details of employees' unions
- Copies of confidentiality/non-competition agreements between the company and the employees and/or copies of collective labor agreements
- Copies of the company's own bylaws or internal regulations ratified by the Manpower Office
- Copies of evidence of fulfillment of Mandatory Manpower Report (*Wajib Lapor Ketenagakerjaan: WLTK*)
- Minimum payment details (*Upah Minimum Regional: UMR*)
- Copies of work permits and immigration documents (only in the case where the company employs any expatriate), including:
  - Expatriate manpower utilization plan (*Rencana Penggunaan Tenaga Kerja Asing: RPTKA*)
  - Limited stay visa details (*Visa Izin Tinggal Terbatas or VITAS*)
  - Temporary stay permit cards (*Kartu Izin Tinggal Terbatas: KITAS*)
  - Work permits (*Izin Mempkerjakan Tenaga Asing: IMTA*)
- Regarding pensions particularly:
  - Details and copies of all documents relating to the enrollment of Manpower Social Security (*Jaminan Sosial Tenaga Kerja: Jamsostek*) program, particularly the old age security program

- Details of any non-compliance by the company with Law No. 3 of 1992 regarding Jamsostek and its implementing regulations
- Details of any additional pension schemes that the company has participated in other than the Jamsostek

2.4.9. *Tax*

Copies of tax registration documents must be examined including:

- Tax registration letter (*Surat Keterangan Terdaftar: SKT*)
- Taxpayer registration number (*Nomor Pokok Wajib Pajak: NPWP*)
- VAT number for taxable companies/entrepreneur (*Pengusaha Kena Pajak: PKP*)
- Taxable entrepreneur confirmation letter (*Surat Pengukuhan Pengusaha Kena Pajak: SPPKP*)

In Indonesia, due diligence in respect of tax-related matters is normally handled by a tax consultant.

2.4.10. *Legal dispute and litigation*

The documents and records regarding legal disputes and litigation are as follows:

- List of any pending litigation, arbitration, mediation, disputes, settlements, or any other legal proceedings
- Every document related to potential future disputes

The following items must be examined with the above documents and records:

- The content of cases and date of occurrence
- Current proceedings and management's intention (whether to settle in the near future or continue to the bitter end)
- Potential cost of unwanted results
- Estimated potential losses

Of course, a company hoping to attract investors is reluctant to disclose any pending dispute. Thus, if a lawyer working on due diligence has no particular proof, but a strong suspicion that a legal dispute exists, asking a question such as "there is a dispute, isn't there?" is unwise. No one will say "Yes, there is." Instead, the lawyer is better off checking the breakdown of costs and expenses. Then, a commission or fee spent to law firm may be found, whereby the lawyer can ask relevant employees the reason for the spending. Either way, the lawyer should request written confirmation that the party has provided details of all known disputes and legal proceedings and that there is no other legal dispute or litigation either pending or likely.

As a part of the standardized procedure, the due diligence team normally does a fact check by asking courts and the tax office whether there is any pending suit.

Often, the court or tax office requires the lawyer to follow an unwritten internal policy, such as submission of original articles of association or a signed copy of establishment deed, etc. Coping with public institutions takes a lot of perseverance.

If the target company has a legal dispute pending, each proof obtained from the company and law firm should be cross-checked. The most commonly used method to obtain a proof from a law firm is to send a request for information bearing the signature of one of the target company's signatories (sometimes, the law firm may even enclose a self-addressed and stamped envelope). The items to include in this request are any information on:

- Date of due diligence
- Any pending litigation or other dispute
- Potential claims not yet raised
- Other opinions made available to the client
- Reasons for a lack of detail if none is supplied

An example of this letter of request is as follows:

[Letter Head]	(Kop Surat)
[Date]	(Tanggal)
[Name of law firm] [Address]	(Nama Kantor Hukum) (Alamat)
Gentleman:	Yang terhormat,
In connection with a due diligence for potential investment, management of our company has decided to prepare and furnish to the potential investor with a description and evaluation of certain contingencies, including those set forth below involving matters with respect to which you have been engaged and to which you have devoted substantive attention on behalf of our company in the form of legal consultation or representation. These contingencies are regarded by management as material for this purpose (management may indicate a materiality limit). Your response should include matters that existed at [Date] and during the period from that date to the date of your response.	Sehubungan dengan uji tuntas untuk investasi yang potensial, manajemen perusahaan kami telah memutuskan untuk mempersiapkan dan menyediakan kepada investor yang potensial, suatu deskripsi dan evaluasi atas kemungkinan-kemungkinan tertentu di masa depan, termasuk hal-hal yang ditetapkan di bawah ini melibatkan hal-hal sehubungan dengan hal mana anda telah diikutsertakan dan terhadap hal mana anda telah mencurahkan perhatian sungguh-sungguh atas nama perusahaan kami dalam bentuk konsultasi atau perwakilan hukum. Kemungkinan-kemungkinan ini dipandang oleh manajemen sebagai hal penting untuk tujuan ini (manajemen dapat menyatakan suatu batas kepentingan).

[PENDING OR THREATENED LITIGATION (EXCLUDING UNASSERTED CLAIMS)

Ordinarily management's information would include (i) the nature of the litigation, (ii) the progress of the case to date, (iii) how management is responding or intends to respond to the litigation, (iv) an evaluation of the likelihood of unfavorable outcome and an estimate, if one can be made, of the amount or range of potential loss.

Please furnish to our investor such explanation if any that you consider necessary to supplement the foregoing information, including an explanation of those matters as to which you view may differ from those stated, and an identification of the omission of any pending or threatened litigation, claims, and assessments or a statement that the list of such matter is complete.

UNASSERTED CLAIMS AND ASSESSMENTS

Ordinarily management's information would include (i) the nature of the matter, (ii) how management intends to respond if the claim is asserted, and (iii) an evaluation of the likelihood of unfavorable outcome and an estimate, if one can be made, of the amount or range of potential loss.

Tanggapan anda diharapkan termasuk hal-hal yang telah ada pada *(Tanggal)* dan selama waktu sejak tanggal tersebut hingga tanggal tanggapan anda.

LITIGASI YANG MENUNGGU KEPUTUSAN ATAU MENGANCAM (DILUAR KLAIM YANG TIDAK TEGAS)

Umumnya informasi manajemen akan termasuk (i) jenis litigasi (ii) perkembangan terkini atas suatu kasus (iii) bagaimana manajemen menanggapi atau bermaksud untuk menanggapi litigasi (iv) suatu evaluasi atas kemungkinan hasil yang tidak diharapkan dan suatu estimasi terkait. Jika salah satunya dapat dibuat dari nilai atau cakupan potensi kerugian.

Harap menyediakan bagi investor kami suatu penjelasan jika hal tersebut anda pertimbangkan perlu untuk menambah informasi yang telah disebut sebelumnya termasuk suatu penjelasan atas hal-hal yang mana anda memandangnya mungkin berbeda dari yang dinyatakan dan suatu identifikasi dari kelalaian atas suatu litigasi yang menunggu keputusan atau mengancam, klaim-klaim dan pemeriksaan-pemeriksaan atau suatu laporan bahwa daftar hal-hal tersebut telah lengkap.

KLAIM-KLAIM DAN PEMERIKSAAN-PEMERIKSAAN YANG TIDAK TEGAS

Umumnya informasi manajemen akan termasuk (i) jenis persoalan, (ii) bagaimana manajemen bermaksud untuk menanggapi jika klaim ditegaskan, dan (iii) suatu evaluasi atas kemungkinan hasil yang tidak diharapkan dan suatu estimasi terkait, jika salah satunya dapat dibuat, dari nilai atau cakupan potensi kerugian.

Please furnish to our investors such explanation, if any, that you consider necessary to supplement the foregoing information, including an explanation of those matters as to which your views may differ from those stated.

We understand that whenever, in the course of performing legal services for us with respect to a matter recognized to involve an unasserted possible claim or assessment that may call for financial statement disclosure, if you have formed a professional conclusion that we should disclose or consider disclosure concerning such possible claim or assessment as a matter of professional responsibility to us, you will so advise us and will consult with us concerning the question of such disclosure. Please specifically confirm to our understanding is correct.

Please specifically identify the nature of and reasons for any limitation of your response.

The investor may request the client to inquire about additional matters, for example, unpaid or unbilled charges or specified information on certain contractually assumed obligations of the company, such as guarantees of indebtedness of others.

Very truly yours,

[Company name]

Harap menyediakan bagi investor kami suatu penjelasan, jika ada, bahwa anda mempertimbangkan perlu untuk menambah informasi yang telah disebut sebelumnya, termasuk suatu penjelasan atas hal-hal yang mana anda memandangnya mungkin berbeda dari yang dinyatakan.

Kami mengerti bahwa sewaktu-waktu, dalam melaksanakan jasa-jasa hukum bagi kami sehubungan dengan persoalan yang diketahui akan melibatkan suatu kemungkinan klaim atau pemeriksaan yang tidak tegas yang dapat meminta pengungkapan laporan keuangan, jika anda telah membuat suatu kesimpulan profesional bahwa kami perlu mengungkapkan atau mempertimbangkan pengungkapan mengenai kemungkinan klaim atau pemeriksaan tersebut sebagai bentuk tanggung jawab profesional terhadap kami, anda perlu menasehati kami dan berkonsultasi dengan kami mengenai persoalan pengungkapan tersebut. Mohon secara spesifik mengkonfirmasi bahwa pemahaman kami benar.

Mohon secara spesifik mengidentifikasi sifat dari dan alasan atas suatu pembatasan pada tanggapan anda.

Investor dapat meminta kepada klien untuk meminta keterangan tentang hal-hal tambahan, contohnya, beban-beban biaya yang belum dibayar atau ditagih atau informasi yang dispesifikasi pada kewajiban yang timbul berdasarkan kontrak tertentu atas perusahaan, seperti jaminan-jaminan atas utang pihak lain.

Hormat kami,

(Nama Perusahaan)

Whether in-house counsel or legal firm's lawyer, no one is willing to provide detailed information about his client's pending disputes to an outsider. Thus, they are more likely to remain silent for reasons of confidentiality, or other persuasive reasons. However, it is important to seek out these reasons.

Lastly, many Indonesian commercial disputes rely on BANI or SIAC for final settlement of disputes, as both are regarded as clearer than regular Indonesian courts. If a target company is on the verge of a commercial arbitration process as an applicant, it may incur substantial legal costs since the applicant should cover the entire amount of any deposit and fee, none of which the other party has to pay. The arbitration center unilaterally decides the arbitration fee. This must be explained to the investors in sufficient detail.

Likewise, apart from the detail in substance, timeframes, and struggling to deal with public institutions, the general procedures in Indonesian legal due diligence are not greatly different from those in other countries.

Advice related to legal due diligence

While some well-known Chinese Indonesian corporate groups have systematic data management systems, many Indonesian companies or groups do not seem to have one. Because it is simply impossible for a single in-house counsel to know all the details and background of all BKPM permits,[19] real estate permits,[20] environmental permits,[21] customs permits,[22] tax registrations,[23] financial statements, variable insurances, and other data, the in-house counsel's main work is to coordinate with the right department or person to provide that relevant information, and to effectively summarize data into a consistent format after understanding each issue and answer. As a series of questions repeatedly comes one after another, the heavy work schedule for this process goes on and on. To smooth this process, it is better to clarify which department or which person is responsible for what work, and how to cope with questions at the earliest possible moment.

Also, the schedule and pace of due diligence are important. If financial and legal due diligence can be harmoniously brought together, involved persons do not need to repeatedly answer the same questions over and over from lawyers and accountants. Also, relevant data can be quickly obtained. That is because a certain portion of legal due diligence is undeniably repeated within the scope of financial due diligence. Nonetheless, a target

---

19 *Surat Persetujuan Penanaman Modal Asing, Izin Prinsip Penanaman Modal, Izin Usaha Penanaman Modal, etc.*
20 *Izin Lokaasi, Surat Keputusan Pemberian Hak Guna Usaha,* etc.
21 *Izin Lingkungan, Izin Gangguan, Izin Pembuangan Air Limbah,* etc.
22 *Angka Pengenal Importir-Produsen,* etc.
23 *Surat Keterangan Terdaftar* (Tax Registration Certificate), *PKP* (VAT Number), etc.

company's request to skip any overlapping portion is unacceptable, because the nature of each due diligence check is fundamentally different.

In the meantime, the key point of a law firm's work in legal due diligence is not the rigorous reading of thousand-page documents (as every young and ambitious lawyer would do), but instead pointing out only the significant issues. The reason why this is so important is that there are numerous Indonesian lawyers magnifying surprisingly trivial and normally inconsequential issues, whether or not they work in a reputable firm. This is thought to be a combination of a poor legal education, which does not effectively teach how to detect an important issue, and a poor legal system, which actually often makes trouble over very minor issues. Of course, if the target company is in an utterly disastrous state and should not be acquired or merged with under any circumstance, the lawyer can point out every single detected issue with highly charged passion.

The following are typical examples over which a passionate but dull lawyer often unnecessarily makes trouble:

- The absence of state gazette showing the establishment of the company or any amendment to the articles of association: it is the MLHR's responsibility to issue this, not the company's responsibility to list this in the state gazette. Nor is a company legally required to keep this document in the office.
- The absence of a special list of shareholders in Article 50 Paragraph 2 of the 2007 Company Act: there is no sanction or penalty against this draconian requirement. The reason why this requirement is draconian is explained in the section *List of Shareholders*. Also, it is virtually impossible for a company to update the list in real time, for directors to take responsibility for any damages incurred evidentially because of the absence of a special list of shareholders.
- The absence of a letter regarding the eligibility of any director or commissioner: this is nothing but formality. There is no sanction or penalty for lacking this letter. Even if the company keeps it, the company would still be liable for the actions of an ineligible director or commissioner from the time the eligibility is lost, and other directors or commissioners noticed about such a fact to the time of their official dismissal. The details are explained in the section "Director."

Generally, a merger and acquisition involve a great number of people. Thus, it is easy to be confused with namesakes, similarly named people, and charge accordingly. Lawyers should be very careful. To resolve any issues, some team leaders in legal due diligence divide the work among associates depending on the contact person immediately after the pre-DD conference. Although it does not sound very agreeable, it is understandable. In any case, the entire team and opponent parties should quickly update one another's respective progress.

2.5.   *Merger plan*

In the case of a merger, the target company's board of directors must prepare for a merger plan, and the board of commissioners must permit it. In the case of an acquisition of shares from a certain shareholder, this plan is not required.

2.6.   *Merger agreement*

While acquisition is freely made as a share sale and purchase agreement between seller and purchaser with variable conditions contemplated, a merger agreement is a strictly formal contract between the merging company and the target company, with a condition precedent of resolution for merger and the following mandatory items (Article 123).

2.6.1.   *Mandatory items*

- The name and domicile of each company in the merger transaction
- The reasons and explanation by each companies' board of directors and the merger conditions
- Procedures for the valuation and conversion of shares in the merging company into shares of the surviving company
- The draft for any amendment to the articles of association of the surviving company
- The financial reports covering the last 3 financial years from each of the companies in the merger
- The plans for continuing or terminating the business activities of the companies in the merger
- A *pro forma* balance sheet of the surviving company in accordance with accounting principles generally accepted in Indonesia
- Method of settlement of the status, rights, and obligations of the members of the board of directors, board of commissioners, and employees of the merging company
- Method of settlement of the rights and obligations of the merging company against third parties
- Method of settlement of the rights of shareholders who do not agree to the merger of the companies
- Names of the members of the board of directors and board of commissioners and the wages, honoraria, and allowances for members of the board of directors and board of commissioners of the surviving company
- Estimated period for implementation of the merger
- Report on the circumstances, development, and results achieved of each of the companies in the merger
- Main activities of each company in the merger and changes which occurred in the current financial year
- Details of any problems arising during the current financial year which affected the activities of the companies in the merger

2.6.2. *Factors to take into account in drafting a contract*

First, there are some different aspects between the 2007 Company Act and foreign corporation law as follows:

- In Indonesia, the date of the shareholders' meeting to approve the merger is not a mandatory item to write in a merger agreement (however, it is desirable to set forth a proper date.)
- The maximum interim dividends or dividends because of the merger is not a mandatory item to include in a merger agreement (however, it is recommended to explicitly state these because the initially determined ownership rate can be later altered.)
- Because the effective date of merger is an issuance date of MLHR's approval or declaration (*Surat Keputusan*), the consolidated financial statement should be made on basis of this date. This is because this date is when an acquired or merged company's assets are absolutely conveyed and transferred to a surviving company, a surviving company's shares are allocated to the previous shareholders of the acquired or merged company, and thus the companies finally become one company.

Second, a merger transaction brings out substantial changes such as the name of the company, changes or additions to business purpose, a surviving company's increase of authorized capital to issue new shares to shareholders of the target company, the removal of shareholders who exercise appraisal rights, etc. Even if a merger agreement specifically states these changes and the shareholder meeting approves them in writing, the articles of association must still be formally amended including notice to or approval from the MLHR and a notary's drafting.

Third, the following matters should be advised in terms of capital allocation: due to the merger transaction, the surviving company's capital increases as much as a total amount of nominal value of the newly issued shares proportionally distributed to shareholders of the target company. Because the total value of these new shares is based on the transferred assets from the target company, in principle, it generally does not exceed the value of net assets of the target company. In the absence of a relevant clause or regulation for a closely held company, the value of the target company's net assets, less the total par value of new shares, is deemed as a gain from the merger, and earmarked for reserves.

The surviving company's stock allocation to shareholders of the target company is decided on the basis of the ratio of acquisition and valuation of the target company. Generally, calculation of the value per share is based on the company's assets and profitability.[24] If the decision process is deemed intolerably

---

24 See Section 8.4.4.1 on whether a surviving company can acquire as much treasury stock as it previously owned. In sum, treasury stock is not permitted pursuant to Article 36 Paragraph 1, and share acquisition by bequest (*kepemilikan saham babah wasiat*) is only

unfair, it can cause nullity, invalidity, cancellation, or termination of the merger or acquisition.

To adjust the allocation of new shares, or for distribution of the profits earned before the target company is extinguished in the financial year (if the accounting period ends after the date of merger), the surviving company may in theory pay cash to shareholders of the target company. Nonetheless, it is very rare in practice.

Lastly, if another option is sought, using variable kinds of shares is not recommended. Although it is possible in theory, the BKPM and MLHR are not familiar with variable types of shares and, thus, inefficiency and risks are large. If a complex capital structure with variable types of shares is inevitable, parties commonly use offshore companies in a jurisdiction that is familiar with such a complex structure.

2.7. Notification to employees and public disclosure prior to merger

While a pension trust fund is a significant factor to consider in mergers and acquisition in some other countries, the most important issue concerning labor in Indonesian transactions is the settlement payment.

Employees have a right to resign due to an M&A. According to the 2007 Company Act (Article 127 Paragraph 2), the board of directors must give notice in writing to employees regarding any merger, consolidation, acquisition, or separation, and do so at least 30 days prior to the notice for the shareholder's meeting resolving the issue. This Article seems to be included not in employees' interest, but also that of the acquirer, because it would harm the company's interest if a majority of employees or key employees resigned after any change of majority shareholder. Also, Indonesia has a custom that an acquirer provides employees of the target company with written confirmation or assurance that it will continue the employment relationship after the merger or acquisition.

In addition, the summary of such a plan should be announced in at least one newspaper (Article 127 Paragraphs 2 and 3). This is to protect interest holders. As stated earlier, since a newspaper is defined as "a daily newspaper in Indonesian language with national circulation," an electronic newspaper would suffice.

2.8. Protection of creditors

If creditors do not submit an objection within 14 days of the public announcement, the merger, consolidation, acquisition, or separation is deemed agreed

---

exceptionally permitted. However, whether this exception includes share repurchase due to merger and acquisitions is unclear, since neither corporate tax law nor Indonesian accounting principle sufficiently specifies it. Therefore, all the legal documents must be carefully drafted in a way that the parties cannot later claim nullity, invalidity, cancellation, or termination of the agreement, merger, or all related transactions.

(Article 127 Paragraph 4). In the event that a creditor objects, the company may either pay the creditor, provide a security, or entrust certain assets to a trust company.

2.9. Resolution for M&A and appraisal rights of minority shareholder

- The resolution of the shareholders' meeting requires the presence or representation of three-fourths of the total shares issued with voting rights, and approval by more than three-fourths of the total votes cast at the meeting (Article 89).
- Appraisal rights of minority shareholders:

Article 126 (2)

The shareholders who disagree against the resolution of general shareholders' meeting in regard to the Merger, Consolidation, Acquisition, or Separation . . . shall only use their right stated in Article 62.

Article 62

(1) Each shareholder shall have the right to request the Company to purchase its shares with a reasonable price if such a shareholder does not agree with the action of the Company which harm the shareholders of the Company in the form of: (a) amendments to the articles of association; (b) the transfer or the encumbrance of the Company's assets, having a nominal value of more than 50 percent of the net assets of the Company; or (c) Merger, Consolidation, Acquisition, or Separation.

(2) In the event that the share requested to be purchased as stated in Paragraph (1) exceeds the limit of the buy-back requirements by the Company as stated in Article 37 Paragraph (1) letter b, the Company is obliged to make an effort so that the remaining shares be purchased by a third party.

Article 37 (1) b

The Company may buy back the outstanding shares if the nominal value of all shares bought back by the Company and the pledge of shares or the fiduciary security on shares held by the Company itself, and/or other company whose shares are directly or indirectly owned by the Company does not exceed 10 percent of the issued capital in the Company, except otherwise regulated in the capital markets.

2.10. *Mandatory bid rule for public companies*

A mandatory tender offer in Indonesia means "an offer through mass media for acquisition of equity securities through purchase or exchange with other securities."[25] Basically, a mandatory bid rule is the strongest and most controversial expression of the sharing principle, which requires the acquirer of shares to make a general offer to the other shareholders once it has acquired sufficient shares by private contract – either on or off market – to obtain control of the target.[26] That is, the rule provides shareholders with a right to exit the company at an attractive price by imposing an obligation on the acquirer to make a general offer.

This rule has its origins in the United Kingdom, and now applies throughout the EU and in Singapore, Indonesia, Japan, and many other jurisdictions. Most importantly, it is not a ubiquitous rule applicable anywhere. U.S. federal law – or the law of Delaware – has not adopted this rule since any shareholder coordination problems are intended to be dealt with by target management.[27] In plain words, the management of target corporations already have a variety of defensive tactics, such as a poison pill tactic, or a shareholders' rights plan. South Korea also has abolished this rule because a pyramid capital structure is pervasive and widespread; this capital structure operates as a strong control defense, particularly for *chaebol* conglomerates.[28] Even those countries having a mandatory bid rule apply substantially different conditions and triggering percentages, from, for example, as little as 4 percent to as much as 90 percent.[29]

Such a rule has been introduced on two grounds.[30] First, the absence of this rule would permit the acquirer to put pressure on those to whom offers are made during the control acquisition process to accept those offers. In the absence of the rule, the acquirer could threaten, for example: "If you do not accept it

---

25 Bapepam Regulation No. IX.F.1 art. 1(d) (2002).
26 Control is usually defined as holding around one-third of the voting shares in the company.
27 Reinier Kraakman et al., *The Anatomy of Corporate Law: A Comparative and Functional Approach*, 2nd ed., Oxford University Press, 2009, p. 254.
28 "Some maintain that foreign giant acquirers with financial strength are increasing, *Chaebol* can no longer secure safe defensive tactics and, above all, a control defense rule is needed for small and middle enterprises." Soonpeel Chang, *Korea's Unique Resistance against the Control Defense*, Directed Research Dissertation, New York University School of Law, 2012; Stephen J. Choi, The Future Direction of Takeover Law in Korea, *Journal of Korean Law*, Vol 7, 2007; Kwon Jong Ho, The Need for Defensive Measures against Hostile Takeover, *KCI* Vol. 22, 2009, pp. 257–288.
29 "Swiss law requires only that the offer be at not less than the higher of the market price when the mandatory offer is launched, and 75% of the highest price paid for the shares over the previous 12 months. Italy permits partial bids for at least 60% of the shares provided the shareholders other than the offeror and connected persons approve the offer by majority vote and the offeror has not acquired more than 1% of the shares over the preceding 12 months. Japan addresses . . . the mandatory bid rule is triggered only at the two-thirds threshold." Kraakman et al., *supra* note 27, pp. 254–255.
30 Kraakman et al., *supra* note 27, pp. 25–256.

now, I will be prepared to make only a lower offer once I have obtained control of the company." Nonetheless, it can be maintained that the value of shares held by the non-accepting shareholders will be higher after the control shift than before, if the bid increases value. That is, even if they remain in the company, providing the non-accepting shareholders with an exit right is not necessary. Second, allowing the acquisition of control over the whole of the company's assets by purchasing only a certain portion of the company's shares would encourage transfers of control to those likely to exploit the private benefits of corporate control. In other words, the mandatory bid rule gives the minority the option to exit the company, because it anticipates that there is a strong likelihood of majority and minority conflicts after the acquisition of control.

To conduct a mandatory tender offer, the acquirer must firstly submit a draft of announcement of the information disclosure along with its supporting documents to OJK and the target company within two business days after the takeover announcement. Second, it must make a public announcement through one or more newspapers having national circulation within two business days of the OJK's receipt of letter. In practice, the offer price to mandatorily tender is the main issue.[31]

The mandatory offer rule is not applicable to unlisted companies. However, the mandatory tender offer is triggered when a person who virtually controls an Indonesian listed company (e.g. the owner of 50% or more of total issued shares, or a person who can directly or indirectly decide corporate management and policy) is changed.[32]

The mandatory tender offer is exempted for the following transactions:[33]

- Shares owned by the shareholders who conduct an acquisition transaction with the new controller
- Shares owned by other parties who have obtained an offer with terms and conditions from a new controller
- Shares owned by other parties who at the same time are conducting a mandatory tender offer or voluntary tender offer regarding the same public company
- Shares owned by the major shareholder
- Shares owned by other controller of such public company

---

31 This book refrains from expounding on the process of setting the offer price and the detailed process of a mandatory tender offer as it is beyond the scope of this book. For details, see ABNR, *Merger and Acquisitions in Indonesia*, Law Guide, 2015.
32 Because this regulation applies to all the parties likely to plan, regiment, and cooperate for a certain purpose, all shareholders (either over 50% or not) are considered able to judge who a virtual controller is. For example, an investor having less than 50 percent voting rights may be appointed by other shareholders to work as a proxy or may have an appointment right. Alternatively, a shareholder resolution may provide a condition that other shareholders are required to appoint a director in favor of such a minority shareholder.
33 Bapepam Regulation No. IX.H.1 (3)(a)(2) (2011).

Also, the mandatory bid rule is not applied in the following cases, where acquisition occurs

- Due to marriage or inheritance
- By parties having no previous share ownership in a public company resulting from the purchase or acquisition of the public company's shares within the previous 12 months, in the maximum amount of 10 percent of the number of shares with legal voting rights in circulation
- Due to the implementation of duty and authority of government, state agencies, or institutions under the law
- Due to a direct purchase of shares owned by and/or controlled by government or state agencies or institutions as an implementation of the provisions as intended in the third point
- Due to a stipulation or decision of a court having permanent legal force
- Due to a business merger, a business dissociation, a business consolidation, or the implementation of liquidation by the shareholders
- Due to a grant that constitutes a transfer of shares without an agreement to obtain compensation in any form whatsoever
- Due to a specific liabilities security having been stipulated in a liabilities and receivables agreement, and a liabilities security in the framework of restructuring the public company stipulated by government or state agencies or institutions under the law
- Due to an acquisition of shares as an implementation of Regulation No. IX.D.1 and Regulation No. IX.D.4
- Due to an implementation of policies on government or state agencies or institutions
- Through a mandatory tender offer, that if it implemented will contradict the laws and regulations
- Due to the implementation of a voluntary tender offer under Regulation No. IX.F.1

Capital market regulations further govern a target company's defense measures and voluntary tender offer. Nonetheless, these defensive tactics are rarely used in practice.

2.11. *Principal license (Izin Prinsip) and Registration of Capital Investment*

Prior to BKPM Regulation 13/2017, an *Izin Prinsip* was required according to the BKPM Regulations 2015, and in the case of a merger, it was issued within 7 days from the date of submission. Now, *Izin Prinsip* is no longer required under the BKPM Regulation 13/2017. Instead, it necessitates Registration of Capital Investment for certain businesses as discussed earlier.

2.12. *Registration and the effective date of merger*

Contrary to the practice of other countries, registration alone does not effectuate a merger or consolidation in Indonesia. According to Article 133 and its elucidation, the effective date of merger or consolidation is the date of

- MLHR's approval of an amendment of the articles of association in the case of a merger (this approval is given as a declaration letter called *Surat Keputusan*)
- Receipt of notification by the MLHR in the case of an amendment of the articles of association as intended in Article 21 Paragraph 3
- If there is no amendment to the articles of association, the ratification of the deed of establishment of the company by the MLHR in case that a consolidation has been conducted.

However, the transfer of shares is regarded as occurring on the date recorded on the share transfer deed.[34]

2.13. Ex post *public announcement*

The result of a consolidation or merger must be publicly announced through one or more newspapers within 30 days of the effective date of the merger or consolidation (Article 133). The effective date of merger or consolidation is the date explained in the preceding paragraph.

2.14. Ex post *notice*

If conditions stipulated in Law No. 5 of 1999 (Prohibition of Monopoly and Unfair Business Competition), are satisfied, along with the implementing regulation and Government Regulation No. 57 of 2010 (Merger or Consolidation and Shares Acquisition Which May Cause the Monopoly Practice and Unfair Business Competition, Business Competition Supervisory Agency), the transaction must be reported to KPPU either through voluntary prior notice or mandatory ex post notice. The conditions are either:

- Such a transaction is an acquisition (acquiring 50% or more of voting rights, attaining appointment rights of a majority of directors, retaining a veto right or exclusive right on major issues, obtaining substantial influence over management, etc.).

---

34 "The transfer is effective on the date of the share transfer deed. However, there are subsequent requirements to notify or make registrations with the MOLHR and other government agencies (including in some circumstances changes in licensing)." Baker & McKenzie, *Global Private M&A Handbook*, September 2016, p. 259.

- The value of the asset after merger is more than IDR 2.5 trillion (IDR 20 trillion in the case of a bank), or the value of sales is more than IDR 5 billion.
- The transaction is a merger, consolidation, or acquisition among non-affiliated companies.

In other words, a transaction which does not fit these any of these criteria does not need to be reported to KPPU. Otherwise, an acquirer must notify the authority within 30 days and, if this deadline is not met, a penalty of IDR 1 billion per day is imposed, up to a maximum of IDR 25 billion).

2.15. *Laws and regulations governing takeovers*

A number of laws and regulations other than the 2007 Company Act also govern mergers, consolidations, and acquisitions in general.

- Government Regulation No. 27 of 1998 Regarding Mergers, Consolidations, and Acquisitions of Limited Liability Companies
- 2007 Capital Investment Act and its Presidential Regulations (amended almost annually)
- 1999 Prohibition of Monopoly and Unfair Business Competition Act

  - Government Regulation No. 57 of 2010 Regarding Merger, Consolidation and Shares Acquisition Which May Cause the Monopoly Practice and Unfair Business Competition
  - KPPU (*Komisi Pengawas Persaingan Usaha*: Business Competition Supervisory Commission) Regulations Regarding M&A (currently being amended and expected to be issued shortly)

In the case of a public company, a merging or acquiring company should provide information about the pending transaction to KPPU, who will then investigate the possibility of monopoly practice or unfair competition. Also, in the event that a public company attempts to make a mandatory tender offer, the offer and supporting documents must be submitted to OJK, and the offer price must strictly follow the regulations. For these transactions, a public company is governed by the following laws and regulations. (Note: Although the function and work of BAPEPAM have been transferred to OJK, the BAPEPAM-LK regulations are still effective and binding.)

- Law No. 8 of 1995 regarding the Capital Market
- BAPEPAM-LK (*Badan Pengawas Pasr Modal dan Lembaga Keuangan*; Capital Market and Financial Institution Supervisory Agency) regulations

  - Rule No. IX.F.1 on Voluntary Tender Offers as an attachment to the Decree of the Chairman of BAPEPAM-LK No. Kep-263/BL/2011

- Rule No. IX.G.1 on Mergers and Acquisition of Public Companies or Issuer Companies as an attachment to the Decree of Chairman of BAPEPAMLK No. Kep-52/PM/1997
- Rule No. IX.H.1 on Public Company Acquisition as an attachment to the Decree of the Chairman of BAPEPAMLK No. Kep-264/BL/2011
- Rule No. IX.E.2 on Material Transaction and Change of Main Business as an attachment to the Decree of BAPEPAM-LK No. Kep-614/BL/2011
- Rule No. X.K.1 on Disclosure of Information Which Must Be Announced to Public Immediately as an attachment to Decree of BAPEPAM-LK No. Kep-86/PM/1996

Apart from the above laws and regulations, a number of tax laws govern M&A transactions, and specific business regulations place additional layers depending on the nature of business field, such as banking, mining, or forestry.

2.16. *Material documents and necessary agreements*

The main documents to obtain and keep relating to merger, consolidation, and acquisition transactions are the

- Announcement of the summary of the merger, consolidation, or acquisition plan to the public through at least one newspaper having nationwide circulation (electronic newspapers allowed)
- Written announcement to the employees
- Resolution of the shareholders' meeting, or the circular resolution of shareholders, of the company. This resolution should be restated in a notarial deed within 30 days of the effective date of the resolution. (For public companies, the approval through shareholders' meeting is required in case of the company's merger or consolidation according to Rule IX.G.1, while it is not mandatory in case of acquisition according to Rule IX.H.1)
- Notarized acquisition/merger/consolidation deed in Indonesian language
- Approval or receipt of notification to the MLHR
- BKPM approval of the transfer of shares acquiring the PMA
- *Ex post* announcement of the acquisition, merger, or consolidation in at least one newspaper having nationwide circulation
- Updated list of shareholders showing the result of acquisition, consolidation, or merger
- Share certificates showing the result of the acquisition, consolidation, or merger
- Updated company registration number (*Tanda Daftar Perseroan:* TDP)

The main agreements or approvals to retain are as follows:

- Shareholder's agreement as a resolution of the shareholders' meeting
- Settlement or agreement with labor union (if applicable)

- BKPM approval (in case of a PMA)
- OJK's approval (in the case of financial companies)
- Creditor's approval
- MLHR's approval or receipt of notification

3.   Types of takeover

It is certainly complex to proceed with any transaction, contract, or supplementary and auxiliary work given the need to understand Indonesian import and export regulations, competition law, and transfer tax rules as well as dealing with governmental agencies. Nonetheless, other than those issues, Indonesian takeover regulations are comparatively simple in the absence of the stipulation of a variety of types of takeover used in modern company law in a variety of foreign jurisdictions.

The United States leads the fashion of law and cases regarding takeovers and has developed a variety of types, tactics, and techniques such as a short-form merger,[35] the 20 percent rule,[36] triangular mergers, reverse triangular mergers, squeeze-out mergers, reverse asset sales, and more. Indonesia has not codified these types of takeovers, nor has it enacted the regulations anticipated in the 2007 Company Act.[37]

Thus, drafting a contract is particularly important, as making an agreement is the only way to protect the party's interest when using a type of takeover not stated in law. This is particularly so given when, as explained earlier, the laws of Indonesia are required as a governing law in many cases, even if using common law jurisdiction is a trend.

Like codified law, legal practice also does not widely use the variety of types of takeovers seen elsewhere. In theory, not only cash but also bonds, securities, services, labor, and many other types of assets should be allowed as consideration, since the definition in Article 1 and Articles 122–137 in the 2007 Company Act do not limit the type of consideration in stock purchases. However, due to appraisal matters in practice, the value of labor or other services is difficult to measure, and are not allowed as a consideration for stock subscription. Cash accounts for the most sizable stock takeovers.[38]

While the most popularly used takeover methods in the United States are mergers or public offers, the most commonly used type in Indonesia is a

---

35 Section 253 of the Del. Gen. Corp. L.; Section 11.04 ABA Rev. Model Bus. Corp. Act (1999 rev.).
36 Section 251(f) Del. Gen. Corp. L.
37 While Article 134 reads "Implementing provision regarding the Merger, Consolidation or Acquisition of the Company shall be further regulated with a Government Regulation," it has not implemented the provision since enactment of the 2007 Company Act.
38 The 10 largest-size takeover cases from June 2012 to June 2013 were all cash for stock. Baker & McKenzie, *Passport to Indonesia-Inbound Investment Trends and Tips*, 2013.

majority shareholder's direct sale of controlling shares to a specific person off the market. An outright hostile takeover without the target company's consent is extremely rare in the Indonesian market.[39]

Given these tendencies, therefore, this section aims to explain the basic take-over types and their related regulations.

3.1. Transfer of business by asset acquisition: cash for assets with the selling company dissolving

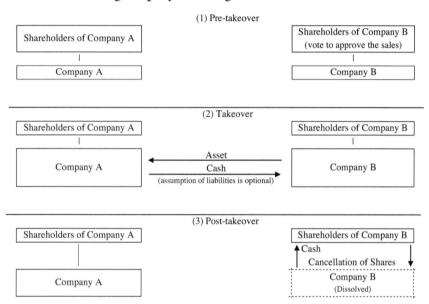

Figure 8.1 Transfer of business by asset acquisition: cash for assets with the selling company dissolving

3.1.1. Introduction

The 2007 Company Act does not have a separate provision regarding business transfer, conveyance of substantially all assets, or sales of material assets. It merely regulates a transaction of providing a security value of which is more than 50 percent of a company's assets as a condition of borrowing money.

Thus, for closely held companies, the main differences between a takeover by stock acquisition and takeover by acquisition of material or substantially all assets are as presented in Table 8.1.

---

39 "In practice, there have been no instances of hostile takeovers in the Indonesian market." Yozua Makes, Indonesia, *The International Capital Markets Review*, 3rd ed., Law Business Research, 2013, ch. 13, p. 163.

Table 8.1 Comparison of the main differences between takeover by stock acquisition and takeover by acquisition of material or substantially all assets

	Merger, consolidation, and acquisition	*Acquisition of assets*
Nature	A scheme governed and regulated by the 2007 Company Act and other relevant regulations	Private contract
Effect	Automatic transfer of all rights and obligations and blanket coverage of target company's comprehensive assets	Individual and separate disposal of each asset (automatic exclusion of assets not written in the agreement)
Dissolution and employment	Target company dissolved, and its employees absorbed (in case of merger).	No dissolution or transfer of employee
Protection of creditor	Mandatory	Optional
Party	Limited to company	Not limited to company
Seller	The seller becomes a shareholder of a surviving company (optional).	The seller does not become a shareholder

3.1.2.   *Formalities triumph over substance: an asset sale is just an asset sale, whether of the material asset or substantially all assets*

One advantage of asset acquisition over merger or consolidation is that the laws and regulations concerning merger and acquisitions do not govern the transaction. For example, the asset purchaser does not need to assume any liability or obligation of the target company. Also, any employment relationships are not automatically transferred to the surviving company.[40] Rather, the terms of fresh employment with the buyer, including whether the purchaser shall be treated as the successor employer, entirely depend upon any agreement between the employee and purchaser. Otherwise, the obligation to pay wages is not automatically assumed. Therefore, the asset seller should know that responsibility for a mandatory severance package still remains with the seller, unless otherwise agreed with the purchaser. There is no exception for transactions between affiliate or group companies.[41]

---

40 This is contrary to many foreign countries. For example, in South Korea, although a mere transfer of all assets with all employees dismissed is not legally regarded as a transfer of business (Supreme Court 1991.8.9 91Da15225), the dissolved company's previous obligation to pay retirement fees to its dismissed employees is automatically transferred to the purchaser of substantially all assets (Supreme Court 2005.2.25. 2004Da34790).

41 For detailed employment issues on a transfer of business by sale of assets, see data from law firm SSEK. At http://blog.ssek.com/wp-content/uploads/2013/01/02-ssek_client-note-Employment-Issues-on-a-Transfer-of-Business-2012-AsiaIndonesia_RDE-RL.pdf.

3.1.3. Cautions

There are some factors which substantially discourage a purchaser from proceeding with a takeover via asset sales than stock sales.

First, a purchaser should thoroughly list every asset, without omission.[42] The seller should also decide on the transfer of every single legal or contractual right and obligation one by one, checking the formalities applicable to the type of each asset.

Second, the purchaser should obtain every relevant license and permit for the business. Hence, even if a purchaser buys a certain production machine at a low price, he should retain the seller's licenses to import a material, and to produce, sell, or export the product. Since ceasing operations until all licenses are obtained is not only unprofitable, but also likely to be harmful to the machine itself from a maintenance perspective, an asset purchaser often operates key machinery without licenses in the seller's name.

Third, when transferring the products at book value, tax benefits in M&A are not applicable.

Fourth, asset sales in Indonesia generally require far too much time and stricter procedural formalities than share transfer sales require. The formalities are more prescriptive and stricter depending on the subject matter, such as real property or intellectual property transfers. It is therefore necessary to include a provision in the contract for the relevant formalities. Due to these formalities and procedures dealing with public officers, conducting an asset purchase in Indonesia takes considerable time to conclude the transaction.

Despite these disadvantages, an asset purchase is sometimes used to transfer business ownership. For example, a foreign company may hope to transfer its entire business to Indonesia due to regulative difficulties in its home country, or for another business purpose aiming at the Indonesian market. It is common for these investors to seek a native partner to create a joint venture company.

3.1.4. Procedures

In the event that the seller is a domestic party selling 50 percent or more net value, it should obtain a shareholders' resolution according to Article 102 of the 2007 Company Act. Simply, even if the property to be sold is a material asset such as an operating system, or a key asset such as a very core technology, brand, or other type of intellectual property, a seller does not need to obtain shareholders' approval insofar as the value of such an asset does not exceed

---

42 Since it is extremely difficult to specify all the subject matters (such as documents, erasers, paperclips, etc.) without any omission or deviance, a contract is often drafted by writing "all the items located in the address" or "all the items stated in certain accounts in the most recent financial statement." Indonesian lawyers interviewed for this book explain that this expression generally does not matter in the event that an executor later executes a court's judgment.

50 percent of the company's net value, and its articles of association also do not specify otherwise. Furthermore, even if the value of sold assets exceeds 50 percent of the company's net assets, the sale becomes effective inasmuch as the assets are sold to a *bona fide* purchaser who did not know the company's failed to obtain shareholders' approval.

For public companies, any of the following transactions with a transferred value of more than 20 percent of the company's capital – either in one transaction, or a series of transactions with the same purpose or activity – are deemed material according to OJK Regulation IX.E.2.[43]

- Acquisition of certain enterprises, projects, and/or business activity
- Purchase, sale, transfer, exchange of asset, or business segments
- Lease of assets
- Borrowing of funds
- Providing an asset as a security
- Providing a corporate guaranty

A company that undertakes any of these material transactions must disclose this information to the public through a daily newspaper and submit supporting documents to OJK in a timely manner. If the transaction is valued at more than 50 percent of its equity, the company must also obtain the approval of a shareholders' meeting at which at least three-fourths of total voting shares is represented, and more than three-fourths of votes cast approve of the transaction. Public companies are required to ensure they follow all exemptions and appropriate timeframes.

3.2. *Transfer of business by asset acquisition: stock for assets with the selling company dissolving*

While this stock-for-assets acquisition is virtually a de facto merger,[44] it is still nothing but asset acquisition, and thus cannot be maintained as a legal merger or consolidation.[45] Therefore, M&A regulations are not applicable to this transaction, including the automatic assumption of rights and obligations, or any transfer of employment relationship. Therefore, acquiring another's business by

---

43 Rule No. IX.E.2 on Material Transaction and Change of Main Business as an attachment to the Decree of BAPEPAM LK No. Kep-614/BL/2011.
44 A so-called forward triangular merger is another type of asset purchase in the United States, which allows Company A to establish a subsidiary company, capitalize it with its own shares, and give these shares to Company B shareholders in consideration of the B assets. However, this forward triangular merger is not allowed in Indonesia due to Article 36 Paragraph 1 against cross-stockholding between a parent and subsidiary company.
45 Even in the United States, only minor states, including Delaware, apply merger-related regulations *mutatis mutandis* to the *de facto* merger. See *Drug, Inc. v. Hunt*, 35 Del. 339, 168 A/87.

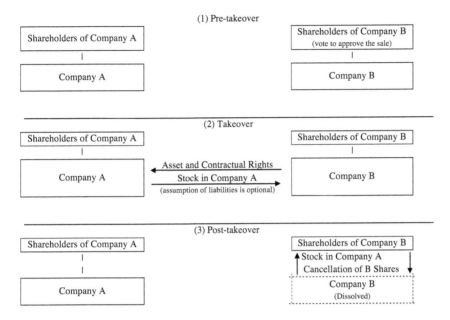

Figure 8.2 Transfer of business by asset acquisition: stock for assets with the selling company dissolving II

asset acquisition needs to take into account generally the same factors as explained in the previous cash-for-asset transaction.

As mentioned earlier, a public company should separately follow a separate OJK Rule No. IX.E.2 (Kep-614/BL/2011) as a material transaction.

If one of the Company B shareholders is a foreign entity, Company A should convert to a PMA. Then, it will end up having more burden in the process, such as observing the Negative Investment List, and calculating and comparing tax amounts depending on various sale scenarios, in addition to the already expensive procedures in asset acquisition. Thus, asset acquisition has comparatively little merit.

If a minority shareholder in Company A opposing this transaction type alleges indemnification of damages after the transaction is completed, his burden of proof regarding the exact loss due to the transaction is considerably heavy.

3.3. Cash for stock

This cash-for-stock transaction is the most widely used method in Indonesia, because it is simple and clear. After the share acquisition, Company A becomes the parent company, and owns the shares in Company B, which becomes a subsidiary. Irrespective of whether the board of directors of Company B approves or not, its shareholders can sell their shares.

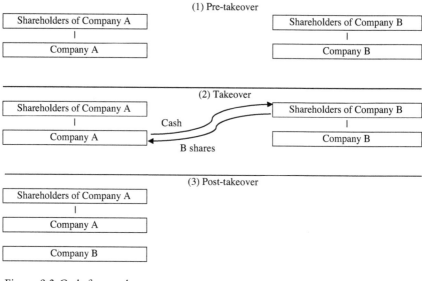

Figure 8.3 Cash for stock

3.4. Stock swap

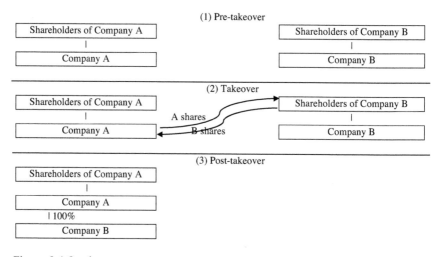

Figure 8.4 Stock swap

Company B shareholders can sell the shares, as whether Company B's board of directors approves or not is irrelevant. No matter how small Company B may be, Company A should undertake all the required procedures, including investing the considerable time and cost involved, as Indonesia does not recognize a short-form merger.

Also, to swap the shares, the fair value of Company B must be appraised and reasonably matched to the value of A shares. This process requires substantial time and cost.

4. Separation of a company

4.1. Definition

Separation means a legal action taken by a company to separate its businesses, which causes all assets and liabilities of the company to be legally transferred to two or more companies, or part of the assets and liabilities of the company to be legally transferred to one or more companies (Article 1 Paragraph 12).

Indonesia names the former (viz. complete separation with extinction of previous company) as "pure separation" (*pemisahan murni*) and the latter (viz. quasi-complete separation without extinction) as "impure separation" (*pemisahan tidak murni*) (Article 135).

4.2. Other types of separation

The classification at Article 153 is just one way to define types of separation, while there are a variety of types recognized and used in practice in Indonesia and other countries. Because the 2007 Company Act does not have a provision to explicitly limit or restrict other types of separation, and the government regulations that Article 136 anticipated have not been promulgated,[46] there

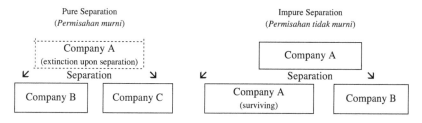

Types, depending on whether the company survives

Figure 8.5 Types of company separation depending on whether the company survives

---

46 Although Government Regulation No. 27 of 1998 regarding Mergers, Consolidations and Acquisitions of Limited Liability Companies still exists, it has no particular merits for use in modern practice. The promulgation of new regulation seems to be continuously delayed. See the MLHR's website: www.djpp.kemenkumham.go.id/component/content/article/63-rancangan-peraturan-pemerintah/2899-rancangan-peraturan-pemerintah-tentang-peng-gabungan-peleburan-pengambilalihan-dan-pemisahan-pers.html.

seems no reason to restrict the following classifications, so far as they do not harm creditors of the company.

4.2.1.   *Spin-off and split-off*

The English terms spin-off and split-off, as commonly spoken by Indonesian lawyers, have different meanings in the SEC's definition and in common usage. Technically speaking, a *spin-off* refers to a type of corporate separation where a parent company distributes shares of a subsidiary that is being spun-off to its existing shareholders on a *pro rata* basis in the form of a special dividend. As a result, the subsidiary becomes a separate and independent company, and the shareholders of the parent company benefit by now holding shares of two separate companies after the spin-off. A *split-off* means a type of separation where shareholders in the parent company can choose either an option to continue holding shares of the subsidiary, or an option to exchange all or some shares held in the parent company for new shares in the subsidiary. Consequently, the distribution of the subsidiary shares is not *pro rata* as is the case with a spin-off.

4.2.2.   *Classification depends on whether shareholders split*

A company can continuously retain shareholders by simply establishing a new company with its preexisting assets (see the left-hand table on separation with shareholders unchanged). By contributing some assets for the establishment of the new subsidiary and allocating the entire shares in the new company to some of its shareholders, a company may help some of its shareholders exit (see the right-hand table on separation with shareholders divided).

4.2.3.   *Classification depends on the combined transaction*

Depending on the combined transaction, separation may be classified into (i) separation for new establishment, (ii) separation by way of acquisition, and

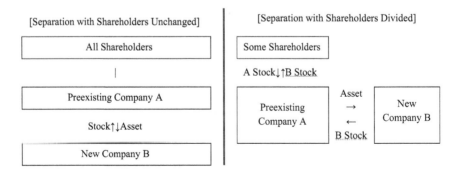

Figure 8.6 Types of company separation depending on whether shareholders split

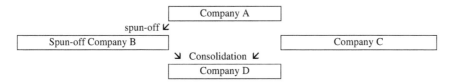

Figure 8.7 An example of separation by way of consolidation

(iii) separation by way of consolidation. If no other transaction is combined, the separation will create a new company. Should the separated company segment be integrated directly to another existing company, such a separation is deemed to be part of a merger scheme (viz. separation by way of acquisition). Provided that a spun-off division is consolidated with another division spun-off from another entity, such a separation is then deemed as a part of consolidation (viz. separation by way of consolidation).

4.2.4. De facto *separation*

There is an issue whether the rules and regulations regarding separation can be applied *mutatis mutandis* in the event that a company uses a roundabout or indirect approach for the same economic effect. For example, a preexisting company may gratuitously transfer part of its business to a newly established company. In the absence of an explicit ruling, it is thought to be hard to apply the separation regulations to these transactions in Indonesia.

4.3. *Purpose*

Corporate separation is used for variable purposes. These include seeking to explore a promising business sector, surviving by cutting off insolvent or bad company divisions, defending control from an external takeover attempt, securing funds for business expansion, resolving an internal dispute, creating a joint venture company with a third party, expansion through consolidation of two split-off divisions, and so on.

4.4. *Procedures*

4.4.1. *Contract draft*

A separation plan generally defines the transferred asset as, for example, all assets, rights, and liabilities, including those that fall within the scope of a certain division according to a separate list or financial statement. If it is unclear to which division a certain asset belongs, the draft must be interpreted and amended considering the totality of circumstances with filed registrations, internal reports, shareholders' resolutions, the parties' intent, etc.

Also, the draft must reflect the normal fluctuation of the spun-off division's assets from the date of separation plan – or the date of shareholders' resolution – to the closing date of separation.

Once a separation plan is approved by the meeting of shareholders, it requires another meeting to approve any change to the plan, whether trivial or not. Otherwise, any change can constitute a reason to invalidate separation.

4.4.2.   File to OJK

Although there is no explicit regulation concerning separation through consolidation between a listed company and a closely held company, OJK indicates that filing is required for such a transaction.

If a separation is exercised by a way of an IPO, it requires special approval from the Director General of Tax, and the IPO registration process must be finalized with OJK within a year, under the assumption that such a special approval will be obtained. If the company faces any uncontrollable circumstance, it may apply to extend the period.

4.4.3.   Public disclosure

A company can satisfy advance disclosure requirements by placing a notice at least 30 days prior of the terms of the separation plan through a newspaper (Article 127 Paragraph 2). It does not need to keep the notice at headquarters or directly contact creditors, as often required in foreign countries.

4.4.4.   Protection of creditors

Nonetheless, the 2007 Company Act in Indonesia contains public announcement procedures for protection of creditors:

- The board of directors should make a public announcement about the separation plan in at least one newspaper and circulate the written announcement to employees (Article 127 Paragraphs 2 and 3).
- A creditor can submit an objection to the company within 14 days from the public announcement, otherwise creditors are deemed to have agreed to the separation plan. If any objecting creditor and the board of directors fail to settle the issue, the objection should be declared to a meeting of shareholders to seek settlement (Article 127 Paragraph 4 to 6).

There are several problems in these provisions.

First, this procedure alone is significantly insufficient to protect a company's creditors. Because a company alienates a part of its assets that could have been used for pay off the company's creditors, the critical issue is how the creditors can be protected. This issue is weighty because (i) after separation, a creditor may retain a receivable only from an unreliable division, while a comparatively strong division becomes free from the liability, (ii) a company may avoid its responsibilities, and (iii) diversification of the business renders risk control impossible.

To resolve this issue, modern company laws in other countries generally stipulate certain creditor safety factors, such as personal delivery of a notice to each individual creditor, mandatory joint and several liabilities between separated companies, providing considerable securities or entrusting considerable assets in a trust company for debts accrued before the due separation date, direct payment of overdue debts to creditors, or other compulsory procedures.

Nevertheless, creditors to an Indonesian company have no such options but must merely rely on a public notification that they may miss noticing. People do not read every type of newspaper on a daily basis (even the employees of newspaper companies). Given that the only legal protection for creditors is to insert a small notice in one newspaper, and provide them only 14 days to object whether the announcement was seen or not, these provisions seem merely a formality rather than a true attempt to inform creditors. Thus, the risk that a company may decide how to transfer liability without agreement from all or some creditors is very high. This is particularly so, given that each creditor has contrary interests each other (given that all want to be at the head of the payment list), and the law does not stipulate how to resolve this matter.

Second, Article 127 Paragraph 7 merely stipulates that "to the extent that the settlement . . . has not been obtained, the . . . separation cannot be performed." In the absence of a milestone court ruling, it is unclear whether a separation already performed without the public announcement is either void, voidable, or remains effective. Other provisions in the 2007 Company Act makes this clear. For example, Article 148 Paragraph 1 states: "In the event the notification to creditor and the MLHR as stated in Article 147 is not implemented, the company's dissolution shall *not be valid to the third party.*"

Let us suppose that a company has already performed a "pure separation" (viz. extinction of the previous company after separation) without a public announcement, the two separate companies have then conducted independent business respectively for 2 years, and a creditor of the previous company finally realized the lack of a public announcement in the separation process 24 months ago.

- If the separation is per se void due to Article 127 Paragraph 7, the existence of the two separated entities is naturally void, and therefore all the independent business, procedures, and contracts formed under the name of the new companies during the 2-year period are void. This may result in a worse economic situation if one of the separate companies has yielded better economic returns thanks to the separation, and the company which became stronger also keeps the payables to the creditor in the financial statements.
- The separation may be cancelable or voidable either by the court's interpretation of Article 127 Paragraph 7, or the creditor's right to revocation of an illegitimate process against himself pursuant to the Indonesian Civil

Act. In this case, the creditor is entitled to cancel the separation at his sole election and, if he does elect to cancel, the court should order restitution for restoration. Therefore, in this case the creditor would have greater bargaining power with the involved parties.

- If the separation remains effective despite Article 127 Paragraph 7, the creditor should seek simultaneous remedy against the previous directors, commissioners, and shareholders in tort. That would be unjust if any individual had insufficient assets to pay off the creditor's receivables to the extinguished company, while the new companies retain the assets which should have been paid the creditor originally.

For self-protection, the creditor objecting to the separation plan within the notice period should request immediate payment in full, or alternatively a security and joint and several liabilities among the separated companies.

4.4.5.   *Approval of separation at the meeting of shareholders*

The resolution to approve a company's separation at the meeting of shareholders requires three-fourths or more holders of total voting-right shares to be present or represented, and approval by at least three-fourths of the total votes cast. If a second meeting is held due to the lack of a quorum, then two-thirds or more holders of total voting-right shares must be present or represented, and the issue approved by at least three-fourths of the total votes cast (Article 89).

While the law remains silent, a company that desires to do away with joint liability would be safer to obtain shareholders' approval of a separation plan and/or separation contract that explicitly states that the separated company exclusively assumes liabilities. Since an Indonesian company does not need to give a separate notice to each creditor, nor is it required to provide the creditors with all the details, the substantive and procedural burdens to separate the entity seems substantially lower in comparison to those for foreign companies.

4.4.6.   *Splits and reverse splits of shares and capital reduction*

In the event that a separated company proceeds to a split or reverse split of shares for capital reduction or any other reason, a certain procedure should be observed.

A company does not need to reduce capital after separation, even though the assets of the existing company decreases, or even perhaps the capital is impaired due to deficits. Thus, if the company does not want to reduce capital despite a decrease in the company's value, it can simply include in the separation plan and/or agreement a clause that it will not reduce capital.

Nevertheless, if a company survives separation, and the value of its net asset is short of capital thereafter, reducing capital may become an issue. Hence, this issue should be detailed in the separation plan and/or agreement in such a case. In the event that the company decides to reduce capital, a simple small-sized spin-off – with shareholders unchanged – should still follow the procedures for protection of creditors pursuant to Articles 27, 44, and 46.

4.4.7. *Appraisal right of a shareholder opposing separation as a way of consolidation or acquisition*

A shareholder opposing a merger or consolidation may exercise an appraisal right (Article 126 Paragraph 2). However, in the case of a spin-off without a change of shareholders, this right will not be recognized.

4.4.8. *Inaugural meeting*

As explained earlier, the 2007 Company Act does not separately regulate a split-off with shareholders changed from separation by way of consolidation or acquisition. In other words, an Indonesian company does not need to follow any specific procedure for the inaugural meeting of the new company after separation as other countries often require.

4.4.9. *Registration of separation*

Articles 29 and 30 on public notice and registration are applied to a closely held company's separation and, thus, it must be registered with the MLHR, and a public notice must be issued. If convertible bonds, or bonds with warrant, are transferred, the registration of these securities should be separately made.

4.4.10. *Licenses and permits*

To assume and continue the business, the separated company should finalize all the required processes for permits and licenses including *Izin Usaha, API umum, API produsen, API Terbatas*, etc. at BKPM or BKPMD. Upon submission of the required forms and evidential documents, the transfer and assumption of these permits and licenses seem not to be difficult as long as the specific items being transferred remain as they were with the original business.

However, if the permit or license is highly specific and exclusive, an advance consultation with authorities would be needed for new issuance due to the nature of such a permit or license.

4.5. *Effect of separation*

4.5.1. *Effect on legal status*

Only a division split from the main corporate body may obtain a separate legal entity status independent from the previous company in the case of "impure separation," while all companies after "pure separation" retain an independent and separate legal entity status separately.[47]

4.5.2.   *Transfer of rights and obligations*

A new company's responsibilities may be limited in proportion to the size of capital pursuant to the separation plan or contract. Unless otherwise regulated by other laws or regulations, the separated company can be also exempted from the previous obligations after following the process outlined in Article 127. Likewise, the assets of a previous company are partially or entirely transferred to the new company.

In the event that joint liabilities are not applied, each spun-off company is liable solely for the assumed amount and matters, and free from other liabilities. Even if the company survives the separation, it can be free from any liability absolutely transferred to the new company.

4.5.3.   *Transfer of assets*

A transfer of assets due to separation is generally based on market price and may be exempt from tax imposition depending on the transaction.

According to the regulation of the Ministry of Finance No.43/PMK.03/2008 (Use of the Value of the Book of the Transfer of Business in the Framework of Company, Mitigation or Business Expansion), business expansion means both "pure separation" and "impure separation." In other words, separation (*pemisahan*) of a company is regarded as expansion (*pemekara*) under tax law, and this regulation is applied to a transfer of assets within divisions of a business.

The technical application of appraisal of fixed assets, real estate acquisition tax, tax basis, taxable object acquisition value (NPOP), and other matters must be studied by professional tax consultants.

4.5.4.   *Allocation of shares*

If the preexisting company has treasury stocks, it can allocate these as capital to the new spun-off company. The new company can then be a subsidiary automatically upon the separation. Depending on the case, the preexisting company may acquire shares in the new company through in-kind contribution or a purchase in the market.

In the event of separation by way of consolidation or merger, the preexisting company may have already retained shares in another constituent company in a consolidation or merger. That is, the preexisting company may have shares in

---

47 "In the case of a bank following Sharia law, banks are still regarded as one entity according to Sharia law and yet many argue in contrary." M. Saiful Ruky, *Menilai Penyertaan Dalam Perseroan*, Gramedia Pustaka Utama, 1999, p. 68.

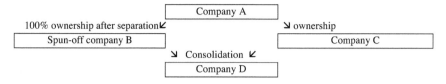

Figure 8.8 Another example of separation by way of consolidation

both its own separated company and another company with which it is consolidating or merging as the following shows.

Then, the newly consolidated Company D can allocate previous shares in Company C to Company A as well, much like in a regular consolidation.

4.5.5. Status of employees[48]

In the event that a company hopes to no longer retain employees, or an employee seeks to leave the company due to the separation, the employment relationship may be terminated pursuant to Article 163 of Employment Act No. 13 Year 2003. Article 156 of the Employment Act covers the details of compensation to the employees.

4.5.6. Annulment of separation

Once 14 days from the public notification pass, a creditor cannot oppose any type of separation including spin-offs, split-offs, and separations via consolidation or merger. Furthermore, as explained earlier, it is unclear whether a violation of procedures in Article 127 Paragraphs 4–7 automatically annuls the already performed separation. Still, there are a number of reasons to seek nullification of separation, such as a wrongful separation plan or agreement, a defective resolution for the approval of separation, grossly unfair substance or procedures, large damages against creditors, etc.

A shareholder, director, commissioner, trustee in a bankruptcy, liquidator, or creditor who has not approved the separation can be a plaintiff in a claim of annulment of separation, and the company will be the defendant. Where it is unclear whether exclusive jurisdiction or not exists under civil procedure law, the plaintiff can file a claim at a regional court having a jurisdiction over the seat of the company.

If the court decides the separation is null and void, relevant procedures such as amendment of the registration of preexisting company, recovery of the

---

48 For details, see this webpage: www.hukumonline.com/klinik/detail/cl3149/status-karyawan-spin-off.

registration of the extinguished company, and dissolution of the new company should be immediately followed. Upon such a court's confirmation or decision to invalidate a company's separation, the constituent parties must bear joint and several liability to the debts, and the assets acquired after separation will be deemed jointly owned by the constituent parties. In a nutshell, although the law is not explicit, the court's decision must bind not only the parties in the litigation, but also all related parties for consistent and coherent consequences.

5. Dissolution and liquidation

5.1. Definition

In the United States, dissolution is generally regarded as the very last stage of liquidation, the process by which a company is brought to an end, and the assets and property of the company are redistributed. However, in Indonesia, the term dissolution (*pembubaran*) means the *first* stage of liquidation, the occurrence of an event stipulated in Article 142 Paragraph 1. Nor does dissolution (*pembubaran*) cause the company to lose its legal entity status, which is maintained until liquidation is completed and a shareholders' meeting or the court accepts the liquidator's submitted report (Article 143 Paragraph 1). That is, dissolution of company merely satisfies one of the conditions for termination of a company's legal entity status.

If a company dissolves, it cannot perform the aim of its existence and thus, naturally, cannot continue business. While a dissolved company may lose the ability to perform business, it still has rights and capacity within the scope of liquidation for stakeholders in and out of the company.

Should the company dissolve due to reasons other than consolidation or merger, the liquidation process begins, and the legal entity status is extinguished upon the completion of the liquidation process. However, if the company is consolidated or amalgamated, the legal entity status is immediately terminated.

5.2. Reasons of dissolution

The stipulated reasons for dissolution of company are as follows (Article 142):

- A resolution of shareholders' meeting
- Termination of the company's existence period as stipulated in the articles of association
- A court order
- A revoked bankruptcy statement based on a binding order of the commercial court, where the assets of the bankrupt company are insufficient to pay the bankruptcy cost
- The condition that the bankrupt assets of the company has been declared in the condition of insolvency as regulated by the law regarding bankruptcy and the suspension of debt payment

- The revocation of the company's business permit, so that the company is obliged to conduct liquidation in accordance with prevailing regulations

Dissolution may be sought by a resolution of shareholders' meeting, the board of directors, board of commissioners, or shareholders holding 10 percent or more of total voting shares. To dissolve a company at a shareholders' meeting, the presence or representation of at least three-fourths of the total voting-right shares, and approval of at least three-fourths of the total shares with voting rights is required (Article 89). In the event that a shareholders' meeting fails to reach a quorum, a second shareholders' meeting must be held with the presence or representation of at least two-thirds of total voting-right shares and should obtain the approval of at least three-fourths of the total shares with voting rights. In sum, 75 percent of the total voting-right shares is needed. Again, according to Articles 142 and 143, the time of dissolution of a company is the date of resolution at shareholders' meeting, not the time of extinguishment of legal entity status.

In a case of dissolution due to termination of company's existence period as stipulated in the articles of association, the dissolution becomes effective upon the lapse of the existence period. If the articles of association do not state the existence period, but instead a condition subsequent to the company's existence, or a condition precedent to dissolution, occurrence of such a condition will effectuate dissolution.

A court order under Article 142 means a court's dissolution order sought by any of the following parties (Article 146 Paragraph 1):

- Prosecutor's office, because the company has violated the public interest, or the company has committed a violation of regulations
- Relevant party, because the deed of establishment is found to be defective
- Shareholders, board of directors, or the board of commissioners, because it is no longer possible to run the company

Dissolution due to a defective deed of establishment is thought to be a court's affirmation of invalidity of establishment, or an order to cancel the establishment. Theoretically, if the defect is so material that it is difficult to regard the company as established in the first place, and such establishment is decided not as material enough to regard it as null and void, but material enough to cancel establishment, the establishment should be cancelled and relevant parties must be restored. However, current Indonesian practice does not differentiate between them.

Therefore, the issue from a plaintiff's perspective is the company's activity until the court's final decision of dissolution. Thus, the plaintiff must seek a provisional disposition to prohibit the company's activity and an order to freeze the company's bank account (*conservatoir beslag*).

In a situation where a binding order of the commercial court revoking bankruptcy brings about dissolution and the bankrupt assets of the company are insufficient to pay the bankruptcy costs, the costs and expenses in bankruptcy are found to be so burdensome after obtaining the commercial court's bankruptcy order that a company would rather undergo a general dissolution and liquidation process than go through bankruptcy. Then, the commercial court will dismiss the curator (Article 142 Paragraph 4). Alternatively, should the value of a company's assets outweigh the amount of obligation, the liquidator should submit a request for the company's bankruptcy (Article 129 Paragraph 2)

5.3.   Effect of dissolution

Once a company dissolves through any of the events mentioned above, the liquidation process should begin (Article 142 Paragraph 2 Item a), where the company automatically becomes incapable of conducting any legal act except where it is required to settle all business issues for the purposes of liquidation (Article 142 Paragraph 2 Item b). As of dissolution, any letter sent externally by the company should include a title "in liquidation" (*dalam likuidasi*) (Article 143 Paragraph 2).

Within 30 days of dissolution, the liquidator should make a public announcement through a newspaper and the state gazette and notify the MLHR for deregistration in the company registry. The public notification must include the company's dissolution and its legal basis, the liquidator's name and address, procedures to submit any claim, and the period in which claims can be submitted.

Again, the company does not need to contact its creditors individually and separately. However, even if a creditor did not claim his receivables at the time of liquidation and thus remaining assets were distributed to shareholders, creditors can still make a claim to the court within 2 years for a refund or compensation from shareholders.

Therefore, to avoid this risk, shareholders should not feel safe when only a public notification is made. A liquidator should settle with not only regular creditors, but also all holders of any conditional debts, pending debts, unfixed debts, or debts with undetermined duration. This is particularly so given that there is no provision at all regarding these debts in the 2007 Company Act or any rule, for example, that an amount appraised by a person appointed by the court should be repaid.

5.4.   Liquidation

5.4.1.   Liquidator

A liquidator (*likuidator*) is the officer appointed to wind up or liquidate a company, and with responsibility for collecting all company assets and settling all claims against the company before putting ending the legal status of the company.

In the event that dissolution occurs due to a resolution of shareholders' meeting, lapse of company duration as set forth in the articles of association, or by the revocation of bankruptcy based on the commercial court's order, and the shareholders' meeting fails to appoint a liquidator, the board of directors should act as liquidator (Article 142 Paragraph 3). The provisions about the board of directors are applied *mutatis mutandis* to appointment, suspension, dismissal, authority, duty, responsibility, and supervision of a liquidator, other than as stipulated under Chapter X (Article 142 Paragraph 6).

Therefore, the appointment and dismissal of a liquidator is to be registered similarly to the appointment and dismissal of a director.

If a company's existence period lapses, or one of the stipulated reasons of dissolution in the articles of association occurs, a shareholders' meeting should determine the appointment of liquidator within 30 days (Article 145 Paragraph 2). Since the term of liquidator is not limited, it is deemed as continuing up to the ultimate closure through liquidation, unless the court views that the liquidator's incapacity prevents him from reasonably performing his obligation even after a hearing (Article 151).

As there is no particular provision regarding a representative director, there is no need to appoint a representative liquidator of the board of liquidators. Since there is no particular restriction, a company can appoint a number of liquidators or co-representative liquidators.

A liquidator has a duty of care and fiduciary duty in the scope of liquidation. The responsibility to the court stipulated in Article 152 Paragraphs 1 and 2 is limited to the submission of an accountability report on the liquidation they carry out (Elucidation of Article 152).

5.4.2. Curator

A curator is a person with responsibility for implementing the company's liquidation (Article 152 Paragraph 2) to the supervisory judge, and informing the MLHR and making a public announcement of the final result of liquidation in a newspaper after the shareholders' meeting discharges the liquidator, or the court receives the appointed liquidator's report (Article 152 Paragraph 4).

A curator is particularly needed when the company is dissolved due to insolvency in accordance to Insolvency and Suspension of Debt Payment Act. According to the MLHR Regulation No. 18 of 2013 (Requirement and Registration Mechanism of Curator and Administrator), one of the requirements of becoming a curator is to be a lawyer, public accountant, or have a bachelor's degree in economics or law, in the latter case must also have at least 3 years' work experience at a law firm.

5.4.3. Procedures

A liquidator should clear up business pending at the time of dismissal, collect receivables and pay debts, realize properties, and distribute all remaining assets.

The collection of receivables includes not only receiving repayments, but also receiving payment in substitutes, selling or transferring receivables, and setting aside and settling pending executory contracts.

For this purpose, a liquidator must notify all creditors within 30 days that the company has been dissolved by way of announcement in newspaper and the state gazette. This public notification should include the company's dissolution and its legal basis, the liquidator's name and address, procedures to submit a claim, and the period in which claims can be submitted the claim. As mentioned earlier, it is not mandatory to contact each creditor, but this is recommended because of the possibility that any creditor may seeks a return of distribution within the subsequent 2 years.

Also, a liquidator should notify the MLHR with evidence of the legal basis of the company's dissolution, and a copy of the public newspaper announcement.

Then, any opposing creditor should submit a written objection within 60 days of the public announcement. If a liquidator ignores or rejects the objection, the creditor is able to submit a claim to the district court within 60 days of the rejection date.

As mentioned earlier, the 2007 Company Act should have been armed with more specific provisions. There is no specific provision in the Act regarding how to collect or settle conditional rights and obligations, unfixed amounts of debt, executory contracts, unscheduled payments, or immature receivables. Because of this, liquidation may substantially drag on for some time to wait for a pending payment due date, or face difficulty settling each receivable and payable. For example, a dissolved company should be entitled to prepayment of debt before the due date, and deduction of interest thereby, or an acceleration of unscheduled payments. Also, the 2007 Company Act should have provisions that conditional rights and obligations, and unfixed amounts of payment, are to be determined by an independent appraiser appointed by the court.

Article 150 Paragraphs 2–5 are noteworthy. If a creditor does not claim in liquidation process but later claims within 2 years of the public dissolution announcement, the court should instruct the liquidator to recollect the assets divided to the shareholders. Then, the shareholders should return the assets in proportion to the amount received over the amount receivable. Therefore, it is better for the liquidator to contact each individual creditor to avoid such a long-term risk.

Lastly, the curator and liquidator must submit a liquidation report to the court. Then, within 30 days of the liquidation report submitted to the court, they must obtain an acquittal and discharge of the liquidator from a shareholders' meeting, notify the MLHR of the result of the liquidation process, and make a public announcement through a newspaper having national circulation (Article 152). Subsequently, the MLHR registers the termination of the company's legal entity status, deletes the company's name in the company registry, and announces this through the state gazette.

5.5.   *Other issues*

5.5.1.   *Tax*

If a company has already decided to withdraw from business, it is usually cannot afford to repay its debts. To exempt the debt, however, the exempted liability is viewed as profit, and thus the tax authority may impose tax over the exempt liability. If a shareholder is also a creditor, it may swap the debt to equity. In any case, it is better to discuss this issue with a tax consultant.

5.5.2.   *Labor*

Generally, all employees are regarded as superior creditors. Still, it is better to consult with an expert because the calculation of outstanding bonus or long-service allowance is different depending on each case, such as whether dissolution is sought for improvement of efficiency, or a case of dissolution due to continuous financial losses over 2 years (Article 164 of No. 13 Year 2003 Labor Act).

Before giving notice of termination, the term of notice and calculation of payment must be prepared. If it is hard to observe the notice period or pay the amount calculated, the company should check whether it can resolve this issue through a documented settlement with employees.

5.5.3.   *Administration*

Upon dissolution, all relevant business licenses and permits must be returned to the authorities, a report on the final account of liquidation must be submitted to tax office, the taxpayer registration must be cancelled at the tax authority, and confirmation should be obtained after tax office due diligence.

On the one hand, it is natural for a dissolved company to be unable to afford to cope with each ineffective administration one by one. On the other hand, nevertheless, it is recommended to properly finalize the liquidation with each administration if any shareholders or directors continuously reside in Indonesia, or the parent company operates business in or out of Indonesia. One of the reasons for this recommendation is the parent company's consolidated financial statement. Modern company laws in most countries in the twenty-first century do not recognize simply firing its employees and closing its bank account and office as a legal dissolution. Even if the company has fully protected its creditors while irretrievably closing the business, its legal entity status still exists, and will go on until the legal liquidation procedures have been completed. If the company survives, its parent company's obligation to complete consolidated financial statements also remains, even if the financial data of the subsidiary company have been scattered.

9   Capital Investment Act

The 2007 Capital Investment Act (*UU No.25 Tahun 2007 tentang Penanaman Modal*) is a law unifying both the PMA Act (*UU No.1, 1967 tentang Penanaman Modal Asing*) and the PMDN Act (*UU No.6, 1968 tentang Penanaman Modal Dalam Negeri*). The combined portion of the former regulates inbound investment for business in the territory of Indonesia by a foreign investor, while the portion of the latter governs an investment in the territory of Indonesia by an Indonesian citizen, business entity, or government.

A dominant part of the face of the 2007 Company Act is covered by many abstract principles or general statements that the specific act does not necessarily stipulate. For example, it merely states that the government shall ensure business certainty and security, administer the affairs, delegate this administration to a district governor or assign it to the district government, accord equitable treatment to all investors of any countries, guide and enhance micro, small, and medium enterprises, increase competitiveness, provide information, coordinate investment policies among the governmental agencies, and so on.

This chapter analyzes the principles of investment that this 2007 Capital Investment Act brings forth and subsequently explains the material practical issues.

1.   Investment principles

Article 3 of the 2007 Capital Investment Act stipulates the principles of the investment activity for business in Indonesia.

1.1.   *Legal certainty*

According to elucidation of Article 3 Section 1 Subsection a, the principle of legal certainty means "a principle that the rule-of-law state lays down law and provisions of laws and regulations as the foundation of any investment policy and measure."

From an international perspective, this principle is not an exclusive matter of the Investment Act, but a general principle applied to any law to be made, interpreted, and applied. Particularly in civil law tradition, legal certainty is defined in terms of the maximum predictability of official behavior. In other words, laws must be certain and precise enough so that their implications are foreseeable, because those who act in good faith on the basis of law as it is, or seems to be, should not be frustrated in their expectations. For the same purpose, laws must be made public, and any retroactivity of laws and decisions must be limited under this principle. The elucidation of this article seems fitting, as this is a generally accepted principle around the world.

Nonetheless, the Indonesian Court frequently applies this principle against a bureaucratic abuse of power beyond this meaning. That is, even if the face of law made in public is sufficiently certain and clear, the Court frequently determines a violation of legal certainty where an executive branch wrongfully takes an administrative measure or does not provide an administrative support arbitrarily.[1]

Supreme Court's decision to annul a local administration chief's declaration due to violation of principle of legal certainty. (No.347K/ TUN/2013)

Summary

The plaintiff in this case was PT. Fairco Agro Mandiri ("FAM"), who was operating a palm oil planation pursuant to an investment license (*Izin Prinsip*) and was rejected by a local administration chief when applying for an extension of location permit (*izin lokasi*) to continue the business. It claimed the administrative declaration of rejection constituted a violation of the principle of legal certainty, as the plaintiff had already obtained other necessary licenses and permits to enjoy the palm oil plantation business. The Court decided that such a declaration of rejection violated the principle of legal certainty and overturned the original judgment.

Details

FAM (i) obtained a location permit for the use of a 14,830 hectare farm from a regional administrative chief (*Bupati*) at Kutai Timur in 2005, (ii) obtained a positive declaration of *Bupati* concerning an extension of the location permit to 13,903 hectares of palm oil farm in June 2007, (iii) obtained a plantation business license (*izin usaha perkebunan*) in 2007, (iv) retained a mandatory environment report AMDAL and related permit from Bupati (v) built up a palm oil mill after obtaining a construction license called an IMB, (vi) satisfied all other relevant requirements including HGU, plasma plantation, and reports for palm oil business at the specific region.

---

1 "Court's verdicts issued by the judge ideally contain aspects of legal certainty. . . . A judge does not have to stick on one principle whenever examining and deciding a case . . . the judge is facing a deadlock whenever written stipulations cannot answer. . . . The judge in his argument and legal consideration must be able to accommodate any stipulations." Fence M. Wantu, Mewujudkan Kepastian Hukum, Keadilan dan Kemanfaatan Dalam Putusan Hakim di Peradilan Perdata, 2011, Fahultaks Hukum Universitas Gadjah Mada.

FAM duly applied for an extension of location permit in 2011 before it would expire. Furthermore, a team of environmental experts conducted a land survey and issued a mandatory report in 2012. Nevertheless, *Bupati* issued a declaration rejecting the applied extension of license permit, basing this on "FAM has not begun plantation development and there is no support from regional society."

FAM refuted this, stating the reason it had not begun plantation development was simply because a license called IPL has not been issued by the administration.

FAM further maintained that it already had three regional permits, and that the regional society did not disagree, there was no law or regulation requiring such mandatory written support from regional society, nor did the above permits and reports mention such a problem.

The Supreme Court ruled that the Bupati's declaration of rejection violated the principle of legal certainty, found at Article 3 Section 1 Subsection a of the 2007 Capital Investment Act. The Supreme Court quashed the judgment of the Appeal Court, which affirmed the declaration as valid and ruled issuance of the applied permit extension to FAM.

Study

Through the long history of legal theories and studies, this principle has developed many branches. In a broad sense in theory, thus, legal certainty may mean that an administrative officer should not misuse power. For example, the general principle in European Union law holds that a lawful power must not be exercised for any other purpose than that for which it was conferred. In *Giuffrida v Commission*,[2] the European Court of Justice held that a European Union institution has misused its powers, and therefore violated the general principle of legal certainty.

Similarly, under the principle of legal certainty, an executive and judicial branch must not change or cancel its decision *ad libitum*. If administration or court can randomly change its measures or decisions, the legal implications of an individual's specific act will be rendered unforeseeable and uncertain.

Unless a universally acceptable ruling is required, as in the European Court of Justice or Constitutional Court, nonetheless, the court is required to refrain from relying on this sort of general principle. Even the European Court of Justice should accept this kind of plea only in exceptional circumstances. *Giuffrida v Commission* is regarded as a very rare example of the Court annulling a decision on this ground.[3]

2 Case 105/75 *Giuffrida v Commission* [1976] ECR 1395.
3 Damian Chalmers, *European Union Law: Text and Materials*, Cambridge, 2006, p. 456.

One reason is that reliance on the general principle rather than specific laws and regulations confers too much power to the judge. This kind of abstract principle is called the "royal provision" (*königlicher paragraph*) in the civil law system, meaning that such a provision can govern over so wide a range of cases that it makes the clause itself and the judge *royal*. That is, applying the royal provision rather than specific and detailed regulations resultantly impairs the principle of legal certainty, because such a provision is polysemic, ambiguous, uncertain, indeterminable, and abstract.

In this case, if *Bupati* has evidentially no valid reason to reject the applicant's administrative request, the unfair rejection could be redressed under specific laws and regulations. For example, Regulation of Ministry of Agrarian and Special Affairs Concerning Location Permit explicitly stipulates the eligibility of a location permit at Article 4 Paragraph 1, and also sets forth that the grant of location permit should be based on consideration of stipulated factors at Article 9 Paragraph 1. Furthermore, Law No. 13 Year 2006 (Guidelines on Regional Financial Management, superseded by Law No. 23 Year 2014 of Regional Government) charges *Bupati* with a duty to strictly follow laws and regulations in exercising his authority. Thus, in this case, the affirmation of FAM's rights could have been easily made with these specific regulations, which prove its eligibility for extension of the location permit and the administrative fault in judging it. Nonetheless, the case directly runs into the general principle of legal certainty, when it could have equally quashed the original judgment based on the specific laws and regulations.

1.2. Accountability

Accountability is not limited to responsibilities in accounting activity. According to Elucidation, accountability includes all the responsibilities to the public or people as the holders of the supreme sovereignty in every activity and end result of investment.

An investor's duties and obligations, as stated in Article 15 and 16, seem to be the substantiated examples of this accountability.[4] Although dominated by general provisions – such as having good corporate governance, respecting the cultural tradition of the community, and complying with laws and regulations – it has two notable obligations: corporate social responsibility and reporting to the BKPM.

Here, corporate social responsibility means only general obligations as a soft law. It should be differentiated from Article 74 of the 2007 Company Act which

---

4 Although "all the responsibilities to public or people as the holders of the supreme sovereignty" implies the government's accountability to investors as well, there is no actual case against the government based on this article.

requires any company doing business related to natural resources to perform social and environmental responsibilities. These s responsibilities under the 2007 Company Act are specifically substantiated in regulations for each business field. For more details, see the earlier section, "Corporate Social Responsibility."

In practice, as the main function of BKPM is to assist and facilitate investment, the report obligation is not as burdensome as it is in an audit or report to the tax authority.

1.3. Equitable and nondiscriminatory treatment against country of origin

The principle of equitable treatment is reconfirmed at Article 6. According to Article 6 Paragraph 2 of the 2007 Capital Investment Act, nonetheless, this principle does not apply to investors of a country that has acquired privileges by virtue of a treaty with Indonesia. That is, equitable and nondiscriminatory treatment depends on bilateral investment treaties between Indonesia and the investor's country.

Importantly, foreign investors can lodge a complaint against a host country for alleged treaty violation under the Investor-State Dispute Settlement (ISDS) provisions of bilateral investment treaties. ISDS is a system through which an individual company can directly sue a country for alleged discriminatory practices. As is often the case with international arbitration under the rules of Washington-based International Centre for Settlement of Investment Disputes – a unit of the World Bank – the size of claims is generally enormous, commonly exceeding US$1 billion. Naturally, from the Indonesian Government's view, ISDS is thought to give rise to significant financial risk. The Coordinating Economic Minister, Cabinet ministers, senior government officials, and lawmakers have mentioned the significance of this when reviewing more than 60 bilateral treaties since early 2014.[5] As a result, Indonesia recently cancelled many of its bilateral investment treaties.

However, this is not the end of the story: at the same time, Indonesia has agreed to ISDS under the ASEAN Comprehensive Investment Agreement and ASEAN's five agreements with Dialogue Partners. Besides, President Joko Widodo has expressed strong interest in joining the Trans-Pacific Partnership, which contains provisions for ISDS.[6]

In sum, the principle of equitable and nondiscriminatory treatment should be understood not only within the domestic regulatory framework, but also in Indonesia's international obligations with respect to ISDS.

5 Vincent Lingga, The Week in Review: Investor-State Dispute, *The Jakarta Post*, May 17, 2015.

6 Stephen L. Magiera, *International Investment Agreements and Investor State Disputes: A Review and Evaluation for Indonesia*, Economic Research Institute for ASEAN and East Asia Discussion Paper Series, ERIA, 2017.

1.4. Others

Transparency is re-stipulated at Article 14 Section b. Elucidation defines transparency as the principle to provide the public with access to true, honest, and nondiscriminatory information on investment activities. To be more specific, as a one-stop service provider (*Pelaranan Terpady Satu Pintu*), the BKPM should equally provide any potential investor with truthful information and guidance about relevant administration, laws, and regulations necessary for investment. Certainly, other authorities have the same duties.

Efficiency in justice is now being stressed. For example, since 2016, a fast-track capital investment process is available for those investors having 1000 or more employees, or investment of IDR 1 billion or more. This is significant, particularly given the massive administrative burden in establishing such a business.

Article 3 further stipulates other principles such as togetherness, sustainability, being environmentally sound, independence, balanced advancement, and national economic unity.

2. Warnings against the attempts to end-run regulations in direct inbound investment

From a foreign direct investor's perspective, the main points of the 2007 Investment Act are as follows:

- Direct inbound investment is possible only in a company (PT) (Article 5 Paragraph 2 of the 2007 Capital Investment Act).
- The maximum of a foreign investor's shareholding rate is limited depending on the business field.
- Any agreement or statement to circumvent this limitation is per se void by operation of law (Article 33 Paragraph 2 of the 2007 Company Investment Act).

In the event that an investor attempts to use an entity other than a company, administrative sanctions may be imposed in the form of a written warning, a restriction of the business activity, and freezing or closure of the business activity and investment facilities (Article 34 Paragraph 1). Other sanctions may be imposed on the business entities or sole proprietorships (Article 34 Paragraph 3).

While the current trend of the Negative Investment List is to open wider fields for inbound investment through the amendments of 2014 and 2016,[7]

---

7 Reuters & Jakarta Globe, Revisions Made on the 2014 Negative Investment List, 12 February 2016, *Jakarta Globe*, http://jakartaglobe.beritasatu.com/business/revisions-made-2014-negative-investment-list/, accessed on 19 March 2018.

many business fields still maintain strong investment barriers. Does this barrier actually prevent a foreigner's investment in the Indonesian market? According to a news article in *Tech in Asia*,[8] some venture capitalists managing foreign funds from the United States and Japan reply in the negative to this question. This article takes an example of Sequoia and Softbank's US$100 million investment in Tokopedia in 2015, and introduces three ways to circumvent the barrier.

From the cold legal perspective, nonetheless, all these introduced methods are ostrich-like and highly risky. This chapter reviews the methods mentioned in the *Tech in Asia*'s article.

2.1.   Convertible note

2.1.1.   How it works

A foreign investor may establish a company in an offshore country and allow the company to advance investment to a target Indonesian company in consideration of convertible notes.

A convertible note is a form of debt that can be converted into equity, typically in conjunction with a future financing round. Of course, convertible bonds can be also used. However, the reason why convertible notes are widely used nowadays instead of traditional convertible bonds is that the historical way of financing is thought obsolete in the twenty-first century's e-commerce and IT industry. Many startup companies nowadays assume that they will need several investment rounds over a few years while deliberately leaving the company's source of revenue be decided later. The film *The Social Network*, describes a scene where Saverin, a co-founder of Facebook, argues for implementing instant cash income by starting advertising, while Zuckerberg and Parker reject the idea for leaving Facebook being cool. A startup making money by inserting ads after only a couple of years of development is regarded as "like throwing the greatest party on campus and someone's saying it's gotta be over by 11." The investment-and-development-only period without any cash income was explained in the movie: "You don't know what the thing is yet. How big it can get, how far it can go? This is no time to take your chips down. A million dollars isn't cool. You know what's cool? A billion dollars." Although this is just a script of a Hollywood movie, the core value

Figure 9.1 Convertible note process

***

8 Nadine Freischlad, How Foreign VCs Are Sneaking Past Indonesia's E-Commerce Laws, *Tech in Asia*, September 11, 2015.

of Indonesian e-commerce activity works in a similar way.⁹ Many focus on how to change and dominate people's lifestyles through applications, sites, or services, rather than being bent on how to instantly raise profits.

Hence, in contrast to convertible bonds, a convertible note does not force the issuer and investors to determine the value of the company, when the company does not have much on which to base a valuation, because "you don't know what the thing is yet." The *Tech in Asia* article explains that it can get around the Negative Investment List as well, as the investor may later sell the convertible notes to a third party upon liquidation. However, the actual practice gives many variable options to an investor. Typically, it offers a discount rate and valuation cap as additional rewards to compensate the angel investor for investing in the earlier round or for the additional risk in its investment. It also more often than not accrues interest to the principal invested as well, increasing the number of shares issued upon conversion.

Despite these advantages, the catch lies in decision-making. The article explains:

> If it comes to this arrangement, another venture capital added, typically a second agreement is set up that defines the foreign venture capital's influence on [the] decision-making process. A convertible note itself would exclude the foreign venture capital from being involved in strategic decisions.

This second agreement regarding the decision-making process is an ostrich-like makeshift approach.

2.1.2. The catch

This type of contractual arrangement is termed a voting agreement. It typically requires shareholders' voting rights to (i) be exercised for certain substantive matters or in certain procedures, (ii) to be exercised at a specific third party's direction, and (iii) not to be exercised in certain events. That is, the stockholder who carries voting rights virtually transfers that power to the investor for voting purposes. At the same time, it more often than not has a so-called procure provision, for shareholders to procure the company to do and not to do certain things. A stronger version of this arrangement includes the Indonesian target company as a contractual party and requires the company to acknowledge that it understands the investor's intention and promises to assist and aid so that the shareholders observe the agreement.

The problem is that, in whatever countries having modern company/corporation law, whether in common law or civil law jurisdictions, the validity

---

9 For example, the well-known local startup Gojek competes with Silicon Valley rivals in emerging markets. So far, armed with more than US$550 million from its latest fundraising, Gojek is valued at US$4 billion. The Limits of Silicon Valley: How Indonesia's Gojek is Beating Uber, *The Conversation*, November 24, 2016.

of this kind of voting agreement is greatly challenged.[10] This is because the concept of this arrangement flies directly against the principle of modern corporation law. A voting agreement and procure provision has been widely used since the nineteenth century in the development of modern corporations. At the same time, its validity and enforceability has been frequently challenged, and decided negatively in numerous cases.[11]

Notably, a voting trust which entrusts voting rights to a third person must be differentiated from voting agreement. Both a voting trust and voting agreement operate to prevent a free exercise of the voting rights of each participant therein if he subsequently desires to vote independently of the terms of the trust or contract. However, even in the United States, where a voting trust is valid as far as the separation of voting power from ownership is less complete, a voting agreement completely separating voting power from ownership is generally regarded as invalid.[12] In Indonesia, even voting trust is extremely rare in comparison to the United States, while proxy voting is very common for geographical reasons.

Due to the high legal risk in Indonesia, investors often use an offshore company, often in Singapore or Hong Kong, and rely on the law there. Nonetheless,

10 The courts in varied jurisdictions resist specifically enforcing the voting right agreement or determine its unenforceability from common law jurisdictions such as states in the United States (*Ringling Bros-Barnum & Bailey Combined Shows, Inc. v. Ringling* 53 A. 2d 441, [Del., 1947] and *West v. Camden*, 135 U.S. 507 [1890]) to civil law jurisdictions such as South Korea (Seoul Central District Court, ruled on 9 July 2010 [2009Gahab136849] that shareholders' agreement cannot bind corporation or a corporate organ's decision, while it remains valid only among the contractual parties) and Japan (Tokyo District Court ruled on 12 June 1981 that a voting agreement executed by 42%–62% of ownership is deemed as a mere gentlemen's agreement and not legally binding).

11 In an earlier period, the Illinois Supreme Court agreed the contract was enforceable where only a majority of stockholders combined for the purpose of electing directors because: "If they increased the value of their own stock, they also increased the value of all other stock. If they destroyed the stock of others, they also by the same act destroyed their own. It is absurd to suppose that a sane man will ruin himself for the mere pleasure of ruining others." *Faulds v. Yates*, 57 Ill. 416,421 (1870). In the meantime, *West v. Camden*, 135 U.S. 507 (1890) held that directors cannot contract away the power to exercise their independent judgment. The Delaware Supreme Court also refused to specifically enforce the voting right agreement – *Ringling Bros-Barnum & Bailey Combined Shows, Inc. v. Ringling*, 53 A. 2d 441 (Del., 1947) See also, The Validity of Stockholders' Voting Agreement in Illinois, *The University of Chicago Law Review* Vol. 3, No. 4, 1936, article 6. A voting agreement is instable not only in the United States, but in other civil law countries, too. For details in this line about Japanese cases, see 稲庭恒一, 判例にみる株主間契約, 明治大学法学部創立百三十周年記念論文集,二〇二-二-二, 59–85面) and for the details regarding South Korean cases, see 이동건 류명현 이수균, 주주간계약의 실무상 쟁점, BFL 제67호(2014.9).

12 The Delaware Supreme Court upheld the validity of a voting trust while refusing to specifically enforce a voting agreement – *Ringling Bros-Barnum & Bailey Combined Shows, Inc. v. Ringling*. See also Recent Cases: Specific Enforcement of Shareholder Voting Agreements, *University of Chicago Law Review* Vol. 15, No. 3, 1948, article 13.

no one can guarantee that choosing the laws of Singapore or Hong Kong as governing law of the voting agreement keeps the parties safe. If any lawyer or venture capitalist does so, or assure its client this is a simple matter rather than giving careful advice, watch out for a con.

First, there is an indispensable likelihood that an arbitrator or judge in these countries may reject the enforceability of the voting agreement for the same reasons as explained above. It should be considered that the demands of investors and shareholders are varied and complicated case by case, and that the case laws developed in these jurisdictions are highly delicate and sophisticated. It is rash and unwise for a lawyer or financial specialist to simply say "I have experience and know that it works" without any reference to any actual case directly relevant to the specific demands of a client.

Second, a foreign court or commercial arbitration center's decision may not be binding in Indonesia. Once a dispute arises, the parties' attempts to circumvent the 2007 Capital Investment Act and Negative Investment List is exposed. In other words, once the court recognizes the validity and enforceability of such an agreement in contemplation of an end run, such a court's recognition automatically frustrates the purpose of the laws and regulations of Indonesia. Therefore, even if a foreign court decides that a party should observe the voting agreement, an Indonesian court may subsequently decide not to execute the agreement against the Indonesian company, as the execution of such a voting agreement directly contradicts Indonesian law. This risk skyrockets with the general reluctance of Indonesian courts in enforcing foreign arbitration awards,[13] and domestic parties' strategies to avoid the execution.

Notably, a new BKPM regulation explicitly states that all indirect ownership and disguised investment in Indonesian public companies will then deem the companies to be a PMA and oblige them to follow the Negative Investment List.

Article 25 of BKPM Regulation No. 6 of 2016

(3) Any change in the company's capital for a PMDN company listed at the capital market resulting in a registration of a foreign investor in the deed of the company, the status of such a company shall be changed to a PMA.

(3a) In the event that the capital of a PMA company listed in the capital market is changed indirectly or through a portfolio at domestic capital market, such a company shall still observe the Negative Investment List.*

* free loose translation

---

13 See PNB Law Firm Jakarta, *International Arbitration through SIAC*, April 2015. At www. indonesia-investments.com/id/business/business-columns/bani-vs-siac-indonesian-or-international-arbitration/item5442.

Another way to circumvent foreign investment rules

To solve the problem mentioned above, one may attempt to use proxy voting, whereby investors have shareholders delegate their voting power to the investors. Indonesian courts require a very specific proxy appointment which explicitly states the agenda at certain shareholders' meeting; otherwise they do not recognize the validity of a broad delegation.

Nevertheless, this does not fundamentally iron out the issues in all management decisions or on voting rights. In principle, such a delegation or appointment can be cancelled or withheld at any time the shareholder wants. Unless the share was issued without voting right in the first place, a voting right is a shareholder's inherent right and privilege, one which make its holder a true shareholder and thus cannot be restricted from exercising these rights, even through the articles of association.

Due to the problems explained above, parties often knowingly or unknowingly somehow settle the issues that cannot be ultimately solved merely with drafting skills. The parties then somehow rely on the justification that other sophisticated lawyers do the same, and on mutual good faith (or a good-faith provision). This good faith implanted by the individuals in charge at the time of executing the contract, however, may disappear with changes of directors over several years, particularly when the opponent party is a big corporation.

2.2. Create multiple entities

2.2.1. How it works

Tech in Asia explains that in the case where there is more time to finalize an investment, the preferred method is to split the companies into multiple entities. That is, the target company may segregate a certain part of the business which a foreign shareholder cannot own because of the Negative Investment List, and implant it to another entity.

For example, if a target business sells products through an internet site, it may establish two separate companies: a company owning the inventory and handling everything related to delivery of products, and the other company holding the IP and being registered as a web portal. Subsequently, they make an exclusive contract. By owning one of the two entities that the Negative Investment List allows, the foreign investor may feel more comfortable to hold equity. This article stresses that this method is legal under Indonesian regulations. However, the problem is not that it is legal.

2.2.2. The catch

First, as the article also indicates, this method takes a lot of money and time to establish. For example, if the entities are separated, the transactions between these companies incur additional tax burdens. That is, dual taxation becomes quad taxation. Besides, many startups in Indonesia create a holding company headquartered out of Indonesia, with skyrocketing costs and expenses in preparation of the business.

Second, if a foreign investor holds only one entity in the project, it cannot perfectly secure the other entity purely owned by a third-citizen Indonesian party. To solve this problem, often the investor keeps up the masquerade by implementing a nominee as described below. Thus, this method has an inherent risk that may be incurred in the typical problems explained in the section "Inspection of the company" or the third option, "Use a nominee" below.

2.3. Use a nominee

Tech in Asia further explains that a third way to circumvent the ban on foreign direct investment in retail e-commerce is to work with a third-party local nominee. That is, this local entity holds the shares on paper. Even some lawyers and guidance book openly give the same advice.[14]

To be more specific, this practice is conducted with a combination of other devices, such as the power of attorney to sell the nominee's shares at any time of the appointee (investor)'s choice, a pledge of the nominee's shares to the investor, the appointment of the investor as a president director, and the acknowledgement and confirmation of facts.

Nonetheless, using a nominee itself is extremely risky. Even *Tech in Asia* notes that foreigners purchasing land in Bali through a nominee arrangement have learned the hard way that it's risky. Australian writer Phil Jarratt, the author of *Bali: Heaven and Hell* says: "If you think you hold land in Bali or anywhere in Indonesia through a local nominee, you'd better make sure you stay on the right side of the local, because you can't win in court."[15] Nothing is different when using a nominee for business share ownership.

In principle, stock ownership through a local nominee is per se void according to Article 1320 of the Civil Code and Article 33 of the 2007 Capital Investment Act. The actual owner cannot exercise any rights as a shareholder, nor can he claim a return for the shares. Article 33 of the 2007 Capital Investment Act absolutely bans a use of a nominee in Paragraph 1 and stresses the invalidity of such a contract again in Paragraph 2. For the same purposes, the BKPM Reg. 6 of 2016 demands a strict observance of the Negative Investment List.

14 An Indonesia Nominee Trading Company Is a Legitimate Way to Conduct Business in Indonesia, and Is Often Used as a Legitimate Vehicle for eEntrepreneurs to Overcome Foreign Investment Restrictions, *Indonesia Company Laws and Regulations Handbook*, International Business Publications, 2009, p 46. Sadly, these kinds of dangerous advices are pervasive in the market. One must understand that using a nominee is simply illegitimate.
15 Jewel Topsfield, A Nightmare in Paradise, *The Sydney Morning Herald*, July 12, 2015.

2.4. *Conclusion*

Although a number of devices to circumvent the ban have been widely used in practice, the Indonesian government is paying sharper attention to this practice, and the trend of laws and regulations is also imposing more and more harsh thresholds against it.[16] The investor should be aware that once the end-run plans begin to not work in a way that he or she expected they would, substantial problems arise such as a dispute with the nominee, the impossibility of returning the investment, administrative sanctions, even criminal punishment, and so on.

3.   Company's rights on land

In relation to the use of land, Article 22 of the 2007 Capital Investment Act allows a company to have only three types of rights, which consist of:

- Right to cultivate (Hak Guna Usaha or HGU)
- Right to build (Hak Guna Bangunan or HGB)
- Right to use (Hak Pakai)

A company can appropriate land within the territory of Indonesia only based on these rights. Although its literal translation is "right," it is better to view these merely as government permits or licenses. For example, these are protected only with a government's official approval for the explicitly granted years.[17]

- HGU may be initially granted for 95 years, extendable for an additional 60 years, and subsequently renewable for 35 years.
- HGB may be initially granted for 80 years, extendable for an additional 50 years, and subsequently renewable for 30 years.
- HAK PAKAI may be initially granted for 70 years, extendable for an additional 45 years, and subsequently renewable for 25 years.

The Indonesian Government explains that (i) the extension of land use is to give incentive for economic participants, (ii) evaluation must be conducted in advance, (iii) any issuance, extension and renewal more than the stipulated years is null and void, (iii) only Government can cancel or terminate the rights, (iv) expansion of right forms Government's guarantee regarding the use of stated years.[18]

---

16 Indonesian experts have the same understanding. For details, see *Pemegang Saham "Nominee" Dilarang* Suparji, *Penanaman Modal Asing Di Indonesia Insentif v. Pembatasan,* Universitas Al Azhar Indonesia, 2008, pp. 242–243.

17 For details, see Peraturan Menteri Negara Agrarian/Kepala Badan Pertanahan Nasional No.40/1996 Tentang Hak Guna Usaha, Hak Guna Bangunan Dan Hak Pakai Atas Tanah.

18 For details, see Jawaban Pemerintah R.I Atas Pertanyaan Hakim Mahkamah Konstitusi R.I Dalam Persidangan Permohonan Pengujian.

Importantly, a company is not allowed to enjoy *ownership* of land. Here, ownership means absolute proprietary right which the holder can exclusively, completely, and directly control, use, and dispose of specified land. A company is merely allowed to have a lease-like right, which allows the holder to use the designated land only for a permitted purpose for the approved time period.[19]

In the meantime, if the company has a business in natural resources, such as forestry or coal extraction, its use of land for such a business must be based on a separate right/permit issued by relevant authorities. This is because the country owns the land, according to Article 33 of the Constitution.[20]

Because these rights are virtually mere permits or licenses, the holder may be afraid of the risk that the country arbitrarily terminates or withholds them. In principle, the Government must not nationalize or expropriate an investor's proprietary rights, including the above land rights, unless provided by law (Article 7 Paragraph 1 of the 2007 Capital Investment Act). However, exceptionally, it may enact special laws for nationalization or expropriation, satisfying the principle of equitable treatment (Article 6 Paragraph 1 of the 2007 Capital Investment Act) and paying compensation of fair market price established by an independent appraiser named by the parties (Article 7 Paragraph 2 of the 2007 Capital Investment Act). Should the compensation be insufficient, the settlement must be through arbitration outside of a court of law (Article 7 Paragraph 3 of the 2007 Capital Investment Act). Nonetheless, foreign investors can still lodge a complaint against the Indonesian Government under the Investor-State Dispute Settlement (ISDS) provisions of bilateral investment treaties.

The in-depth discussion regarding this provision requires understanding of Indonesia's laws and regulations over real estate, which are extremely difficult and complex.[21]

19 In addition, as a treasure house of natural resources with a history of colonization and exploitation, Indonesia does not allow ownership of real property for a foreigner, whether as a residence or industrial land.
20 Article 33, Paragraph 3 of the 1945 Constitution of Republic of Indonesia: "The land, waters and natural resources shall be under the powers of the State and shall be used to the greatest benefit of the people."
21 For details, see Suparji, *supra* note 16.

Index

Note: Page numbers in *italic* indicate a figure and page numbers in **bold** indicate a table on the corresponding page.

For Product Safety Concerns and Information please contact our EU
representative GPSR@taylorandfrancis.com
Taylor & Francis Verlag GmbH, Kaufingerstraße 24, 80331 München, Germany

www.ingramcontent.com/pod-product-compliance
Ingram Content Group UK Ltd.
Pitfield, Milton Keynes, MK11 3LW, UK
UKHW020959180425
457613UK00019B/748